Praise
Dare to I

"Bruce Kodish presents an emin⟨
to both scientific and ethical inquiry ⎯⎯ ⍺⍳gues that these forms of
inquiry are profoundly interconnected. He provides a compelling program for the unification of science and ethics."
> —John Allman, Ph.D., Hixon Professor of Neurobiology,
> California Institute of Technology

"I regard *Dare to Inquire* as a great achievement. One might say,
looking at the world, "What a mess!" But unlike many books that only,
in the end, list our problems, *Dare to Inquire* points to practical (or at
least possible) solutions. It's as if a master architect had laid out the
blue-print of one way we might proceed. I did not find a phony moment in it; brave, it does not compromise to curry favor, nor will it
shrink from challenging assumptions, even basic ones. Yet, if we disagree on some point, that seems OK too. Inquiring readers will discover that this well-written book educates and, for some, inspires, and
has many facets of interest—and like most good books, really sets you
to thinking."
> —James D. French, Editor-in-Chief, *General Semantics Bulletin*

"A gutsy antidote for befuddlement—if you feel confused by contradictory belief systems, or by your own linguistic habits, philosophical
fence-sitting, fear of chaos, or an unhealthy craving for perfect answers,
then you might *Dare to Inquire*. Bruce Kodish offers a method through
the madness. You'll discover that you don't need an external authority, metaphysical or otherwise, for you to live an ethical and rewarding life."
> —Paul Dennithome Johnston, Executive Director, International
> Society of General Semantics; Managing Editor, *ETC: A Review
> of General Semantics* ; Author of *The Clone Chronicles*

"According to the philosopher Charles Peirce, there is only one
commandment worth following - 'thou shalt not block the road to inquiry.' Bruce Kodish does an exemplary job of defending this 'commandment', and shows how the principles of general semantics can
help one lead a rich and fulfilling life, free from dangerous illusions
and rigid thinking. I particularly found rewarding his discussion on
how one can leave a life's legacy of which one can truly be proud."
> —Timothy J. Madigan, Chairman of the Editorial Board
> of *Free Inquiry* Magazine

"As an example of honest, rigorous scholarship, I'd recommend Bruce Kodish's latest book *Dare to Inquire* anytime. Prepare yourself for an intellectual adventure."

—Jeff Mordkowitz, Director, Institute of General Semantics; Originator, The SevenSimpleStepsMethod™

"With *Dare to Inquire* Dr. Bruce Kodish has established himself at the forefront of writers in general semantics, neuro-evaluational linguistics, and humanistic philosophy. His formulating is plain in the sense of being open and clear, his tone compassionate throughout, but with flashes of slightly wicked wit when required. Bruce Kodish's main purpose herein is to present general semantics as a humanistic system, explanatory of and applicable to the broad range of human problems related to how we 'size things up' (evaluate); he places Korzybski's system in its historic-derivative context and, in so doing, gives the reader a handy, economical handbook of neuro-philosophy. Earthlings concerned with scholarship, teaching, or just plain being thoughtful about what they're going to be up to in the 'Third' Millenium, will, I predict, greatly enjoy and benefit from this masterful work."

—Robert P. Pula, Director Emeritus, Institute of General Semantics; Author of *A General Semantics Glossary: Pula's Guide for the Perplexed* and *Knowledge, Uncertainty and Courage: Selected General Semantics Writings of Robert P. Pula*

"In *Dare to Inquire*, Bruce Kodish tackles head-on many of the key issues which confront and confound modern society. Any thinking person would find something challenging and stimulating in this book. Dare to read it."

—Jim Underdown, Executive Director, Center for Inquiry-West

"This seems to me a revolutionary book on how to transcend prejudices, evade the currently fashionable lunacies, open yourself to new perceptions, new empathy and even new ideas, free your living total brain from the limits of your dogmatic verbal "mind," and generally wake up and smell the bodies of dead children and other innocents piling up everywhere. In a time of rising rage and terror, we need this as badly as a city with plague needs vaccines and antibiotics. If I had the money I'd send a copy to every delegate at the UN."

—Robert Anton Wilson, Author of *TSOG: The Thing That Ate The Constitution*

Dare to Inquire

Sanity and Survival for the 21st Century and Beyond

Bruce I. Kodish, Ph.D.

Pasadena, CA

Dare to Inquire: Sanity and Survival for the 21st Century and Beyond
by Bruce I. Kodish
Copyright © 2003 by Bruce I. Kodish

Published by

Extensional Publishing
330 Cordova St. #178
Pasadena, CA 91101-4654
Fax: 626-795-0954 Tel: 626-795-0959
Email: ExtensionalPubl@aol.com

Publisher's Catalogue in Publication Data

Kodish, Bruce I.
Dare to Inquire: Sanity and Survival for the 21st Century and
Beyond/ by Bruce I. Kodish
Pasadena, CA: Extensional Publishing, © 2003
400 pp. includes index
ISBN 0-9700664-7-3 (paperback: acid free paper)
Library of Congress Control Number: 2002096100

1. General Semantics 2. Practical Philosophy 3. Applied Psychology 4. Science and Religion
I. Title. II. Kodish, Bruce I.

LC Classification B820
Dewey Decimal Classification # 149.94

Cover Design by Edward Dawson

Figures on pp. 100, 110, 128, and 130 used with permission of the Institute of General Semantics and *General Semantics Bulletin*.
Extensive quotations from the works of Alfred Korzybski used with permission of the Institute of General Semantics and the Alfred Korzybski Literary Estate.

For more information go to www.driveyourselfsane.com
You may contact the author at DriveSelfSane@aol.com

Contents

About the Author

Upon this first, and in one sense this sole, rule of reason, that in order to learn you must desire to learn, and in so desiring not be satisfied with what you already incline to think, there follows one corollary which itself deserves to be written upon every wall of the city of philosophy:

Do not block the way of inquiry.[1]

— CHARLES S. PEIRCE

(Do Not Skip This) Preface:
Why I Wrote This Book

This book is about the need for adult humans to 'grow up'. Especially now, more than a year after the debacle of 9/11/2001, it is not hard to denounce intolerance and fanaticism and want to uproot it. The question remains, "How?"—"How do we do it?" Can we stop an apparently accelerating, world-wide movement toward fundamentalism, despotism and despair? I want to share with you here one of the main sources of my personal urgency about this question.

Although not about Judaism, this book comes out of my lifetime quest to make sense of my life as a Jew, of the history of my people, and of antisemitism (hostility toward Jews and Judaism). My grandparents came to America less than 100 years ago (in the early twentieth century) to escape antisemitic oppression in Eastern Europe. I grew up in the nineteen-fifties and nineteen-sixties in a traditionally observant though religiously non-orthodox Jewish household in Akron, Ohio and then Pittsburgh. We went to synagogue often. I studied Hebrew and Jewish history from a young age. More significantly for me, I was immersed in the transplanted secular culture and language of Russian-Polish Jewry. My first language was Yinglish—in my case the Upper Midwest Ohio English of my parents and the speech of extended family and friends, which was peppered with Yiddish words, phrases, syntax and attitude.

When the destruction of European Jewry by the Nazis emerged fully into my pubescent awareness, I decided that 'God' as I had understood 'Him', the benevolent, personal creator of the universe, was either not benevolent or not 'God'. Since then I have sought to define a meaningful life-stance for myself, one without a personal (person-like), supernatural 'God' to sustain it. In that search, a not uncommon one for Jews, I discovered humanism and general semantics and have used these approaches to evolve a flexible set of commitments for myself.

The title of this book simply states my basic theme—*Dare to Inquire*. However far I've gone from orthodoxy, I've maintained the questioning and inquiry which play a major role in the Jewish culture and religious teaching that I grew up with. But, of course, the philosophy of inquiry, which I label humanism, is not exclusive to Judaism or any other particular culture/civilization. In Part I of *Dare to Inquire*, I survey humanist viewpoints from many cultures and expressed by many individuals, while focusing on European and American sources. I then seek to clarify different forms of humanism and show what distinguishes a humanist approach from others.

Part II provides an introduction to the far-reaching applied science-philosophy of general semantics originated by Alfred Korzybski. General Semantics grew out of the humanist tradition. It provides a system for applying an attitude of inquiry in everyday life and possibly fulfilling the as-yet undeveloped promise for a more humanistic future. While various writers have emphasized and popularized bits and pieces of this system, one of the remarkable things about general semantics remains the scarcity of writings which show the comprehensiveness and fruitfulness of this approach to science and daily life. *Dare to Inquire* follows on the previous book by my wife and me, *Drive Yourself Sane*, which provides a practical introduction to the system. In Part II of this book, I focus on the broader scientific-philosophical background, assumptions and formulations of general semantics. I show how general semantics can help you become aware of your personal 'reality tunnel'—the way that you perceive the world. This personal awareness can give you greater power to expand your perceptions, solve problems, and improve your life.

Part III focuses on some applications of general semantics to science, religion, ethics and social policy. In it I give my present responses to some perennial questions about the nature of the world and of humans, the role of science in society, the 'meaning' and purpose of life, and how we humans can get along with one another. Whether or not you agree with my conclusions, I hope they inspire you, the reader, as you formulate answers for yourself. The material in Parts I and II provide a foundation for better understanding Part III.

There are no 'facts' about the future. The fate, indeed the survival, of humanity seem highly unpredictable to me. My concern for humanity-as-a-whole has grown with and been colored by my concern for the uncertain fate of the Jewish people and the survival of Israel, the Palestinian Jewish State. An unapologetic Zionist, I lived in Israel from 1975 to 1977. I've sat for hours in a bomb shelter with Katyusha rockets (fired by Palestinian Arab guerrillas) flying overhead, laid concertina barbed-wire on the Israeli-Lebanese border, and carried a rifle on guard-duty for community self-defense. Unfortunately the Israeli fight for survival still continues (2003).[1]

For me, Jewish particularism, including support for the Jewish homeland, has always been intertwined with Jewish universalism. My humanism began with the readings of the Torah that I heard in the synagogue of my youth: "Love therefore the stranger, for you were strangers in the land of Egypt." "Seek the peace of the country where I have carried you and pray unto the Lord for it, for in its peace shall you have peace."[2] I'm a typical Jew and Zionist in that regard. Despite whatever you may have heard or read to the contrary, Israel remains an island of democracy and of freedom for minorities in a boiling sea of Middle-Eastern tyranny. Unrepresentative acts by a small number of out-of-the-mainstream Jewish fanatics have disturbed me as much as they do most Jews and Israelis.

I am also disturbed by the oppression, torture, and killing of peace-loving, freedom-seeking Arabs and Muslims by their fanatical 'brothers' throughout the Arab-Islamic world. Tyrants and fanatics use Militant Islamic ideology to blame outsiders (Israelis, Jews and Americans) for the troubles of their societies. This use of 'the religion of peace' promotes lowered expectations, unfruitful victimhood, and the oppression of women and minorities. It incites terrorism. The consequences of such attitudes and practices have spread beyond the Middle East and the Islamic world, as we know. They represent the broader problem of fundamentalism, by no means exclusively Arab-Islamic, which imperils the entire planet.

We humans appear to be in a mess. We've gotten stuck in a phase of arrested development. This 'stuckness' seems very much a problem of 'philosophy'—a problem of prevailing fundamentalist doctrines, i.e., habits of thinking-feeling which keep individuals and humanity as a whole from moving into something that might more resemble 'adulthood'.

Such dogmatic doctrines and habits encourage us to confuse our limited perceptions of the world with the world itself. We confuse our fallible symbols and word maps with the ever-changing objects of experience. We eat the menu instead of the meal and starve ourselves by feasting on phantoms in a world more abundant than we realize.

Our dysfunctional doctrines and habits lead us into an ever-expanding maze of seemingly unresolvable conflicts and difficulties. They account for a large portion of the *potentially preventable* human-caused disasters that continue to plague our planet at a seemingly ever-accelerating rate.

Are there ways out of this mess? Can humanity put away its childish things and move toward adulthood? The solutions I propose in this book do not start with attempting to change humanity as a whole. Rather, what I suggest requires a change of personal philosophy, a change which happens in one individual at a time—perhaps you, when you dare to inquire.

Applying the humanistic tools of general semantics and related approaches, you can learn to question your favorite doctrines. You can develop new habits of thinking-feeling. Daring to inquire, you can wake up from belief-sleep and develop a more mature philosophy of life which can help you find maximum probability of predictability within the wisdom of accepting uncertainty.

At the very least, you will have some tools for living a more interesting and productive personal life. In addition, you may also have an effect on other individuals in some surprising ways. When sufficient numbers of adults begin to think-feel in ways more suitable to adults (as defined in this book), this may perhaps lead to more visible changes in the larger society.

A saner, more positive, and sustainable future for the people of planet Earth does not seem inevitable. However, I consider it possible and worth working toward. On that basis, I offer this book as a potentially useful guide for "Tikkun Olam" (Hebrew for "repairing the world"), a map for moving out of our present childish mess of difficulties and toward the adulthood of humanity.

    — Bruce I. Kodish
      Pasadena, CA
      January, 2003

A Language Note

One of the main points in this book is that a language as a form of representation is not a 'transparent', neutral medium that simply contains and conveys 'meaning'. Rather, a language (with its associated evaluations) structures how we represent things in various, often unnoticed ways that influence our ongoing behavior. Here, I'd like to call your attention to some of the conscious uses of language that I make throughout this book.

I apply double quotes according to standard usage to indicate direct quotes as well as terms/phrases typically used by someone but not necessarily indicating a direct quote. I use single quotes throughout this work, not only in the standard usage to indicate a quote within a quote. I also use them when I wish to indicate terms and phrases that I'm using playfully, metaphorically or with caution. The single quotes can serve as "safety devices," to prevent us from getting misled by the evaluational 'baggage' of terms, i.e., certain false-to-fact implications of typical usage.

I also make frequent use of the term "et cetera" (etc.), which comes from the Latin for "and so forth." I find that explicit use of "etc." and related terms reminds me to retain a non-finalistic, non-allness attitude in my statements. Such an attitude encourages looking for and enumerating examples when speaking and writing. After doing this, I still haven't said it all. Whenever I see a period I find it useful to remember "etc." and thus avoid a "period and stop" attitude.

My use of "et cetera" as well as "some," "to me," "as I see it," "from my point of view," "seem(s)," "to some degree," etc., may seem too indefinite or "wishy-washy" for some readers. Despite such objections, this language represents my conscious effort to practice EMA, English Minus Absolutisms, which was formulated by general-semantics scholar and distinguished lexicographer, Allen Walker Read. EMA is based on Alfred Korzybski's general principle of uncertainty in regard to *all* statements about the non-verbal world (yes, I said *all*—legitimate here). In keeping with EMA, the reader can take any positive statement I make in this book about the non-verbal world as only probable to some degree, at a particular date.

In relation to dates, I use the common Gregorian calendar. However, since I am not a Christian, I apply the labels originally used by Jewish scholars—BCE (Before the Common Era) instead of BC (Before Christ), and CE (Common Era) instead of AD (Anno Domini, the Latin for "Year of the Lord," i.e, Jesus Christ).

The term "general semantics" does not refer to some sort of generalized semantics. Rather "general semantics" is the name of a particular discipline. I abbreviate general semantics as "GS" with capital letters. When using the term as a modifier, as in the phrase "a general-semantics approach," I use a hyphen to emphasize its unitary nature.

Acknowledgements

This book reflects what my parents taught me before I could read a book. My mother of beloved memory, Dorothy Berson Kodish, instilled in me her own down-to-earth, humanistic Jewish values, which will never leave me. My father, Morris 'Mashe' Kodish, continues to inspire me with his hearty, tough, and loving presence.

Much gratitude also goes to my uncle, the late Sam Berson, for the inspiration of many long walks and talks. My gratitude also goes to my in-laws, the late George Samuelson and Bea Samuelson, for their interest, support and Jewish humor.

My wife, Susan Presby Kodish, provided invaluable motivational, formulational and editorial help. This book would not exist without the considerable love, inspiration, and perspiration which she contributed.

Thanks as well go to all of those who read and commented on the evolving manuscript. Special thanks go to James D. French, Paul Dennithorne Johnston, Timothy J. Madigan, and Robert P. Pula, who provided considerable editorial help. Additional thanks to the members of my doctoral committee at the Union Institute and University including Peter Fenner, Bethe Hagens, Stuart Jordan, and Maxine Theodoulou. Their enthusiasm, encouragement and criticism helped me shape what became the core of this book.

Numerous discussions with friends from the Washington Area Secular Humanists and the Council for Secular Humanism stimulated my formulating about humanism, religion, individual and social ethics, etc.

Numerous friends and colleagues at the Institute of General Semantics, the International Society for General Semantics and the Baltimore Society for General Semantics have encouraged me in my study and teaching of general semantics. In particular, I have benefited from discussions and interactions with the following general-semantics scholar-teachers, among many others: the late Dorothy Berleth, Sanford I. Berman, Milton Dawes,

James D. French, the late Helen Hafner, the late Kenneth G. Johnson, Paul Dennithorne Johnston, Homer J. Moore Jr., the late Stuart A. Mayper, Jeffrey A. Mordkowitz, Thomas E. Nelson, Robert P. Pula, the late Allen Walker Read, the late Charlotte Schuchardt Read, Steve Stockdale and Ralph Wesselman.

I feel a particular debt to dear Charlotte, who gently showed me the major importance of organism-as-a-whole-in-environment approaches, sensory awareness, and silence on the un-speakable level, in the approach to living that Korzybski taught. She first suggested to me the possibility of studying the Alexander Technique.

The influence of Robert P. Pula also permeates this book. I have benefitted from many years of contact and conversation with Bob, one of the most important general-semantics formulators since Korzybski's death. Bob's teaching, writing, and creative 'spirit' exemplify the humor, rigor, and depth inherent in the general-semantics discipline.

Friends and colleagues in the community of Alexander Technique teachers, especially Ron Dennis and the late Troup Mathews, have helped me to internalize my knowledge about the embodiment of human consciousness and culture.

Discussions with friends at the School of the Natural Order have helped me to draw out and express some further implications of time-binding and human connectedness to the larger whole. Much thanks as well to Elan Z. Neev, peace visionary, who has helped me gain a deeper understanding of the universal, humanistic aspects of Judaism. Thanks also to Max Sandor who has helped me gain insight into some realms of philosophy that I might have otherwise ignored.

My sister, Marilyn Kodish Sutherland; my brother-in-law Chuck Sutherland; my step-children, David Presby and Joan Presby, and my son-in-law Larry Adler have provided consistent love and encouragement. My granddaughter, Rebecca Chaya Adler, and my nieces, nephews and grand-nieces give me nakhes[1] and inspire me to do what I can to help create a safer, saner, world.

Introduction

The chief obstacle to the progress of the human race, is the human race.[1]

— DON MARQUIS

Chapter 1
The Present Mess

A Problematic World

Something like 6.1 billion humans presently (2003) live on planet Earth, almost 4 times the number of people who lived 100 years ago. This growth has been exponential. Like bacteria growing in a Petri dish, as the total number of humans has increased on Earth, the rate of increase has increased—accelerating as it goes. In 1800, the estimated world population reached 1 billion for the first time in human history. By 1900, this had increased to 1.6 billion. Biologist Edward O. Wilson notes, "people born in 1950 were the first to see the human population double in their lifetime, from 2.5 billion to over six billion now." [1] By the year 2050, reasonable estimates predict that world human population may reach about 10 billion. It seems time to seriously consider a notion long emphasized by environmentalists: the resources of the world are not endless. After a point, which we already may have reached, more people is not better.

Indeed, the sheer number of human beings contributes to a complex of interacting problems. Human population size affects, and is affected by, food supply, pollution levels, natural resource and energy depletion, political-ethnic-religious conflicts, etc. Urban sprawl is increasing. The climate is changing. Irreplaceable plants and animals become endangered or extinct at an alarming rate. Wilderness is getting paved over with freeways, parking lots, and other forms of development. The distance between the haves and the have-nots becomes wider and seems more unbridgeable, even in the "affluent society" of the United States.

The encroachments and benefits of the globalized consumer/information economy—which political scientist Benjamin Barber calls "McWorld"—is faced with a counter-

The Unfulfilled Promise of Humanism

Urgings to expand the scope of scientific inquiry have been blocked by the attitudes of some scientists, philosophers and humanists. Speaking in the name of science, some scientists and skeptics have embraced a narrow view which restricts scientific inquiry to particular types of research methodology or particular established fields of study. Some important types of inquiry may thus get labeled as "unscientific" even if researchers in these areas are careful not to claim more than their evidence merits. By using "unscientific" or "pseudo-science" as name-calling epithets, so-called skeptics can thus prematurely block potentially valuable pathways of study.

Another factor has blocked the expansion of a scientific, naturalistic attitude of inquiry into the broader culture. A certain amount of sentimentality and formulational toothlessness has characterized many of the philosophers who have espoused a scientific, naturalistic outlook. Thinkers who could be considered naturalistic humanists, such as John Dewey, Sidney Hook, Ernest Nagel and Willard Quine, have done some good by espousing the extension of scientific inquiry to broader areas of life. However, they have had little in the way of a general teachable system for actually bringing scientific attitudes of evaluating to the woman and man in the street. Without such a teachable system, a scientific approach to living may remain mostly verbal chatter and out of reach for most people. The promise of humanism has thus, to a great degree, remained unfulfilled.

The failure to provide a teachable system on the part of these individuals may have had something to do with the academic culture within which they functioned. This culture has perhaps too readily encouraged overspecialization and impracticality. However, I suspect that something even deeper than academic custom underlies the relative unworkability of much of the humanist agenda up to now. Humanists say that they support the use of scientific methods in everyday life. But what version of these do they support? Different views of reason and science yield different results.

Modern humans have eaten abundantly from the 'tree of knowledge'. However, living within the fruits of science, humanist philosophy, etc., are 'worms'—underlying out-of-date assumptions about the world, how we evaluate, etc. These assumptions, embedded in moment-to-moment linguistic habits and codified by Aristotle and his followers, I label (after Korzybski) "aristotelian."

Unexamined aristotelian assumptions have prevented some 'sciences' from becoming truly up-to-date scientific disciplines. They have prevented humanists from extending an attitude of science to other areas of human life. These unexamined assumptions, embodied in their language use, have kept the scientists, humanists and others who hold them ensnared by doctrines unsuitable for a modern (2003) scientific outlook, no matter what they say about supporting 'science'.

Humanist philosopher Corliss Lamont asserted that Aristotle's "laws of thought remain definitive for valid reasoning...." [5] In his book, *The New Skepticism*, humanist philosopher Paul Kurtz declared that "No one can argue or make sense if he violates the rules of identity, contradiction, and the excluded middle." [6] What happens to a scientific, humanistic view of reason if these rules do not have universal application? Indeed, I argue that in their traditional form they don't. They require revision and restatement in order to cover a more thoroughly up-to-date (2003) scientific attitude.

A systematic analysis of the above-mentioned impeding factors was worked out in the early decades of the twentieth century by philosopher-scientist Alfred Korzybski. The generalized philosophy-science which he formulated, known as general semantics (GS), goes beyond theoretical analysis to offer practical tools for fulfilling the promise of humanism and thus moving toward individual and social adulthood and sanity.

General Semantics

The discipline of general semantics, formulated in the 1920s and 1930s, has a rather short history compared to humanism as a whole. As an applied, scientifically-based epistemology, it focuses on how we know what we know, with knowledge viewed in the broadest possible sense to include 'thinking', 'feeling', 'acting', etc. GS avows a naturalistic orientation and has humanistic values at its base.

Drive Yourself Sane provides a practical guide for applying the system and the tools of general semantics. These tools may seem so startlingly simple that many people have dismissed them without trying them. Please refer to *Drive Yourself Sane* for a basic explanation of the system and how to use it.

Dare to Inquire has a different mission: to provide a broad overview of general semantics, showing how it is embedded in the humanist tradition, and demonstrating its continuing relevance to human problem-solving. Part I presents some background on the humanistic tradition, the philosophical/scientific antecedents in the growth of human inquiry upon which Korzybski built his system. Part II introduces Korzybski's work and his basic formulations, and shows how these fit into the tradition of humanistic philosophy and science while providing methods for use in daily life. In Part III, I demonstrate the use of general-semantics tools to dig up aristotelian 'weeds' in some present-day aspects of science, religion, and ethics/social policy, and to sow nutrition-rich non-aristotelian seeds instead.

This book can thus serve as a useful entry to GS for people interested in philosophy, humanism, social science, psychology, religion, ethics, the humanities and sciences. Such individuals may feel intrigued with the notion that there exist specific ways to increase sanity and expand human consciousness, both individually and collectively, through the application of a general attitude of scientific inquiry. Current students of GS can also find useful background and new ways to view the discipline.

Sufficient research has been done to indicate that use of the system of general semantics has great promise for improving human functioning.[7] I do not intend this book, however, as an academic research summary. Rather I hope to show the continuing merit of Korzybski's relatively unrecognized and still revolutionary approach to human evaluating.

General Semantics supplies a non-aristotelian framework that can provide religious and naturalistic humanists (and perhaps even a few daring non-humanists) with specific means to actually apply an attitude of scientific inquiry to everyday life, not just talk about it. As its particular strength, general semantics provides a general, teachable system for the practice of science-based methods of evaluating. It furnishes a broad framework for connecting the various fragmented pieces of knowledge that continue to accumulate in seemingly separate areas of study. It offers a non-aristotelian approach for science and everyday life. If I can encourage even a few individuals to dare to inquire in some different ways, I will have fulfilled my purpose.

A Modest Proposal

If and when humanity as a whole does manage to 'grow up' and reach something resembling 'adulthood', problems will surely not cease. We will still exist some distance away from Utopia, which I believe lies in the district of Erehwon, i.e., nowhere. In spite of this, many of our difficulties will not, I predict, seem so unavoidable and unresolvable as they presently do.

The adulthood of humanity will require each of us to put away our childish habits of evaluating. It will require each of us to learn how to distinguish many different aspects and levels of our experience. It will require a new awareness of human linguistic behavior and of how the structure of language and 'logic' can structure our behavior for better and worse. The adulthood of humanity will result from a generalized application of a scientific attitude—an attitude of inquiry— to our problems, including those of everyday life. This may involve a sometimes thorough, painful and self-challenging evaluation of beliefs, assumptions and habits from the most personal to the most abstract levels.

Fulfilling the promise of humanism does not mean an arrogant overestimation of human talents by making humans into demi-gods of some kind. Rather, a new modesty will prevail. For the most part, humans will stop passing off their own creations as the work of extra-human powers. Many more individuals will recognize that we *fallible* humans create our own gods, moralities, purposes and possibilities. Adulthood does not mean godhood for humans. It does mean, as I intend it, that only we have the responsibility for our destinies.

Humanism involves recognizing that the human venture remains—for better and worse—inescapably human, all too human. With continuing dire world events, I feel a certain sense of urgency in writing this book. By accepting our fallible humanness more fully than we have before, we humans may have a better chance of resolving problems and conflicts, reducing or preventing avoidable difficulties and nudging ourselves and our world in more desirable directions. Let's see.

Part I
The Humanist Tradition

**If man knew his own greatness
he would not have to rise any higher.**[1]
— STANISLAW JERZY LEC

Chapter 2
Humanist Roots

General Semantics belongs to the wider intellectual tradition of humanistic philosophy,

> ...a doctrine, attitude, or way of life centered on human interests or values; esp. a philosophy that usu.[usually] rejects supernaturalism and stresses an individual's dignity and worth and capacity for self-realization through reason.[1]

In Part I, *The Humanist Tradition,* I present basic background for understanding the humanistic sources of general semantics. In this chapter, "Humanist Roots," I discuss some of the trends and thinkers that have had importance in the development of humanism, mainly in Europe and the West, to the beginning of the twentieth century. In the next chapter, "A Spectrum of Modern Humanism," I treat the different versions, from religious to non-religious, of present-day humanism. In the final chapter of Part I, "Becoming More Fully Human," I provide further details about naturalistic humanism, the particular view of humanism which seems closest to the system of general semantics as I understand it.

Note—I do not consider this survey of humanism as in any way comprehensive. It neglects many essential developments in mathematics, science, technology, art, music, society, politics, religion, etc., which have contributed to a humanist outlook. It overlooks the countless individual mothers, fathers, hunters, gardeners, engineers, miners, merchants, farmers, sailors, artists, musicians, teachers, cooks, etc. (most of them unknown to us), who have added to the development of human knowledge and humanistic values.

The Humanities

The term "humanism" has had a variety of uses over many years. Humanism may refer to a person's humanitarian con-

While Renaissance humanists explored ancient learning and sought to remove church-imposed restrictions on inquiry, the advancement of science still appeared somewhat limited. Renaissance humanists also maintained the Classical and Medieval exclusion of women in their elevation of the City of 'Man'. Nonetheless, the Renaissance humanists helped shine more light into the relatively endarkened world of Medieval European culture.

Humanistic Traditions of Religion

I take a detour here to note once again that humanism is not necessarily opposed to religion. Many religious traditions involve, to a greater or lesser degree, humanistic teachings. For example, the Hebrew Bible declares what has become known as "the golden rule"—"Love your neighbor as yourself." [Leviticus 19:18]—which Jesus quoted. Hillel, a Jewish teacher from the first century B.C.E., was said to have been asked by a non-Jew to summarize the teachings of his religion while standing on one foot. Hillel's reply built upon the above-noted Biblical passage: "What is hateful unto you do not do unto your neighbor. The rest is commentary—now go and study." He is also famous for his own commentary to this, "If I am not for myself, who will be for me, and if I am only for myself, what am I? And if not now, when?" [6]

Something like the "golden rule," based on what Confucius called "Shu" (reciprocity), exists in each of the world's major religious traditions and, it seems, most if not all of the minor ones as well. (The Wiccans have a libertarian-sounding version "An[d] it harm none, do what thou wilt.") Philosophical teachings and folk proverbs from around the world also contain versions of this humanistic principle. Some versions, like Hillel's, are stated negatively. Some are stated positively as in this Jesus quote, "Do unto others as you would have others do unto you." Another positively stated version is this one attributed to Muhammad, "Not one of you is a believer until he loves for his brother what he loves for himself." [7]

These different versions may lead to different results and ought to be looked at critically. For example, when stated in some positive ways, the "golden rule" may lead to not-so-golden results. George Bernard Shaw was not necessarily joking when he said, "Do not do unto others as you would have them do unto you. Their tastes may not be the same." Nonetheless the existence of some kind of "golden rule" within many different traditions indicates the probable existence of a factor or factors that transcend any one tradition. An individual may at least pause to consider that his or her particular tradition does not necessarily provide the sole approach to morality.

Humanists consider it likely that common requirements of human living and social life have led religions to incorporate such teachings into their doctrines. Humanists, whether or not they consider themselves religious, can look for and find wisdom in many religious traditions without emphasizing or accepting the supernatural and dogmatic aspects that often accompany them. "Enjoy the fruit and throw away the rind." Of course, one person's fruit may be another person's rind.

Non-Religious Traditions of Humanism

Since the Renaissance, non-religious (secular) forms and sources of humanism have included non-religious traditions of literature and the fine arts; democratic theory and practice; scientific theorizing and investigation; and the eighteenth-century Enlightenment. A variety of non-religious, humanistic philosophies grew from Classical roots and were nourished by Renaissance and Enlightenment thinkers. These non-religious traditions continued developing new forms as they moved into the nineteenth century.

The Renaissance de-emphasis of religious themes in the arts and literature marked a return to the Classical emphasis on all aspects of life in this world. Since that time the arts and literature have become increasingly secular in outlook.

Democratic theory and practice evolved by criticizing religiously-justified authoritarian governments. Many people now accept that a government constitutes not a divinely-ordained but a humanly-created entity that ought to operate for the benefit of all of its citizens. Seventeenth-century philosophers like Baruch Spinoza and John Locke provided compelling arguments for liberal democratic governments.

The publication in 1543 of Copernicus' work provides a useful marker for the start of what became known as the "Scientific Revolution." The work of the "natural philosophers," i.e., scientists, combined mathematical theorizing with experimental observation to gain precise understanding of the 'physical' world. Others, inspired in one or another way by this new viewpoint, attempted to extend aspects of it into other areas of philosophy and human life. Although the term "science" at one time was used to label any form of human knowledge, by the nineteenth century it had become equivalent with the exact theoretical and experimental work of the "natural philosophers."[8] Since Copernicus, scientific activities have accelerated the movement from supernaturalistic to naturalistic views in biology, geography, astronomy, geology, prehistory, meteorology, chemistry, physics, medicine, philology, biblical studies, and other areas.

The torch of Renaissance humanism and of science was taken up by eighteenth-century writers, artists and scientists of the Enlightenment. They felt emboldened by the Copernican Revolution, which had overturned the geocentric view of the universe, and by Newton's 'universal' laws of physics. As a result, they sought to turn the 'light' of reason onto other areas and to question established authorities and institutions in religion, politics and culture. Enlightenment thinking took a strong hold in eighteenth-century France, where intellectuals such as Voltaire and Montesquieu made bold critiques of religion, politics and culture. In Germany, the Enlightenment was represented by philosopher Immanuel Kant, with his motto "Sapere aude!" (Dare to know!),[9] and aphorism-writing scientist Georg Christoph Lichtenberg, who wrote, "To doubt things which are now believed without any investigation whatsoever, that's the main point everywhere."[10] Meanwhile on the British Isles, the Enlightenment included people like David Hume and Adam Smith. (Note: I don't see the antisemitism of Voltaire and Kant as a failure of humanism. Their prejudice against Jews represents those men's sad failure to shine sufficient humanistic 'light' on their own formulating.)

Humanistic Viewpoints

Non-religious (or mostly non-religious) philosophical viewpoints such as Freethought, Naturalism, Materialism, Skepticism, Epicureanism and Stoicism have also contributed to the humanist outlook. I briefly discuss these non-religious philosophies here.

Inspired by the work of "natural philosophers," the Freethought (Rationalist) Movement—popular terms for skepticism about religion—date back at least to Enlightenment times. Freethinkers have had as their *raison d'etre* the rational criticism of religion, revelation and 'God'. Some freethinkers have boldly expressed their atheism or agnosticism. Others, like Thomas Paine, have considered themselves Deists. Rejecting Christianity, Deists (there are still a few around) formulated that an impersonal God had started the newtonian clockwork and then left its operations to the laws of nature. Still others, following Spinoza, argued for what later became known as Pantheism, a view which sees impersonal Nature as the only reality and sees it as Divine. Schopenhauer, although an admirer of Spinoza, later argued that "to call the world 'God' is not to explain it; it is only to enrich our language with a superfluous synonym for the word 'world'."[11]

views of some humanistically-inclined formulators starting in the latter half of the nineteenth century, including Charles S. Peirce, Oliver Wendell Holmes, Jr., William James, F. C. S. Schiller, and John Dewey. These individuals had in common "...the notion that the world is still incomplete, still in the making, and that man is a real agent in determining the character and direction of developments yet to come." [20] Pragmatism thus labels a number of differing approaches that focus especially on the changing and unfixed aspects of 'meanings', 'truths', 'values' due to the role of human activity in our interpretations of words, symbols and events. Not surprisingly, pragmatism also emphasizes the practical applications of these understandings.

Two nineteenth-century thinkers, Soren Kierkegaard and Freidrich Nietszche, directly inspired the broad movement of twentieth-century formulating known as "existentialism." Existentialism labels a wide-range of differing philosophies which share the attitude that "...philosophy should begin neither with axioms nor with doctrines, neither with ideas nor with sense impressions, but with experiences that involve the whole individual." [21] The humanist theme was struck by Kierkegaard, who, despite his theism, echoed Stirner with his emphasis on the importance of the individual and his/her everyday experience. Nietszche bridged pragmatist and existential approaches, expressing a passionate concern for a critical approach and creative response to a life without God.

Sigmund Freud, who spanned the nineteenth and twentieth centuries, counts as an important naturalistic humanist influence. His formulation of unconscious factors in human behavior and his development of psychoanalysis broadened people's views of human motivation. Recent attempts to portray Freud's work as nothing more than pseudo-science do incalculable harm to the advance of knowledge about ourselves.

Without whitewashing some of the untenable claims and methods of Freud and some of his followers, I assert that Freud made some great discoveries that should not be abandoned because of an overzealous and dogmatic 'skepticism'. According to Paul Edwards, a skeptical humanist philosopher and distinguished editor of the *Encyclopedia of Philosophy*, Freud's great discoveries include parapraxis (slips of tongue), transference and repression. Edwards has also noted the importance of Freud's student, Wilhelm Reich, who discovered how neuroses and other problems can become anchored in a person's musculature, an area that Korzybski explored as well.[22]

By the end of the nineteenth century, there was little doubt about the effects of science on the rest of culture. Historian Andrew Dickson White wrote about "...the atmosphere of thought engendered by the development of all sciences during the last three centuries." White, a founder and the first president of Cornell University as well as a distinguished U.S. diplomat, said "Vast masses of myths, legend, marvel, and dogmatic assertion, coming into this atmosphere, have been dissolved and are now dissolving quietly away like icebergs drifted into the Gulf Stream." [23] Another century has now passed and it appears, as of 2003, that we still have some very big icebergs ahead of us.

Chinese and Indian Humanism

In this sorely incomplete attempt to survey humanist roots up to the start of the twentieth century, I want to at least note non-European humanistic traditions such as those in China and India (among other places neglected by me).

I mention here the tradition of Chinese philosophy, exemplified in this statement from Confucius, "It is not truth that makes man great, but man that makes truth great." [24] Confucianism emphasizes social harmony and rules for moral living. It became the basis of Chinese Classical education.

Should we describe humanism as a religion or not? That depends. "Religion" commonly gets defined in terms such as this: "the service and worship of God or the supernatural."[4] So it may create confusion to try to stretch religious language to include naturalistic, 'materialistic', skeptical and scientific viewpoints. Advocates of such views often experience the language and trappings of religion with distaste.

Religious humanists tend to have a 'stretched', functionalist view of religion. Accordingly, any worldview and its attendant ethical attitudes and community expressions can be called 'religious'. This follows from William James' emphasis on religion's "functional value" as a means by which people derive psychological, moral, group, aesthetic and existential meanings for their lives. By the functionalist definition, 'religion' provides the way that humans cope with these dimensions of life.[5] However, many people understand religion to involve theism, i.e., belief in a personal (person-like) God or Gods. Thus one interpretation of the functionalist view can mistakenly take it as requiring that only those who believe in such a 'God' can fulfill these human needs. Surely, religion related to theistic belief involves *a* way, not *the only* way of serving these needs.

The functionalist definition of religion has thus become subject to abuse and misunderstanding. For example, extreme right-wing fundamentalist Christians in the U.S. have claimed that teaching the theory of evolution in science classrooms constitutes an imposition of the secular humanist religion.

In 1980, responding to attacks on "secular humanism" by the religious right, Kurtz founded the Council for Democratic and Secular Humanism, now renamed the Council for Secular Humanism. He also founded the magazine *Free Inquiry*, and published the *Secular Humanist Declaration*. These provide a fully secular alternative for humanists who find no appeal in the language, form or content of any religion. Kurtz has emphasized that "secular humanism is not a religion—for it does not postulate a supreme being or a supernatural or divine reality, nor does it have a creed, a dogma, or prayers." [6]

Religious humanists, such as the signers of *Humanist Manifesto I* and, more recently, members of the Fellowship of Religious Humanists, the Society of Humanistic Judaism, and Ethical Culture, while professing a naturalistic philosophy continue to find important the appearance and language of 'religion', 'faith' and 'spirituality'.

Regretting the split between religious and secular humanists, religious humanist Howard Radest has expressed the view that "modern Humanism's lack of coherence...might find a more hopeful resolution were polarization over religion settled." [7]

A Humanistic Spectrum

A resolution to the division within the life-stance of humanism can result by accepting rather than regretting the differences between its religious and secular versions.

Among the humanist figures I discussed in the previous chapter—a small sampling based on personal study and preference—one can find a variety of viewpoints toward religion. Montaigne, for example, "saw himself as being a good Catholic and, on a visit to Rome, felt entitled to ask for an audience with the Pope." [8] Thomas Paine, a deist, believed in an indifferent creator underlying the order of the universe. Spinoza, a pantheist, equated 'God' with nature. His naturalistic view of the universe appears atheistic when shorn of 'religious' language. Non-believing humanists include Hume, Mill and T.H. Huxley.

What qualities made these people humanists apart from their religious or non-religious beliefs? The attitude of humanism as I define it here, whether religious or secular, revolves around the style with which we hold our beliefs. Do we hold our basic beliefs or viewpoints tentatively, openly, inquiringly and tolerantly? Do we take a non-fundamentalist, *fallibilist* viewpoint which assumes that *"all of our present interpretations of the universe are subject to revision or replacement"*?[9] Avoiding the closed, dogmatic and intolerant attitude of "the true believer" or fundamentalist seems central to a humanist perspective.

A closed, dogmatic, fundamentalist attitude involves maintaining an underlying view of the world as dangerous and of humans as helpless. It involves looking for absolute authorities treated unquestioningly. With a closed attitude, one accepts or rejects others based on those others' beliefs. A closed orientation includes stereotyping, intolerance and preference for the use of force when dealing with opponents. Dogmatic people tend to overlook internal inconsistencies in their own viewpoints. Concurrently, they seek to protect their views from contradictory evidence.[10]

In contrast, people with open, skeptical, fallibilist attitudes don't view the world as necessarily hostile. An open orientation involves seeing the possibility for humans to exert a limited but significant control over their own lives. Open individuals tend to question authorities and don't require absolute certainty. They avoid identifying people with their beliefs, avoid stereotyping, work to remain tolerant of those with whom they disagree, and justify force only for physical self-defense. Non-dogmatic, skeptical individuals concern themselves with reason and evidence and show a willingness to revise their opinions when necessary.[11]

On the next page, Figure 1 shows a humanist spectrum based on these distinctions (the lines are dotted to indicate a 'fuzzy' or gradient continuum of categories). Religious views—in the sense of theism—postulate a supernatural realm. Non-religious views, on the other hand, accept this world, the natural realm, as the only one we can and do know. The area above the horizontal line represents closed, dogmatic systems of belief, or fundamentalism. Religious fundamentalism includes fanatical systems like Islamism (a militant, totalitarian movement that 'infects' the Islamic world) or extreme right-wing Christianity. Non-religious fundamentalist ideologies include Stalinism and the Khmer Rouge movement. The area below the line represents fallibilism—the open, skeptical area of humanism.

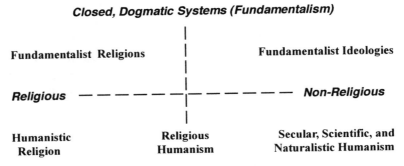

Closed, Dogmatic Systems (Fundamentalism)

Fundamentalist Religions   **Fundamentalist Ideologies**

Religious — — — — — — — — — — *Non-Religious*

Humanistic   **Religious**   **Secular, Scientific, and**
Religion   **Humanism**   **Naturalistic Humanism**

Open, Skeptical Systems (Fallibilism)

Figure 1 Humanist Spectrum

"Humanistic Religion" (as I define it here) includes the views of those tolerant members of religious faiths who, while embracing their beliefs, also admit that they don't necessarily possess the one and only 'Truth'. Major elements of at least some religious traditions, like Buddhism and Judaism, appear to me especially conducive to a humanistic outlook and contain a great deal of secular wisdom. Other religions, such as much of popular, present-day (2003) Islam, seem to make things especially difficult for humanistic believers. Nonetheless, to the extent that religious Muslims question accepted Islamic dogmas and retain a more open outlook, they can behave as humanistic Muslims.

I here use the term "Religious Humanism" to include individuals and groups who wish to retain and redefine at least some of the rituals and language of religion while they more or less embrace a secular, naturalistic, non-theistic point of view. For example, Spinoza, Paine, the signers of *Humanist*

Manifesto I, and the movements of Humanistic and Reconstructionist Judaism belong in this category. Religious humanism thus straddles 'religious' and more clearcut secular approaches.

In the scheme presented here "Secular, Scientific, and Naturalistic Humanism" constitutes the third main grouping. These three terms refer to a similar humanistic outlook, although they bring out different aspects of it. Different individuals may prefer one term over another. The term "secular" refers to non-religious areas of living, in particular aspects of public life and government where the possibility exists of transcending the perspective of one particular religious group. Thus "secular humanism" emphasizes what even religious people do when they are not involved in strictly religious matters.

"Scientific humanism" has been used by various people to emphasize the important relation of a scientific attitude and approach to the secular perspective. In his book *The Promise of Scientific Humanism* (published in 1940), Oliver Reiser made a comment which still seems appropriate (2003):

> Among modern groups the "scientific humanists" stand alone in telling us that we must go forward rather than backward, that we need not less science but more. These newer humanists may agree with our cultural recidivists and crisis religionists that the modern world needs badly a spiritual revolution, but they insist that it will have to be one inspired by a scientific understanding of nature; it must be guided by intelligence.[12]

Both "secular humanism" and "scientific humanism" qualify as *non-supernaturalistic,* or in positive terms, *naturalistic* approaches. Naturalism, as previously noted, refers to the viewpoint which holds that we can best understand nature, i.e., life, the universe and everything, by means of scientific methods. The fact that scientific methods work as well as they do implies that nature, ourselves included, has a certain structure.

Reflecting this, some secular and scientifically-oriented humanists—like me—prefer to label their approach "Naturalistic Humanism." Naturalistic humanism has a broad focus which includes but goes beyond what most people think of as 'science' or 'scientific methods'. It explores the basic assumptions about nature that seem most likely to underlie the success of scientific approaches at a given date. It applies the perspective of philosophical naturalism to humanistic concerns, including what a scientific attitude entails. It extends this outlook to personal, practical, ethical and social problems. It remains open to the importance and influence of music, art, literature, and other aspects of culture and living beyond science.

Naturalistic humanism has at its core a non-dogmatic, probabilistic attitude. This results, to a significant extent, from the fact that we can naturalistically study the scientific approach itself. We can therefore expect science and the philosophy of naturalism to evolve as we learn more about ourselves and the rest of the universe.

As an alternative to "naturalistic humanism" some people prefer the label "humanistic naturalism." Humanist scholar Warren Allen Smith writes:

> If...forced to choose a label for his philosophical outlook and based upon findings of the present research [Smith's book, *Who's Who In Hell: A Handbook and International Directory for Humanists, Freethinkers, Naturalists, Rationalists, and Non-Theists*], the present author would respond "humanistic naturalism" for the following reasons: (a) my basic outlook is naturalistic, not supernaturalistic; (b) the scientific method of reasoning is paramount in my search for truths; and (c) the humanities supply my inspiration for the good life.[13]

Pantheism skirts somewhere along a fuzzy boundary between naturalistic and religious humanism. Pantheists do not accept the existence of a personal 'God'. Like Spinoza, they

ciplines. Although new interdisciplinary fields have evolved, there exists a certain amount of resistance to those who seek a synthesis among fields.

Scientists may hide behind claims of value-neutrality. Philosophers may hesitate to descend to the level of practical life application of their work. Nonetheless, knowledge has human consequences. A continuing need exists for those who can survey and analyze general developments in various fields of scientific knowledge, philosophy, etc., and synthesize them in the context of humanistic values and concerns. A broad view of the relations and general principles among various disciplines can serve scientists, philosophers and laypeople.

A synthesized worldview, at a date, can bring the seemingly separate fields of 'science' and 'philosophy' into a more inclusive framework. Such a framework does not quite qualify as either 'science' or 'philosophy', as these terms have come to be commonly understood. Instead, it involves a 'fuzzy', borderland area of philosophy-science: both a philosophical science and a naturalistic philosophy. This borderland fosters the love of wisdom sought by earlier philosophers. But, rather than expect 'eternal truths', modern practical philosophers recognize that knowledge changes and grows. Therefore the worldview of naturalistic-humanist, practical philosophy needs to be reformulated and communicated to the public in each generation.

Scientific Inquiry

A scientific worldview also provides naturalistic humanists with a method of inquiry that they see as applicable in a generalized form to all aspects of life.

What values underlie a scientific way of life? An openness toward revising one's beliefs, and considering those of others, seems basic. That, and an ardent regard for preserving the freedom to inquire.

Such openness involves examining one's viewpoints and those of others in terms of logic and observable evidence. Naturalistic humanists see as urgent the necessity to enlarge this attitude within the general public. Thus, they have great interest in the educational movement known as "critical thinking." A naturalistic humanist approach to teaching critical thinking seeks to extend the good practice of open-minded inquiry out of the laboratory and into everyday problem-solving and ethical concerns.

Ethical Life-Stance

British humanist Harry Stopes-Roe developed the term *life-stance* to label: "The style and content of an individual's or a community's relationship with that which is of ultimate importance; the presuppositions of this, and consequences for life that flow from it." [5] This seems roughly equivalent to eupraxsophy or practical philosophy.

Ethical consequences that flow from the life-stance of naturalistic humanism take shape from its scientific worldview and its commitment to critical inquiry. That sounds like pretty heavy going. However, for each of us, it can be boiled down to a fairly simple-sounding question: *How do I live the good life without 'God'?* For a start I'd like to clarify the terms of the question:

• "Live...Life": Being alive, in our case, as humans. We enter the world in the middle, like a movie that's already started, and leave before the never-ending non-conclusion. We don't know the length of our lifespan. In the time that we have we interact with and influence whatever and whomever we encounter.

• "*The* Good": may imply that there's one best way of living life; accurate in some respects, which I'll return to. Perhaps, in another sense, it turns out more useful to consider, "*a* good life," since the details of what constitutes such a life will be different for each of us.

• "God": Many people, particularly some religious humanists, "new agers," etc., seem to have a broad and shifting meaning for "God," a vague, higher, 'spiritual' power outside of any particular religion. Here I will use the common definition: a person-like, supernatural entity to whom one prays, on whom one relies for hope and comfort; usually embedded in a religion, which provides rituals, sense of security, community, and a way to deal with death.

Living without 'God'

As humans understand more fully how the world works, there seems less need, at least scientifically, to resort to supernaturalistic explanations. We humans are a part of the universe and, according to the best knowledge presently available, originated as products of natural evolutionary processes. The present (2003) scientific worldview provides no definitive evidence of a cosmic purpose-giver outside of nature.

Many people, perhaps the majority, find this insight too stark and severe. Can human life have 'meaning' without a purpose ordained by a supernatural purpose-giver? If no such 'God(s)' exist, what basis do we have for behaving ethically?

Many theists maintain that ethics, how we ought to act, must be guided by 'God's law' and goaded by the divine 'carrot' and 'stick' of heaven and hell.

Different religions base their divine authority for ethics, the good life, etc., on different revelations as laid out in different holy books. Which 'absolute' authority do we choose? Might not this diversity of religious claims indicate the fallible human origins of religion?

Whether or not a supernatural order-giver exists, its existence cannot provide a basis for morality. Religionists may consider an act immoral because 'God' says so, as interpreted by the religious authorities of their choice. However, making ethical standards solely dependent on God's will makes God into an arbitrary despot with us as his or her oppressed subjects. Must we bow and scrape before the capricious and inconsistent edicts of such a deity, depending on his or her whim to determine 'right' from 'wrong'?

At this point, theistic believers in a personal God typically retreat to arguments about Divine mysteries and the limited nature of human understanding. Where does that leave human reason? As far as I can see, the appeal to divine authority to justify ethical decisions constitutes an abrogation of reasonable ethical decision-making.

The naturalistic humanist proceeds without such a God. We consider that what can be created by humans under the heading of 'God' can be created without relying on such an entity. The 'meaning of life' comes from each individual. Each of us can discover/create our own 'meanings', purposes, etc., for ourselves. An ethical life stance, which includes a view of a good life, can be based on human standards, independent of one's belief or disbelief in 'God'

Living as Humans

Paul Goodman nicely described some individual and social aspects basic to living a good life: he wanted "a society in which children have bright eyes, nobody is pushed around, rivers are clean, and in which there is useful work, tasty food, and occasionally satisfying nookie." [6]

As this quote indicates, human values have their basis in human needs. We live as organisms with others in a world with a particular structure. Given how we and the world in which we live are constructed, some general standards, values, principles, etc., rather than others, appear to provide more of a chance of enhancing our own and others' well-being.

Does the fact that our values have an emotional basis in human needs mean that we can't use rational and up-to-date scientific knowledge and attitudes to deal with questions about values and ethics? Some people seem to think so. They have pointed out that scientific knowledge, involving statements of fact, do not in themselves tell us what we ought to do. True. Yet we create too sharp a division between 'reason' and 'emotion', between what 'is' and what we ought to do, if we place values and ethical decision-making beyond the realm of a scientific attitude.

Propelled by a basic "life force," we can develop individual and social ethical values that do not seem simply arbitrary. Rather, they relate to commonalities that human beings—products of natural evolution—share.

The work of Abraham Maslow seems especially relevant in understanding the values which flow from our common human needs. Maslow, a psychologist and naturalistic humanist, stimulated the development of humanistic psychology in the 1950s and 60s.

Maslow's research led him to formulate a hierarchy of needs. Each level of needs, listed here, is built upon the previous levels (although higher levels may also influence lower ones). Levels include: *Basic Physiological*—hunger, thirst, sex, sleep, etc.; *Safety*—to live, move about without fear; *Belongingness* and *Love*; *Esteem*—strength, competence, independence, recognition, appreciation, dominance, status; *Self-actualization* (less well defined)—to know and understand self and world; aesthetic appreciation and expression; care and nurturing of others.

The term "self-actualization" originated with neurologist Kurt Goldstein. Although used and elaborated by Maslow, he came to prefer the term "full humanness" because many people misunderstood and misused "self-actualization" and it became associated with self-indulgence. For Maslow and for my purposes, self-actualization involves not only developing your idiosyncratic potentials (self), but your cultural potentials—your ability to contribute to world betterment.

Let's further explore the notion of self-actualization, becoming more fully human. In the following section, I discuss some of the qualities that seem to make up the values which come from humans actualizing themselves in society with others.

Becoming More Fully Human

Maslow studied a number of individuals whom he considered self-actualized (or at least close to it). In observing these people, he developed a set of characteristics for describing their behavior.[7] As you can see, individual and social aspects of humanness come together in this list. I detail the characteristics here because they seem to me to serve as useful guideposts for an ethical life-stance, living a good life. As a way of clarifying their interrelatedness, my wife and I have organized them under five main categories of behavior. (Italicized labels are Maslow's. Descriptions are ours.) They include:

I. Reality-based

• *Clear perception of reality*. More efficient and more comfortable relations with it. This includes comfort with the unknown and a capacity to detect sham, i.e. having a good crap-detector. Doubt and uncertainty provide a stimulating challenge rather than create fear.

• *Acceptance (self, others, nature)*. Seeing nature as it is, including ourselves, and enjoying ourselves fully; accepting illness and death as part of reality; and feeling appropriately bad about discrepancies between what is possible and what currently is present.

• *Imperfections*. Being fully human does not produce or rely on "perfection." Imperfections accepted.

II. Connectedness to Others

• *Gemeinschaftsgefühl*. This connotes a feeling of connectedness and kinship with fellow humans (despite their sometimes significant shortcomings) and a desire to help them; also an ability to forgive.

• *Interpersonal relations.* This involves especially close ties with relatively few individuals, in addition to broad kindness and compassion for most others. (Not likely a "social butterfly" or a "glad-hander.")

• *Democratic character structure.* Deep respect for others, with an ability to learn from just about everybody; anti-authoritarian.

• *Problem-centering.* This involves focusing on problems outside of ourselves, with emphasis on contributing to the good of humankind.

III. Connectedness to Self

• *Detachment; need for privacy.* This includes not only the ability to be alone, but liking solitude; an ability to view events, including ourselves, as if from a distance and thus evaluate relatively clearly; and an ability to concentrate.

• *Autonomy.* Independence from culture and environment. This allows for stability in the face of frustrations, deprivations, etc.

• *Resistance to enculturation.* Outward apparent conventionality is combined with an inner-directedness.

IV. Openness to Experience

• *Continued freshness of appreciation.* Experiencing, as if fresh and new, the basic goods of life, which creates a rich, sensual life. Being "with it" in a most direct way. Present, e.g., when eating, walking, listening, reading— are you here now?

• *Creativeness.* A generalized ability to view and react to the world in the open, fresh way of a child.

• *Spontaneity.* Giving free reign to inner thoughts, allowing for an inner unconventionality, which is expressed outwardly in appropriate situations.

• *Playfulness.*

- *Oceanic feeling.* A full involvement and concentration leading to ecstasy, awe and wonder, and self-forgetfulness; what some might call "mystical" experiences, but with no necessary religious (extra-neural, 'transcendent') connection or association.

V. Humanistic Values

- *Philosophical, unhostile sense of humor.* Humor based on poking fun at humans, including yourself, in general—our foolishness or trying to appear bigger than we are, etc.—rather than at individuals. This often is intrinsic to a situation, and spontaneous.

- *Discrimination between means and ends.* Clarity about worthwhile goals, while enjoying the "means" toward those goals as if they were ends in themselves. (E.g., nutritious diet as end; food shopping and preparation as means, also ends as sources of enjoyment).

- *Resolution of dichotomies.* Higher-level resolution leads to internal unity; results in an encompassing wholistic perspective.

- *Values.* Based on acceptance of self, human nature, much of social life and nature and physical realities, they flow from other aspects of self-actualization discussed above.

Finally, I add, humans should not forget an important guideline from cats for living a good life: *sleep is under-rated— take naps!*

What can we make of these characteristics of self-actualized, more fully human people? As I said, I note them here because they seem to me to serve as useful targets for aiming our efforts at living a good life. This list can serve as a stimulus for considering for yourself how you really want to exist in the world—to live "a" and "the" good life. With all of this possible for us humans living our spans of time, do we absolutely need untestable beliefs in a cosmic supernatural being called "God?"

Ethical Decision-Making

The process of critical, scientific, ethical deliberating involves a respect for facts and a commitment to uncovering and criticizing values and beliefs. With such a commitment, the results of an inquiry are not completely predetermined. None of us can approach ethical questions with a completely blank slate. That does not even appear desirable. Yet a humanistic approach to ethics (within which I would include social policy and politics) cannot depend on static answers that have already been set in place by some authority. It requires accepting the duty of questioning, evaluating and revising our beliefs.

The practical philosophy of naturalistic humanism impels us to act not dogmatically and unquestioningly but rather as inquiringly, openly and skeptically as we can. As new developments occur in science, technology and social life, new problems occur, with us as the guinea pigs.

For example, the issues of abortion, euthanasia, informed consent, cloning, genetic and reproductive engineering, etc., have become more pressing as the technology of biology and medicine becomes more effective and powerful. Life and death decisions may depend upon competing theories and values of bioethics. The degradation of the environment appears ever more important, with competing claims or disclaimers of responsibility from government, business, and individuals. Policy decisions that affect the future of our planet depend on competing views of environmental ethics.

Knowledge becomes vital in a naturalistic humanist approach to these and other problems. In line with this, naturalistic humanists support and make use of basic and applied research in the sciences, including social/behavioral sciences. Too many social policy decisions are made on the basis of religious or political ideology. Unfortunately, too many people feel that they already know the causes and solutions of com-

plex social problems. We have much evidence of the consequences of ill-considered laws, social programs and policies
both of the 'right' and 'left'—as well as the 'center'.

From the viewpoint of naturalistic humanism, the political,
social, economic, psychological, etc., causes and consequences
of social problems and solutions need to be studied much more
intensively in a scientific manner. Institutions that make policies
need to have a greater responsiveness to such research and an
openness to change.

Democratic Values

Both in our more personal decisions and in the broader
social sphere, humanist practical philosophy involves a commitment to democratic values, the values of an open society.
I'm not talking about any particular political party or nation
here. I'm referring to values which include dedication to civil
liberties and the rights of free expression and privacy. Religious and cultural pluralism come under these liberties as does
separation of church (synagogue, mosque, etc.) and state.

Philosopher Karl Popper remains perhaps the most well-
known exponent of this view, presented in his two-volume
book, *The Open Society and its Enemies*. However, others before and since have written about the open society, democratic
values and what makes them inseparable from humanism.

Humanists do not and cannot always agree about what
party to vote for and what specific social policies to support.
(However, the practical philosophy of humanism may at times
provide constraints as to what parties and policies *cannot* be
consistently supported from that position.) Political positions
have a close connection with economic issues. American humanism as represented in *Humanist Manifesto I* had allied itself with a vision of "[a] socialized and co-operative economic
order." [8] More recently humanists have debated both for socialist (emphasizing equality) and libertarian (emphasizing individual liberty) positions—and for positions in between.

Humanists may legitimately differ in these areas. However, it behooves them as humanists not to hold doctrinaire positions. Perhaps concern with either liberty or equality does not necessarily require exclusion of the other. Some balance in practice, to be determined by consequences, seems most in keeping with a naturalistic humanist perspective. In any case, the values of democracy and an open society need upholding *in practice* for any political-social-economic position to be considered an ethically humanistic one.

Humanism and General Semantics

Despite its appeal for some, an approach to life that does not necessarily depend on being religious has seemed like 'somewhat thin gruel' for others.

Some of these people may have strong, emotional pressures to look for and find absolute answers and unquestionable authorities, religious or otherwise. However, other basically humanistic individuals may have some 'sense' or 'intuition' of a 'Divine' or transcendental purpose. In addition, for some basically 'rationalist', pragmatic people, a religious affiliation may provide meaningful human connections. They may feel hesitant to drop long-standing connections with their communities of family and friends. Nevertheless, some of these individuals may still find something useful in a study of humanism, particularly naturalistic humanism, whether or not they give up their religion.

Religionists may not be the only ones who find something lacking in the secular, naturalistic form of humanism. This lifestance can seem like a lonely road sometimes. Although atheists, agnostics, humanists, etc., have become more numerous in recent years (at least in some parts of the world), many humanists may experience very little in the way of a community that shares their still-minority views. The growth of the humanist movement both in the U.S. and elsewhere has been a promising development in getting more humanists, rationalists, free thinkers, etc., involved with a fellowship of similarly-oriented individuals.

Both 'religious' and non-religious humanists may also feel frustration that the promise of humanism has not been fulfilled as they may have hoped. World society (2003) seems very far from having much of the critically rational, scientifically-oriented culture of inquiry in which humanists would like to live. Humanists may also experience personal difficulties in bringing the philosophy they espouse into practical application in their daily lives. They may observe these difficulties in the behavior of humanist friends and colleagues as well. How can we actually bring this practical philosophy into practice? Means for doing this might also have some usefulness in bringing a more critical, scientific attitude to the general public.

As I stated in Chapter 1, a significant part of the problem has resulted from narrow, inadequate views of science and a scientific attitude among humanists and within the scientific and philosophical communities. These views have involved, among other things, the restriction of science to particular methodologies or fields, over-zealous and uncritical rejection of new viewpoints and alternative views, insufficient attention to the internal and external effects of language, premature closure upon inadequate theories about insufficiently investigated issues, and the failure to provide adequate teachable approaches to a general orientation of scientific inquiry. General Semantics, the subject of Part II, provides such a teachable approach.

Many people consider it strange to treat *all* of science and mathematics as forms of human behavior. That the truths of mathematics are 'eternal', 'universal' platonic forms still remains a significant belief among many mathematicians, philosophers and scientists. It also still seems common to treat 'reason' as separate from 'emotion', and science and mathematics as worlds apart from human feeling, value and action.

These attitudes run deep. The aristotelian rules of identity, contradiction, and the excluded middle are still considered inviolable by many. Many philosophers and scientists (some of them humanists) reject the notion that our habitual language and associated evaluations entail assumptions (e.g., a separate 'mind' and 'body', 'reason' and 'emotion') which may affect our ongoing perception and behavior in untold significant and unfortunate ways.

In Part II, I take pains to demonstrate the usefulness of the general-semantics approach. I show how the habitual structure of our language and related evaluations contains a key to the problems with which naturalistic humanists, scientists, and others have been dealing. I believe it unlikely that a scientific attitude will ever become a common view unless more people take much more seriously the enormous power of our language use.

The work of Korzybski and related formulators on the relations among the 'world', 'thought', 'language', and behavior represents, I believe, a missing ingredient for humanist inquiry and scientific problem-solving. Korzybski's work and related studies can help humanists turn naturalistic humanism from a 'thin gruel' into a nourishing meal which could more likely deliver its promised possibilities. General Semantics, the non-aristotelian system which Korzybski originated, provides specific tools for making humanism workable.

Part II
Making Humanism Workable

Man is ultimately a doctrinal being. Even our language has its silent doctrines, and no activity of man is free from some doctrines, so that the kind of metaphysics a man has, is not of indifference to his world outlook and his behavior.[1]

— ALFRED KORZYBSKI

Chapter 5
Defining Humanhood

Having established the background of humanism, I present the discipline of general semantics in Part II. General Semantics provides methods for making humanist values workable. In this chapter, I discuss time-binding, the central notion motivating Korzybski's work. The following three chapters (6, 7, and 8) discuss the related assumptions which underlie GS. The remaining chapters of Part II (9 through 14), provide a formulational, practical overview of the GS system.

Korzybski and His World

Alfred Korzybski's work was motivated by deep curiosity and deep concern for his fellow humans. His wife, Mira Edgerly Korzybska, remarked that, "I had never met anyone with such a *capacity to care* for humanity-as-a-whole, as few men are capable of caring for one woman." [1]

He was born on July 3, 1879 in Warsaw, Poland, then governed by a Russian Czarist dictatorship. Both sides of his upper-class family came from the Polish landed nobility. Although some people later insisted on calling Korzybski "Count," Allen Walker Read pointed out that, "Korzybski did not seek out the title in spite of the standing of his family in the Polish aristocracy, but its use was fostered by his wife, a talented American portrait painter, who believed it was useful to her to be called 'Countess Korzybska'." [2] Korzybski's parents owned property in the city and had a farm where Korzybski spent much of his youth. He came from a long line of lawyers, mathematicians, engineers and scientists who were nourished by the long tradition of Polish humanist culture.

Korzybski and his older sister were raised by French and German governesses. They thus learned French and German in addition to Polish and Russian. Korzybski considered this multi-lingual environment significant for his later work since it prevented him from believing in word magic and attaching some special importance to one way of labeling things.[3] He later advocated that children learn at least one foreign language to encourage evaluational flexibility.[4]

The poor clay soil of the Korzybski estate required innovative methods of plowing, irrigation, etc., to be productive. Korzybski's father applied his engineering talents to turn the estate into a model farm. This example of using scientific methods to deal with practical problems likely provided young Alfred with a powerful example of possibilities that he would later apply to general psycho-social betterment.

When Korzybski was five years old, his father also provided him more directly with a "feel" for science by introducing him to the differential calculus and physical-mathematical methods. This feel and the importance of conveying it to others would stay with him for the rest of his life.

Korzybski's family was not religious and he received no religious training, despite the generally Catholic environment in Poland.[5] He remembered with fondness his closest brush with religious study, a class with a Jesuit priest who taught comparative religion in a nominally Catholic religious class. Based on this experience, he recommended the study of comparative religions to provide innoculation against narrow, sectarian dogmas.[6]

From the beginning of his life, Korzybski functioned as a "trouble shooter." Peasant and itinerant workers required supervision in the farm work. Medical problems (since there was no physician nearby), domestic and labor disputes among the workers, etc., became challenges with which the young Korzybski had to deal. These required resourcefulness, and an ability to observe and to look at things from other people's points of view.

The family raised horses and Korzybski developed exceptional skill as a rider and horse trainer. He greatly respected the intelligence of horses and claimed that they taught him a great deal of "horse-sense."[7]

Korzybski performed somewhat indifferently in school. He found that by attending closely in class and getting a broad picture of the subject matter he was able to pass his exams without much studying.[8] He constantly read on his own, however. He had ambitions to become a physicist, a mathematician or a lawyer, but found that the course of study that his parents had put him through, with no Latin or Greek, was geared toward engineering school and so prevented him from getting into a university. This disappointed him greatly. Instead he attended the Polytechnic Institute in Warsaw where he studied chemical engineering.

After engineering school, Korzybski became a teacher at a girl's school, managed his family's estate and Warsaw apartment building and traveled throughout Europe, including Italy, where he lived for a couple of years in Rome.

When he returned from Rome to the family estate, Korzybski felt dismay at the conditions of the peasant workers there and their government-enforced illiteracy. Despite Czarist laws against educating peasants, he built a schoolhouse for them. Only the machinations of his father kept him from getting sent to Siberia for this crime.

At the start of World War I, Korzybski, 35 years old, joined the Second Russian Army, working in the intelligence service. The war proved momentous for him. Assigned to get information on German battle plans, he traveled throughout the Eastern front at great personal risk, sustained injuries (some permanent) and felt deeply unsettled by the suffering he saw.

After a year at the front, he was sent as an artillery expert to Canada, where he oversaw munitions testing at the Petawawa Proving Ground. When this assignment ended,

Korzybski came to the United States, where he involved himself with various war-related tasks. With the Russian Revolution in 1917 and the breakdown of the Russian Army, Korzybski became a recruiter for the French-Polish Military Commission and lectured for the United States Government, selling Liberty Bonds. When the war ended in 1918, he decided to stay in the United States—by the mid-1920s, permanently.

Throughout the period of the war and its aftermath Korzybski wondered at the destruction and social collapse that he observed. How could it happen? What could prevent it from recurring? He was struck as well by the achievements of human civilization, which included the technology used so destructively during the war.

When engineers build buildings, they expect them to remain standing. If ever the buildings collapse, scientifically-based calculations and design principles usually can reveal what went wrong. Yet in our human interactions and social institutions, 'collapse' seems a 'normal' expectable outcome. Periodic wars, revolutions and other disasters seem neither preventable nor correctable.[9]

These concerns reflected a deeper question, "What makes humans human?" In other words, "How do human beings differ from animals?" These became burning questions for him, based on his concern for humanity and its future.

Manhood of Humanity

In New York City with his wife Mira, Alfred Korzybski stood atop the Woolworth Building, then (around 1920) the tallest building in the world. Below he saw the city streets:

> ...I was looking over New York. That enormous city, steaming, boiling with life...And I asked myself the question, how it happens, the physical side of it looking at the street, at Broadway. You saw vermin crawling, and the vermin were humans. They were so small because the height was so great, and a streetcar was a caterpillar...Looking at that,

I was much intrigued. I was fully aware that everyone of those little bits of humans there, everyone was full of joy, sorrows, and what not. And who did that tremendous thing called New York? That vermin did it. I didn't get my answer there, but I was asking how humans, little things like that with such a wealth of personal life, how in the dickens can they do such a thing as New York, London, Paris, wars, revolutions, and what not. That question popped at me, on the top of that building.[10]

(The Woolworth Building, still standing, now (2003) overlooks a gaping hole, the mass grave site of the former World Trade Center towers—definitely done by 'vermin'.)

Korzybski's answer to the question "how in the dickens can they do such a thing?" became the focus of his life work. He presented it in *Manhood of Humanity*, published in 1921. This book, using the accepted terminology of the time, addressed all "humankind–men, women and children." [11]

What did he propose? In the book, Korzybski noted that engineers use scientific-mathematical knowledge and methods to build relatively non-collapsible structures. Likewise, he contended that we might be able to apply scientific-mathematical methods to ourselves and our societies to create 'non-collapsing' social institutions. In this, he was reviving an old dream of Bacon, Descartes, Spinoza, Leibnitz, Locke, Hume and others.

By applying scientific methods to human problems, we could create a new discipline, which he labeled "human engineering," a science of human welfare. The first step in doing this involved answering the question, "What makes humans human?"

The Time-Binding Class of Life

This question asked for a definition of humanhood. Korzybski had a great concern to avoid the armchair metaphysics, with its search for 'essences' that had characterized many previous philosophical attempts to define 'Man'. Rather, Korzybski wanted to understand humans functionally, in terms of what they do. He found it necessary to build a functional definition on the basis of Darwin's naturalistic view of human evolution.

Korzybski accepted that life evolved out of non-life. Life involves specific physico-chemical configurations that emerged out of organic chemical phenomena. What characterizes life? Recognizing the unsatisfactory state of the scientific knowledge of the time (1921), he accepted that life somehow involves "autonomous activities"[12] in which, quoting biologist Jacques Loeb, "the living cell synthesizes its own complicated specific material from indifferent or nonspecific simple compounds of the surrounding medium..."[13]

Korzybski built on this to create a functional classification of life forms. For his purposes he chose to differentiate plants, animals and humans as three major groups. He characterized plants by their ability to chemically "bind" or organize the energy of the sun, storing it and using it to grow. Thus he defined plants as "chemistry-binders."

Animals use plant energy as food, either directly, or indirectly by consuming other animals. Thus they include chemistry-binding in their make-up. Animals transform this acquired energy in order to move through the dimension of space so as to acquire more energy, etc. Their lives involve marking, defending and otherwise organizing their space or territory. Thus, Korzybski defined animals as "space-binders."

Finally, we consider humans. Human beings have their own metabolisms and use plant energy. So in various ways they incorporate chemistry-binding. Humans also incorporate space-binding features. We move through space. We look like animals and share many functional characteristics with them. We domesticate animals and make use of animal products. But we humans differ from any other creature.

We have the ability to symbolize our experiences. We can organize or "bind" this symbolic information so as to receive and transmit it from one time to another at an accelerating rate. Korzybski therefore called humanity "time-binders."

Time-Binding, Culture and Biology

The human dimension of time-binding corresponds to the anthropologist's notion of culture—described by Raymond Firth as "the component of accumulated resources, immaterial as well as material, which the people inherit, employ, transmute, add to, and transmit...it includes the residual effects of social action. It is necessarily also an incentive to action." [14]

I almost agree with Ashley Montagu when he wrote that "Korzybski's conception of time-binding and the anthropological conception of culture are virtually identical in character." [15] However, as he developed his work, Korzybski very carefully eschewed characterizing any aspect of human culture—as some anthropologists did and do—as 'immaterial'. (Another crucial difference between time-binding and the culture formulation is the notion of acceleration—*potential* and actual "accelerating accelerations.")

Korzybski insisted in a very exacting way that, "All phenomena *in nature* are *natural* and should be approached as *such*." [16] He thus forthrightly maintained (in 1921) the importance of speaking and writing in such a fashion so as to keep clear that 'society' and 'culture' do *not* function in a realm separate from 'biology'.

Korzybski considered culture (i.e., 'thoughts', 'languages', 'symbols', 'images', etc.) as the natural product of the "physico-chemical base...of the human time-binding energy" [17] of individual nervous systems in association with one another. A 'thought' gets embodied in a language or some other symbolism. It represents a residual effect or product of time-binding. This effect provides a new incentive for action by modifying the physico-chemical base of the individual who created it or anyone else who interprets it. The physico-chemical base which gets so changed can produce a new 'thought' which may provide yet again some new incentive for action.

This very 'material' process, which Korzybski called his "spiral theory" of time-binding, depends explicitly on a non-linear, circular notion of causality which preceded by some years the notion of "feedback" in control theory and cybernetics. This circular or spiral process of causality has serious implications for all aspects of human culture. These implications have remained unrecognized by many experts on language and human behavior up to the present (2003).

Many scientists now affirm, with Korzybski and Jacques Loeb, *"that all life phenomena can be unequivocally explained in physico-chemical terms."* [18] Yet many people, including scientists, seem surprised by the implications of this which Korzybski clearly noted, "...if we teach humans false ideas, we affect their time-binding capacities and energies very seriously, by affecting in a wrong way the physico-chemical base." [19] As he elsewhere noted, "Neural products are stored up or preserved in extra-neural form [various observable aspects of language, symbolism, culture, etc., e.g., books], and they can be put back in the nervous system *as active neural processes*" for better and worse. [20]

In his later work, Korzybski elaborated on this spiral theory of time-binding in terms of the "self-reflexiveness" of human symbolic processes and the "circularity of human knowledge." In an interesting way, this spiral effect brings out the importance of how we humans define ourselves both as individuals and as members of the human race.

The Symbolic Class of Life

Our time-binding energies very much entail human symbolic abilities:

> The affairs of man are conducted by our own, man-made rules and according to man-made theories. Man's achievements rest upon the use of symbols. For this reason, we must consider ourselves as a symbolic, semantic class of life, and those who rule the symbols, rule us. [21]

Independently of Korzybski, philosopher Ernst Cassirer also saw the defining importance of symbolism in understanding human life. Cassirer published the three volumes of his work, *Philosophy of Symbolic Forms*, in 1923-1929, a few years after Korzybski's *Manhood of Humanity*. In a later work, *An Essay on Man*, Cassirer wrote the following, apparently unaware of Korzybski:

> Man has, as it were, discovered a new method of adapting himself to his environment. Between the receptor system and the effector system, which are to be found in all animal species, we find in man a third link which we may describe as the *symbolic system*. This new acquisition transforms the whole of human life. As compared with the other animals man lives not merely in a broader reality; he lives so to speak, in a new *dimension* of reality....Reason is a very inadequate term with which to comprehend the forms of man's cultural life in all their richness and variety. But all these forms are symbolic forms. Hence, instead of defining man as an *animal rationale*, we should define him as an *animal symbolicum*. By so doing we can designate his specific difference, and we can understand the new way open to man—the way to civilization.[22]

Korzybski, who had read Cassirer's work, dedicated his book *Science and Sanity* to the works of Cassirer, among others, which "greatly influenced my enquiry." Such scholarly acknowledgement was typical of Korzybski. Also typically of Korzybski (trained as an engineer), he formulated the symbolic mechanism in terms of time-binding, which provides a practical way to apply Cassirer's and others' insights about human culture.

Time-Binding and Progress

The GS formulation of time-binding does not aim simply at neutral description. Rather, the time-binding process involves our *potentially constructive* building upon the past, i.e., using the accumulated inheritance of symbolically-generated culture in adaptive, wise and well-informed ways. This implies at least a limited kind of progress measured by the growth of knowledge.

To progress in this way, we must apply our 'reason' to what we inherit, which means to criticize it in order to build upon it. Such progress also depends upon *how* we reason. Writers on progress presented views on the evolution of reasoning that find echoes in Korzybski's work.

For example, Auguste Comte distinguished three phases in the development of human knowledge: the theological, metaphysical and scientific stages. In the theological phase explanations for things are sought in 'God(s)' and 'spirits'. The metaphysical phase tends toward theoretical explanations detached from experience and experiment. In the scientific stage, according to Comte, theory is subordinated to observation and experiment in order to gain knowledge.

In *Manhood,* Korzybski referred to the childhood of humanity and its adulthood. In his later work he distinguished among primitive (one-valued), pre-modern (two-or few-valued, aristotelian) and modern scientific (infinite-valued, non-aristotelian) worldviews. (The first two belong to the childhood and the last to the adulthood of humanity.) These divisions roughly correspond to Comte's threefold division.

Comte's work had a flavor of optimism and a sense of the inevitability of human progress: "In a dynamical view, the progress of the race must be considered susceptible of modification only with regard to its speed, and without any reversal in the order of development, or any interval of any importance being overleaped." [23] Korzybski's work in *Manhood* seems generally consistent with Comte's notion, particularly in relation to the progress in human knowledge that time-binding entails.

Korzybski's work on time-binding, then, has connections with previous writers on 'progress'. What does his work contribute to their discussion? Korzybski's attempt to quantify 'progress', although in some ways unsatisfactory, provides a key.

The Exponential Growth of Knowledge

In *Manhood*, Korzybski formulated a 'scientific' law of progress where "…time-binding power is an exponential power or function of time"[24] expressed by the formula PR^T (P = progress; R = ratio of progress; T = number of past generations). This formula yields ever-increasing acceleration over time.[25]

While he did not adequately define the terms of the formula and while he probably erred in calling it a "law," it does not deserve to be simply tossed out because of this. I agree with Robert Anton Wilson who noted, "The math…was too simple…Nonetheless, Korzybski…was groping toward the truth: acceleration is real, and it is intimately connected with *time-binding*, the passing of signals between generations."[26]

John Allen Paulos has explained, "…a sequence grows exponentially (or geometrically) if its rate of growth is proportional to the amount of the quantity present—i.e., if each number in the sequence comes from multiplying its predecessor by the same factor." In contrast, a "sequence grows linearly (or arithmetically) if its rate of growth is constant—i.e., if each number in the sequence comes from adding the same factor to its predecessor."[27]

Korzybski theorized that the growth of knowledge in so-called physical science and technology constitutes exemplary time-binding. The relatively high rate here readily demonstrates its exponential character, he contended, showing a rapidly-rising curve that grows steeper with each generation of scientists as more and more knowledge accumulates. However, our social/behavioral knowledge, he contended, does not represent successful time-binding. It grows (if not strictly arithmetically) at a slow rate which, in comparison with the more rapidly rising growth curve of physical science, approaches a straight line.

Within the social/behavioral area we can include law, politics, economics, morals, human relationships, etc. These areas of knowledge relate to our personal and social lives. The differential growth rate between our knowledge of the 'physical' world and our knowledge of ourselves and our social relationships continues to lead to disastrous consequences as noted before: collapsing social structures (including bombed buildings and people).

We have the possibility of moving closer to the adulthood of humanity by bridging the divide between science and human affairs. A major step in this direction can occur when we abandon outdated religious and zoological definitions of ourselves. We *cannot* understand ourselves scientifically if we insist on defining ourselves as some combination of supernatural ('soul','spirit', etc.) and 'animal'. We *cannot* understand ourselves scientifically if we insist on viewing ourselves simply as 'animals' destined to play out brutal competitive games of survival of the fittest for goods and territory. (*It's becoming clear [2003] that we can't scientifically understand animals that way either.*) We *can* understand ourselves scientifically and advance human welfare by defining and studying ourselves in detail as a time-binding class of life.

A Time-Binding Organism

The boundary separating animals from humans has become more indistinct as biological study advances. Consciousness, language use (still controversial), technology, altruism, reverence, etc., appear to exist—at least to some degree—in other species such as primates, birds, etc.

Do some animals time-bind? Some non-humans can indeed start where their previous generations have left off. For example, chimpanzees establish life-long relationships within groups and their young learn all manner of things by imitation, including how to find food and use simple tools and medicinal plants. The exact procedure for using a twig to pull out 'morsels' of protein from a termite nest is not in any chimp's genes. Presumably, some past chimp 'geniuses' had to figure out that termites come out of underground nests, that they taste good, don't make you sick (unless you eat too many), and can be extricated with the appropriate tools and techniques. All of this knowledge had to be learned and carried on to the present by other chimps.

Still, as far as I know, as of 2003 nobody has found any chimpanzee libraries, laboratories or universities. (Although chimp tool 'workshops' have now been discovered.) Korzybski preferred not to talk about humans as animals. He acknowledged the difference between humans and animals as a difference of degrees. He considered this "a difference that makes a difference" to such a degree that it seemed justified to designate humans as a separate, non-animal, time-binding class of life. (Perhaps Korzybski was also influenced by his experiences in Poland, where the rights of serfs — which he defended—were devalued by calling the people "beasts.")

Stuart A. Mayper, scientist, philosopher, korzybskian scholar and former editor of the *General Semantics Bulletin*, agreed with Korzybski "that the differences between humans and non-human animals are great enough to justify setting up a third 'Kingdom' of Time-Binders—*evolved from animals*, we should insist." [28] Biological taxonomists, who specialize in classifying species according to evolutionary principles, have not taken up Korzybski's or Mayper's suggestions.

The extent of human, symbolically-based, time-binding efforts does seem to far exceed that of other organisms. Nonetheless, might it still have some usefulness to view humans as 'animals' of a sort— although preeminently time-binding ones? Could it help us to 'bear in mind' our continuity with other forms of life: bacteria, bamboos, bonobos, and buttercups, etc? Remembering our connections with the ecological web to which all organisms belong does seem vital.

Within a few centuries, human time-binding activities have altered human environments, the habitats of other organisms and the larger, ecological network to an awesome degree. Our time-binding activities now affect the immediate and the long-term lives of all creatures great and small. Yet we humans are not immune to the regularities that have been observed to operate within and among other creatures. Our quality of life and survival depends upon humanity-as-a-whole finding some harmony with its larger environment-as-a-whole.

Time-Binding and Cooperation

Because it emphasizes a larger, cooperative context for human actions, viewing humans as time-binders can lead to a greater sense of responsibility toward other humans, other organisms, and the larger environment within which we live .

The notion of time-binding challenges the "Social Darwinist" notion of animalistic "survival of the fittest" as a justification for short-sighted human greed, selfishness, and unqualified competition. Rather,

> ..."survival of the fittest" for human beings *as such*—that is, for *time-binders*—is survival *in time*, which means intellectual or spiritual competition, struggle for excellence, for making the *best* survive. The-fittest-in-time—those who make the best survive—are those who do the most in producing values for all mankind including *posterity*.[29]

Consider these time-binding questions:

• Can you find anything that you have made, arranged, organized, composed, written, etc., that did not in some way depend on the contributions of others?

• Take an object from your pocket, desktop, or around your house or office. How did it get here? Where did you get it from? Trace things back a bit. How was it manufactured? How many people were involved in making it and getting it to the store or place where you bought it or got it from? Did some time exist before that kind of object existed? Who invented it? What other inventions were required to produce it? Et cetera.

• How did you come to be reading this book?

Although each of us can make innovations, none of our creations are made solely on our own. None of us, completely from scratch, invented the language that we speak and write or the tools with which we make things. *Recognizing ourselves as time-binders implies acknowledging our debts and feeling grateful to those who came before us.*

Considering those who will come after us rounds out the cooperative view of time-binding. Nurturing a child, communicating our 'ideas' in writing, teaching, etc., or transmitting them through our personal example or in inventions, artifacts, etc., we establish ourselves as the present link in a chain that connects the past with the future.

What do you want your legacy to be?—a time-binding question formulated by my wife, Susan Presby Kodish, in her personal coaching work. You won't live forever. Usually we think of a legacy as an amount of money or property left for an inheritance. Here I mean something different, although it could include these kinds of things. Rather, by legacy I mean something related to how you would like to be remembered after you've gone. This doesn't have to be by way of some great masterpiece you've left that everyone recognizes or a monument erected in your memory. Rather, by legacy I mean more precisely: what difference you would like your presence to have made on others, on the world (whether or not recognized). Don't think that because your name may be forgotten in a few hundred years—likely sooner— that your existence in the world now doesn't make a difference.

Professor J. T. Shotwell wrote about two kinds of immortality:
...the immortality of monuments,—of things to look at and recall; and the immortality of use,—of things which surrender their identity but continue to live, things forgotten but treasured, and incorporated in the vital forces of society. Thought can achieve both kinds. It embodies itself in forms—like epics, cathedrals and even engines—where the

endurance depends upon the nature of the stuff used, the perfection of the workmanship and the fortune of time. But it also embodies itself in use; that is, it can continue to work, enter into other thought and continue to emit its energy even when its original mold is broken up.[30]

As a time-binder, you will leave a legacy, willy-nilly, whether you do it purposefully or not. What do you want yours to be?

Time-Binding and Economics

Korzybski was not the first to note the cooperative process of time-binding. This process was touched upon by others—in the long-standing tradition of discussion on "the idea of progress"—without getting labeled as such. (See, for example, da Vinci's description in Chapter 2, page 34.)

Another description by late nineteenth-century political economist Henry George, in his work *Progress and Poverty*, showed that he understood the process of time-binding quite well:

> The narrow span of human life allows the individual to go but a short distance, but though each generation may do but little, yet generations, succeeding to the gain of their predecessors, may gradually elevate the status of mankind, as coral polyps, building one generation upon the work of the other, gradually elevate themselves from the bottom of the sea."[31]

What, then, distinguishes Korzybski's work? Korzybski closed in upon the process that George and others had noted and discussed. Korzybski *labeled it* and made it the starting point of a science of humanity. As I later elaborate, we should not disparage the power of labeling.

We can use a new label or term to represent an entire theory. Once we have reached adequate agreement about what we mean by a term (this may sometimes require long, drawn out discussion and study), we can use the single term rather than repeating each time the long, drawn out discussion. A

new term can thus allow us—more easily than before we had
the term—to bring out and isolate new, salient and useful aspects of experience; summarize relations; make new distinctions and draw forth implications. The explicit and general
theory represented by the term "time-binding," has implications that can be drawn forth for a variety of areas including
politics and economics.

What are some of the economic-political implications of the
cooperative view of time-binding? Korzybski defined wealth as:

> ...those things—whether they be material commodities or
> forms of knowledge and understanding—that have been
> produced by the time-binding energies of humanity, and
> according to which *nearly all the wealth of the world at
> any given time* is the *accumulated fruit of the toil of past
> generations*—the living work of the dead.[32]

Economically, money represents but doesn't constitute
wealth. Korzybski warned "against confusing the '*making*' of
money by hook or crook, by trick or trade, with the *creating*
of wealth, by the product of labor." [33]

From this time-binding view of wealth, Korzybski criticized both capitalists and socialists:

> There are capitalists and capitalists; there are socialists and
> socialists. Among the capitalists there are those who want
> wealth—mainly the fruit of dead men's toil—for them-
> selves. Among the socialists there are those—the orthodox
> socialists—who seek to disperse it. The former do not
> perceive that the product of the labor of the dead is itself
> dead if not quickened by the energies of living men. The
> orthodox socialists do not perceive the tremendous ben-
> efits that accrue to mankind from the accumulation of
> wealth, if *rightly used.*[34]

He suggested that " 'capitalistic' lust to *keep* for SELF and
'proletarian' lust to *get* for SELF are both of them space-binding
lust—animal lust—beneath the level of time-binding life." [35]

Korzybski proposed that an alternative political-economic

approach must result from a time-binding perspective. He did not elaborate its details, but at its base it would involve a political-economic order, neither 'socialist' nor 'capitalist' as many people understand those terms, but focused on cooperation which would benefit all humans. Wars represented for Korzybski the disaster of applying time-binding energies to a common aim that goes no further than narrow group political-economic interests.

Time-Binding and Democracy

The relation of time-binding to democracy (government functioning in the direction of a more or less open society) deserves some mention here. Korzybski's student and colleague, Guthrie Janssen, explored this relation and considered democratic values at the heart of a time-binding view. In his article, "Time-Binding: Functional Basis of Democracy," he wrote that in a democracy:

> A primary requirement would seem to be that it should tend to facilitate time-binding. It should tend to foster an optimum flow of communication. It should tend to make communication occur with ever-decreasing limitations, so that each individual may increasingly enjoy the benefits of the functioning of the nervous systems of others, including those of generations past. And it should tend to permit each individual to make optimum time-binding contributions himself.[36]

Scientific activity, when it *actually* functions scientifically and not only in the name of 'science', follows this pattern. The open-ended nature of democratic-scientific communication leaves unobstructed the possibility of more information and revising opinions.

By contrast, in a dictatorship (government, corporation, family, etc.) functioning in the direction of a more or less closed society:

...there is no need for the time-binding contributions of others because, since he [the dictator—an individual or group] has the 'final' answers, what others contribute would either be the 'same', or it would be 'wrong'. So he blocks off others from making their time-binding contributions.... [H]owever the blockage of people's time-binding activities occurs, the situation that results has the character of 'dictatorship' by our definition. There may be even a dictatorship by a majority (e.g., a 'dictatorship of the proletariat'), if it sets up a 'closed system' barring the time-binding contributions of others. Moreover, dictatorships of varying degrees are found in economic, social, religious, and other spheres besides politics.[37]

As Korzybski said:

...from a time-binding point of view a dictatorship of whatever kind won't work, and eventually won't last; it twists the time-binding of humans, and so humans themselves. And a democracy, however imperfect, after all permits us humans to behave like humans in the time-binding sense.[38]

Time-Binding and Piecemeal Progress

One must see behind certain aspects of Korzybski's style in *Manhood of Humanity* to recognize that time-binding implies a *qualified*, piecemeal view of progress. Writing in his new language, Korzybski had not yet developed GS and the formulational carefulness which results from its use. (Korzybski received considerable stylistic help from his friend, mathematician Cassius J. Keyser, which may have contributed to the florid, ornate prose of the book, very unlike Korzybski's later style.)

Korzybski, however, did recognize the tentative, piecemeal nature of progress. A major contribution of his to the "great conversation" about progress was his recognition of its possible pathology. He clearly emphasized that the extent to which we bring forth our time-binding potential is not the inevitable consequence of some absolute cosmic law. Rather it depends on us, subject to the individual and collective choices we make. It depends on our basic values. Korzybski's work is founded on the value of knowledge and the values inherent in its pursuit.

At a time when the notion of the neutrality of science (its supposed value-free nature) received great support, Korzybski showed boldness in emphasizing the 'value-full' foundations and consequences of a scientific approach:

> If those who know why and how neglect to act, those who do not know will act, and the world will continue to flounder. The whole history of mankind and especially the present [1921] plight of the world show only too sadly how dangerous and expensive it is to have the world governed by those who do not know.[39]

At the start of the twenty-first century, many people have questioned the adequacy of a scientific approach. Pessimism seems rampant and many have turned to absolutistic relativism or to equally absolutistic fundamentalist religions and ideologies. Korzybski addressed this kind of movement when he wrote:

> ...it may be proved that undue pessimism is as dangerous a 'religion' as any other blind creed...as long as we presuppose the situation to be hopeless, the situation will indeed be hopeless. The spirit of Human Engineering does not know the word "hopeless"; for engineers know that wrong methods are alone responsible for disastrous results, and that every situation can be successfully handled by the use of proper means. The task of engineering science is not only to know but to know how.[40]

In his work after the publication of *Manhood of Humanity*, Korzybski studied the detailed mechanisms of time-binding. He sought *know-how*. How does time-binding work? What impedes it? How can we enhance the time-binding mechanism in all fields of human endeavor?

Chapter 6
Logical Fate and Freedom

Psychiatry and Mathematics

In seeking to understand the mechanisms of time-binding, Korzybski studied mathematics, mathematical foundations, physics, colloidal chemistry, neurology, anthropology and other fields. He spent two years, 1925 and 1926, studying psychiatric patients at St. Elisabeths Hospital in Washington, D.C., with his friend, the distinguished psychiatrist William Alanson White, M.D.

To understand how time-binding works, Korzybski considered it necessary to study its extremes. One end of the continuum of human time-binding behavior was represented by psychiatric cases—insanity. The other end was represented by scientists, mathematicians and other inquirers when working at their best—sanity. He labeled the so-called 'normal' person, hovering between the two extremes, "unsane," a term suggested to him by psychiatrist Philip Graven.

Considering science and mathematics (including logic) in relation to psychiatric problems and daily life adjustment, as Korzybski did, seemed like a somewhat strange mix to many people (perhaps to some it still does). Writing about Korzybski's work, organizational management theorist F. J. Roethlesberger (who attended a seminar in the 1930s given by Korzybski) wrote:

> At this time there was considerable interest in comparing the way a child thinks (Piaget) with the way a primitive thinks (Levy-Bruhl) and with the way a neurotic thinks (Freud). Only a genius or a nut would have tried to compare the way a mathematician thinks (Russell and Whitehead) and the way a neurotic thinks (psychiatry). Korzybski was such a man.[1]

Korzybski's position may have seemed extreme to those who saw mathematics as dealing with some kind of extra-human, 'transcendental', platonic realm. Even now (2003), this notion pervades much of the scientific-mathematical community. However, as far back as the 1920s Korzybski viewed mathematics as a *language*, a form of human behavior. He emphasized mathematics as a product *created by* and *affecting human nervous systems*, an exemplar of human time-binding effort.

A study of mathematics and especially *how mathematicians evaluate when working at their best* might provide useful data about human evaluative processes in general. These data might have *practical* value in helping the man and woman on the street to become better time-binders. Might this indeed have some relation to psychiatrists' study of sanity? In these concerns, Korzybski was not entirely alone.

Logical Fate

Cassius J. Keyser felt greatly stimulated by, and promoted, Korzybski's work. He seemed particularly impressed by Korzybski's notion about the pernicious effects of specific false assumptions about humans and the need to postulate a new, more accurate, basic view about human potentialities, i.e., time-binding.

It seems likely that this appealed to Keyser, in no small part, because of his own work in *humanistic* mathematics and logic. Keyser had a special interest in the thought processes of mathematicians and especially the role of assumptions in mathematics, science and life. For more than two thousand years, Euclid's geometry had been considered 'the' geometry of this world. Euclid's axioms, viewed as 'self-evident', included this postulate: through any point outside of a line, only one other parallel line can be drawn. This was finally challenged in the nineteenth century by several mathematicians such as Bolyai, Lobachevski, Riemann and Gauss. These men found that they could create consistent and valid non-euclidean geometries where no parallel lines or an indefinite number of parallel lines exist.

The resultant revolution in mathematics entailed a greater recognition than previously of the 'logical' freedom of humans in creating postulates or assumptions in mathematics. The propositions of Euclid represented not 'the' geometry of this world but rather *a* geometry, one among many. Indeed, modern physicists have found that some non-euclidean geometries more closely approximate some features of the world that they study than does the euclidean.

The time-binding shift from euclidean to non-euclidean geometry exemplifies what Korzybski considered the mathematical structure of human knowledge. From our assumptions, premises, postulates, presuppositions, expectations, etc.— often unconscious— conclusions follow. We can, however, revise and change our assumptions. According to Keyser, mathematics (in its 'logical' aspects) involved a consummate effort to *make conscious* and to *work out* the implications of assumptions, premises, principles, etc. "Mathematics is the study of Fate—not fate in a physical sense, but in the sense of the binding thread that connects thought with thought and conclusions with their premises." [2]

This notion of *"logical fate"* helped Korzybski in his writings in the mid-1920s as he sought to understand the general role of assumptions in human time-binding behavior, including sanity. Mathematicians argue with great passion about highly abstract and esoteric problems. Nonetheless, mathematical language, because of its simplicity, allows us to see important aspects of human evaluation, e.g., the fateful role of our assumptions, the importance of structure, etc., in a particularly clear way.

Korzybski's primary interest in developing his formulations lay not in mathematics and science as such. His interest in these as human behavior, in terms of forms of representation and languages, consisted in discovering what methods he could derive from them for improving human evaluation. In this regard, the relation of terminology to assumptions appears crucial. The assumptions, premises, basic postulates, etc., that we live with, and sometimes die by, involve undefined terms.

Every Word a World

In any verbal (including logical, mathematical and scientific) discussion, it is *not possible* to verbally define all your terms, i.e., your words. Take a definition, a verbal delineation of the properties or qualities that distinguish a particular category of objects from any other, e.g., "Man is a rational animal." Take each term and further define it. Define each word of your verbal definition, etc. (I suggest you actually do this, at least for a few minutes, to get a 'feel' for what I'm talking about. Otherwise you will miss something basic that you will not be able to get from just reading these words.)

At a certain point, which will not take very long, you will find yourself 'running around in verbal circles'. You will likely come upon certain terms that appear basic to you in the area under discussion. You will not be able to provide a completely adequate verbal definition of those terms. Keyser and Korzybski called them "undefined terms."

Undefined terms refer to non-verbal experiences. Eventually, with an undefined term, we must leave the crystalized realm of verbal concepts and satisfy ourselves with some unexpressed, amorphous experience that is not words. This may reveal for each of us our *metaphysics*—our basic, usually-out-of-awareness presuppositions, assumptions, etc.

Undefined terms have long been recognized by logicians, mathematicians and others. Such terms seem to correspond to what some philosophers, following Descartes, have called "clear and distinct ideas." Hmm. Undefined terms also seem to correspond to the philosophical "a priori." A great deal of philosophical exertion over the centuries appears to have involved the *end point* of getting to this level: "Now, I've *got* it."

For Korzybski (following Keyser), *stating your undefined terms*, rather than defining all your terms, provided the important *starting point* of basic postulates about any area under discussion. Undefined terms fix the limits of your metaphysics or worldview. It is important to emphasize that these terms point to non-verbal levels of experience, *not* to words, formulas or symbols. This has profound implications for how we understand and deal with our problems:

> He who accepts uncritically the vocabulary made by X, accepts unwillingly and unbeknowingly X's metaphysics. This fact is of very great importance. If we accept the vocabulary made by X and the metaphysics made by Y, we are lost in inconsistency, the world is an ugly mess, unknown and *unknowable*." [3]

Logical Fate in Mathematics and Science

The "celebrated man and woman in the street" as well as those who are called 'scientists' and 'mathematicians', can apply a generalized scientific, mathematical viewpoint (one of the main goals of humanists) by first becoming aware of logical fate.

Not only can we become aware of our assumptions, we can also claim and use our freedom to choose and revise them. Once assumptions have been stated and their consequences worked out at least to some degree, empirical investigation can test them in relation to observations and experiments. This combination of logic and experience makes possible the rejection, correction and revision of assumptions, including those involved with undefined terms. This revision provides one of the most important of the time-binding 'tools' for science and sanity.

In GS, we're concerned with practical consequences. Accordingly, the consequences of a given set of assumptions (embedded and embodied in a set of undefined terms) include attitudes and behavior. Mathematicians and scientists appear notable because, at least in the limited realms of their work, they attempt to search for and explicitly state their assumptions, work out the implications of them, test and revise them. However, even there, problems may result from supposedly accepting the metaphysics (basic assumptions) of modern science while applying the vocabulary and metaphysics (involving structure of language and logic) from a bygone period.

Also in their daily lives, scientists and mathematicians—like the rest of us—often remain unconscious of the frequently inadequate assumptions they've inherited. These inadequate assumptions can therefore continue to 'promote' their undesirable effects, leading to unsanity and insanity. This explains why scientists and mathematicians may not function any more sanely than other people.

Logical Fate in Daily Life

Other people's behavior, as well as our own, may make more sense to us if we can understand the premises or assumptions under which they and we operate. We can learn to avoid blame and bitterness in this way. Those with whom we disagree may not 'be' bad but rather simply acting from a different, though perhaps mistaken, set of assumptions.

Figure 2 illustrates what happens. A1 represents a possibly mistaken set of assumptions. C1 represents the conclusions and consequences, the attitudes and behavior, that follow from A1. A2 represents a different, possibly more accurate set of assumptions, with C2 the consequences resulting from these. The wavy lines indicate the incongruity of trying to get to the more satisfactory consequences without revising the old assumptions. Arrow I shows the revision of assumptions required to get to the new consequences (arrow II).

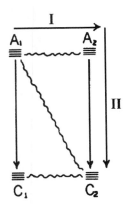

Figure 2 Logical Fate [4]

Keyser's notion of logical fate and Korzybski's elaboration of it predated by many years Thomas Kuhn's notion of
"paradigms." The logical fate model provides a broader perspective than that of Kuhn, since it includes people's everyday 'thinking' as well as the activities of scientists. (Kuhn, de-
servedly in my opinion, is considered by many as one of the
major twentieth-century formulators in the philosophy of science. I view Keyser and Korzybski similarly.)

A particular perspective in science often develops, according to Kuhn, through "puzzle-solving" within a particular
paradigm, the framework of assumptions, beliefs, values, and
techniques that defines a field at a particular time. In terms of
the logical fate model, this corresponds to the movement from
A1 to C1. When such puzzle-solving can no longer account
for significant 'facts', a "scientific revolution" can occur, involving the birth of a new paradigm. This roughly seems to
correspond to the revision of assumptions from A1 to A2.

Some have suggested that Kuhn insufficiently emphasized the criteria for choosing one 'paradigm' or set of assumptions over another and thus provided some enthusiasts with a smokescreen for 'pseudo-science'. In regard to this issue, the GS approach seems clear. We cannot function without assumptions. Our time-binding abilities and logical fate intertwine. We inherit most of our assumptions, premises, postulates, undefined terms, etc. We remain trapped by their consequences, like a fly in a honey jar, unless we can find a way to revise them for our benefit.

This surely doesn't mean that "anything goes." After explicitly stating our assumptions, we can evaluate them on the basis of internal consistency, simplicity, explanatory range, predictivity in relation to new observations and experiments, etc. These criteria provide some basis for judging some assumptions as better than others and thus for revising our old assumptions. Insofar as we can do this, we behave 'scientifically', with a scientific attitude, even in areas of life that have not traditionally been considered 'scientific'. We have some means for making progress, i.e., for time-binding.

Logical Fate in Personal Problem-Solving

Logical fate also has applications in the personal time-binding represented by psychotherapy and personal problem-solving. The notion of logical fate adds new power to the teachings of Epictetus, Spinoza and others. Non-adaptive 'emotions' and dysfunctional behaviors may result not from external events but from the belief-based judgements we make upon events. The use of generalized mathematical-scientific methods of uncovering and challenging assumptions, beliefs, etc., (as well as other aspects of GS discussed later) provides an opportunity for a more satisfactory response to life.

In this regard, Korzybski taught his work to psychologists and psychiatrists. Under the aegis of William Alanson White,

M.D., he did educational/preventive work with the psychiatric patients at St. Elisabeths Hospital. Although he did not provide therapy, he continued throughout his career to do educational/preventive work individually and in seminars with many people who had problems in living. Some individuals were sent to him by psychiatrists who wanted his educational work to supplement their treatments.

Since then many major thinkers and many practitioners in the related fields of psychotherapy, counseling, and consulting have been influenced by Korzybski. For example, in the area known as "Cognitive-Behavior Therapy," the approach of Rational Emotive Behavior Therapy (REBT) was founded by Albert Ellis, who studied and makes significant use of Korzybski's work. Isabel Caro has developed her Cognitive Therapy of Evaluation based on GS. (Her book, *General Semantics in Psychotherapy*, shows some of the extent of GS influence in that field.) Korzybski's work has also been recognized by Lou Marinoff, author of the book, *Plato, Not Prozac*, and one of the leaders in the newly-labeled field of "philosophical practice and consulting."

Logical fate, the effect of assumptions on behavior, is not total or exclusive. People have wonderful abilities to compartmentalize their beliefs: to restrict them to limited areas of their lives or to hold contradictory views concurrently. Sometimes, if they hold 'nutty' beliefs in some areas, this compartmentalizing can actually help them stay relatively sane.

Nonetheless, so-called 'normal' people all too often *do* act on their beliefs sufficiently enough to increase problems and misery for themselves and/or others.

Chapter 7
A Mathematical Approach to Life

Mathematics and Sanity

Korzybski gave a special place to mathematics in his formulating about human evaluation. He had had enough experience with the 'mentally ill' at St. Elisabeths and elsewhere and with mathematicians —including some mentally ill ones—to realize that mathematicians were not "wonders in private life—not at all. But mathematizing seems to be a way of science; it seems, again a way of sanity." [1] What did he mean?

Korzybski used the term "physico-mathematical *method*" to refer to the general attitude/approach of using mathematics to study the 'physical' world. He thought-felt that this approach has something to teach us that might be useful for everyday life. Even physicists and mathematicians have not made full use of it because of the limited ways in which they understand their own activities.

In this chapter, I explore Korzybski's radical, humanistic view of mathematics and physico-mathematical method. In the following chapter, I discuss some of the premises that Korzybski accepted as basic to an up-to-date, science-based worldview. These premises provide the background of assumptions upon which Korzybski built his system, general semantics—which offers means for applying a scientific-mathematical approach to our everyday talking-evaluating-living.

The Unreasonable Effectiveness of Mathematics

At the beginning of the twenty-first century, the question of the status of mathematics in relation to 'reality' is an active one. Many mathematicians and scientists still seem to agree with Nobel physicist Eugene Wigner as to what he called the "unreasonable effectiveness of mathematics" in describing, explaining and predicting events of the natural world. An impressive number of mathematicians and scientists remain platonists. According to this view, the order of the universe 'is' mathematical. This mathematical order exists outside of us and is not created by mathematicians and scientists. Rather, it is revealed to them in the process of discovery.

For example, in 1962, Gell-Mann, Okubu and Ne'eman used the mathematics of symmetry to predict a new elementary particle. The mathematical pattern indicated the place for a new particle and lo...a new particle was found. Something special is going on here, something that some people don't think can be accounted for by simply considering mathematics as a cultural product of human nervous systems.[2]

As science writer Martin Gardner expressed it:

> If mathematical concepts have no locus outside of human culture, how has nature managed to produce such a boundless profusion of beautiful models of mathematical objects: orbits that are conic-section curves, snowflakes, coastlines that model fractal curves, carbon molecules that are tetrahedral, and on and on?[3]

His opinion reflects that of many in the mathematical-scientific community. Nonetheless, from a consistent naturalistic perspective the view that the order of the world 'is' mathematical seems seriously mistaken. To say that "nature [has] managed to produce such a boundless profusion of beautiful models of mathematical objects," reverses the observable facts of human mathematical/scientific behavior. Nature *is not* a model of mathematics. Rather, the mathematical symbols that humans create, insofar as they are given 'physical' content, themselves constitute models which may or may not coincide with the order of nature very well—two gallons of alcohol plus two gallons of water make less than four of the mixture.

Structure, Relation and Order

Korzybski took as a given that an external world (outside the nervous system) existed. He also took as basic the assumption that *we live in a universe of some structure which includes us*. However, *the structure of the universe is not mathematical despite the fact that it can be described mathematically*.

In GS, structure is defined as a complex or pattern of relations. Relations can in turn be described in terms of multi-dimensional order. Order runs the gamut from 'random' to 'non-random' processes and therefore covers a much broader field than what mathematicians and physicists usually refer to when they use this term. Order, in this sense, has no opposite. As Robert Pula has often puckishly said, "There ain't such a thing as 'no order' "—in the way I am using the term here.

Structure, relation and order constitute basic undefined terms in GS. They can be defined in relation to each other and perhaps a few other terms such as difference, similarity, etc. Ultimately, to understand these undefined terms, we must go beyond the words to non-verbal, non-symbolic, non-mathematical experience. They are also multiordinal terms (which I describe in more detail in later chapters). Suffice it to say (for now) that a multiordinal term may be used to refer to different levels of existence and experience, non-verbal and verbal. Multiordinal terms like "structure," "order," and "relation" can be used to describe a variety of 'things' and events.

Stick out your right hand. Notice your individual fingers. With your palm facing you, what you call your thumb will be located on the right. Counting your thumb as first, your index finger as second, etc., there is a structure or order to the fingers that the structure or order of the numbers (mathematics) can describe and point to. If you tell me that you have five fingers, I can make some highly probable predictions about your fingers without seeing your hand. For example, the second digit is between the first and third, the third digit between the second and fourth, etc. The related structurings of the non-verbal order of your fingers nonetheless are not the numbers. The numbers give us predictivity. That we can do this effectively with fingers seems no less unreasonable, though surely a lot easier, than the feats of Gell-Mann, Okuda, Ne'eman, and others.

Mathematics as a Language

Willard Gibbs, the great nineteenth-century American physicist, one of the founders of thermodynamics, was known for *not* saying much at Yale University faculty meetings. At one such meeting, discussion ensued about changing the math and language requirements for undergraduates. People were surprised to see Gibbs stand up to speak. "Mathematics is a language," he said and then sat down again.[4]

What distinguishes mathematics as a language? Numbers and mathematics explicitly deal with structure, relations and order.[5] As I indicated above, we live and have experiences in a world comprised of some structure which consists of a complex of relations of multi-dimensional order. Therefore we can use the numbers and relations of math to accurately 'map' our world.

To a significant extent, the structure of the world can be described with some exactness with the explicit language of relations—mathematical functions. For example, a function of two variables, (x) and (y), can be stated in the form "y is a function of x" or $y = (f)x$. Such a function shows a definite relation between x and y. For every value of x, the formula of the function determines what the value of y will be.

So, for instance, the compound interest that you earn is a function of the length of time that you have your money in an account with a given rate of interest, and the starting amount of money. A map, called a graph, can be made to show a functional curve relating the amount of money the account has accrued (y) to any given point of time (x).

Although the language of mathematics does constitute a cultural product of human nervous systems, this does not make it completely arbitrary. The nature of the mathematical language game, although highly dependent on the human imagination, is constrained by relatively invariant aspects of the world (ourselves included), our daily needs, and the game rules and nature of the mathematizing process. (Mathematical behavior well-nigh definitely constitutes a complex function of both hereditary and non-hereditary factors.)

Nature has indeed managed to produce a boundless profusion of what we call orbits, snowflakes, coastlines, carbon molecules, etc. From a viewpoint of scientific naturalism, the structure, relation, order of nature includes us. If mathematics is a product of our nervous systems, can it be so miraculous and surprising that we can use mathematics, i.e., relational languages of possible structure or order, to model nature so well? From this viewpoint, no—although the process by which human nervous systems mathematize may not yet be adequately understood. Korzybski was surely not trivializing the importance of mathematics, but revealing its power, when he referred to it as a language of a structure similar to the structure of the world and the human nervous system.

The Importance of Asymmetrical Relations

Humpty Dumpty learned that you can't unbreak an egg. Humpty sitting on the wall is not the same as Humpty after his fall. If Humpty-sprawled-broken-on-the-ground is later than Humpty-sitting-happily-on-the-wall, then Humpty, sitting on the wall, cannot be later than Humpty, lying on the ground.

Unlike a symmetrical relation, where equivalent items can be reversed, much of life in general seems to consist of asymmetrical (roughly meaning irreversible) relations. These constitute among the most important kinds of structure to be found in the world. This emphasis on asymmetry is based upon the significance of differences among individual non-verbal phenomena—both differences among spatial dimensions and differences from one time to another.

The practical applications resulting from a focus on differences and asymmetrical relations include the simple yet profound methods of applying index numbers and dates to our daily language; This brings greater exactness into everyday formulating. (See Chapter 14 for further details about indexing and dating.)

The importance of difference and asymmetry which Korzybski emphasized, although difficult to deny, was not in keeping with the apparent governing paradigm of physicists which emphasized—and still does in 2003—similarity and symmetry. For example, in relation to time, the basic 'laws' of newtonian mechanics, relativity, and quantum physics were and are considered symmetrical or reversible in relation to time. The passage of 'time' is considered irrelevant to their operation.

However, life as we experience it does involve asymmetrical, irreversible processes. The science of thermodynamics provides a basis for understanding the irreversibility of the world— life as an asymmetrical function of time. Rather than see this irreversibility as a secondary fluke or, perhaps in some sense, illusory, some physical scientists like chemist Ilya Prigogine have sought to give it a primary place in physical theory. Prigogine's "evolutionary paradigm" for science provides "a new concept of matter, matter that is 'active,' as matter leads to irreversible processes and as irreversible processes organize matter."[6] General-semantics views seem in keeping with this emphasis on the asymmetrical and irreversible aspects of nature.

Physico-Mathematical Methods and the World

So-called 'pure' mathematics deals with validity, the inner, logical consistency of related formulations. In pure mathematics the formulations can be considered 'content'-free. They don't need to refer to any particular thing or process in the non-verbal world but rather may be related or not to any number of perceivable, conceivable processes or things. Because such particulars are not specified, deductions from 'pure' mathematical abstractions seem to work 'absolutely' in the sense that nothing can be left out.

However, even here absolute certainty does not seem possible. Kurt Gödel demonstrated that "no mathematical system can ever be complete in itself, not even theoretically self-sufficient, but must always contain statements not provable within the system." [7]

Physico-mathematical methods involve adapting this pure mathematics in order to understand the observable 'physical' world. This is the realm of applied mathematics, in which mathematical relations are used to model or map particular processes in the world. With mathematical modeling, as with non-mathematical language, particulars do get left out. The use of mathematics lends greater exactness to these models, which, however, can only function as potentially revisable approximations. Scientists and mathematicians seem generally to agree with Einstein's statement that "As far as the laws of mathematics refer to reality, they are not certain; and as far as they are certain, they do not refer to reality." [8]

How this physico-mathematical modeling process works has been described by Einstein and others in what philosophers of science call the hypothetical-deductive method.

In a 1952 letter to a friend, Einstein presented a model of thinking (a model of modeling), pictured on the next page, which shows this method unusually well. [9]

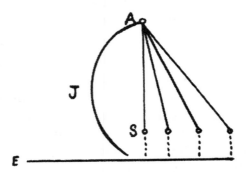

Figure 3 Einstein's Model of Thinking[10]

Stuart Mayper described Einstein's model as follows:
This is a model not just of scientific [scientific-mathemati-
cal] thinking, but of thinking in general....Einstein illustrates
his model this way: first, a horizontal line labeled E, which
represents experience, the world of experience, sense data.
Somewhere above this line there begins an ascending curve,
which Professor Holton has labeled J, for "jump," that's what
[Karl] Popper would call a "conjecture"—not a product of
logical reasoning, but of the imagination. This leads to a point
at a high-level, labeled A: our Axioms, our Assumptions, our
postulates...[often represented by means of a mathematical
model]. From this A point, the axiom system or assumptions,
some straight lines [logically] come down to a number of
Statements marked S, statements which are deductions from
the theories...The last step is to relate these S statements to
experience, testing the theory that way. The whole process we
could sum up as E J A S and back to E.[11]

A and S here correspond to the assumptions (A) and consequences (C) of the logical fate diagram in Chapter 6.
Einstein's model elaborates on how scientists test and revise
their assumptions (theories). We scientifically test our A by
inquiring how well its related Ss predict what we actually find
at E through observation and experimentation at a given date.

As Einstein, Popper, Korzybski and others noted, successful predictions can never utterly prove an A. However, *unsuccessful predictions can falsify A* (indicate that it needs to be revised in some way). What makes a theory scientific? A scientific theory will be stated in such a way that it risks falsification (disconfirmation). The best tests of a theory provide the most rigourous, potentially falsifying challenges. A successful scientific theory, one with better predictivity than others at a given date, survives such attempts to falsify it.

I live in Southern California where there is an abundance of beliefs and practices such as acupuncture, qi gong, feng shui, 'alternative' healing methods, 'mind'-cures, diet systems, etc. Those who wish to make use of such approaches—which in some cases may possibly have some value—would do well to stop looking for proof or confirmation. Those daring to inquire will use a scientific approach to examine how well a system stands up to experimental tests which seek to disconfirm it.

For instance, look for any cases whereby some 'healing' method didn't work. What might this indicate about the method? Alternative explanations for observed phenomena have great importance in fostering healthy doubt about conclusions. Do you feel better because of the method of healing—or might a better explanation for how you feel involve your hopes, your desperation, your belief in its efficacy, the 'authority' of the 'healer', etc.? Some claims may possess a lot more 'maybeness' than their advocates believe.

A minimal 'maybeness' pertains to even the best, nigh certain scientific theories. Even the most rigorously tested theory can most accurately be stated in probabilistic, not absolutistic terms. Mayper suggested that we use "nigh," as I did above, to express "almost but not quite entirely."

Applying this Einsteinian-Popperian model of scientific-mathematical evaluating promotes an orientation of inevitable fallibility which was central for Korzybski, as it was for Einstein, Popper and others. Korzybski was intent on teaching people to apply this model more broadly. He contended that "all verbalism is, ultimately, similar to mathematics in structure." [12]

In pursuing the korzybskian task of bringing ordinary language closer to mathematics, it is not necessary to speak in algebra, however. The chapters "Living Extensionally" and "Extensional Languaging" present simple methods for applying a 'generalized science' and a 'generalized mathematics' to daily language and life.

Mathematics as a Human Activity

Mathematical humanists such as Aristotle, Locke, Hume, Mill and Lakatos preceded Korzybski in viewing mathematics as a form of human behavior. (See Reuben Hersh's *What Is Mathematics Really?*) The move toward understanding mathematics in this way, though still a minority position, has importance if mathematics and science are to become understood on a naturalistic, not a supernatural, basis. An important part of this involves moving away from seeing "mathematics as a clear-cut entity, 'by itself'." [13]

Conventional discussions of mathematics encourage the false-to-fact elimination of the individuals doing the mathematics when considering mathematical statements. However, any kind of mathematical statement has importance only within the context of the social relationships among mathematizing individuals.

This relation of formulations to formulators extends to any other sort of statement as well, including the statements in Bibles, Korans, etc. This fact is often obscured by those who have an interest in keeping well-hidden the particular human origins of their favorite doctrines.

What results from applying a broadly scientific-mathematical approach to any statement someone makes about the world (applying Einstein's, Popper's and Korzybski's attitude of looking for disconfirmation)? As I hope to demonstrate in Part III, we might expect some dramatic effects in the fields of religion, ethics, politics, law—and science, among others. In the next chapter, I elaborate upon the general view of the world that results from taking this seriously.

Chapter 8
A Relational Worldview

The GS worldview can be summarized in six words: *"To be is to be related."* [1] What do these words imply? The primacy of relations/relationships represents one of the most profound shifts in the last few centuries of Western scientific thinking—a shift from thinking in terms of substance (things and 'thingness') to thinking in terms of structure and order, which quickly leads to the study of differences, changes, processes, etc.

Understanding the structure of 'matter', for instance, involves investigating the relations of molecules, then atoms, then the constituents of atoms, i.e., electrons, protons, neutrons, etc. At these 'deeper' levels of what the world seems to be made of, 'matter' (M) has been shown to have a precise quantitative relation to energy (E). According to Einstein's famous equation, $E=MC^2$—where C equals the speed of light. The 'non-thingness' of 'matter' and its equivalence to energy ('action' or 'change') has had a central role in changing our understanding of the world. A practical demonstration—alas—of Einstein's equation occurred with the 1945 detonations of the atomic bombs at Hiroshima and Nagasaki.

In this chapter, I explore how *to be is to be related* and how this understanding connects to other basic presuppositions,undefined terms, etc.,which underly the general-semantics system.

The Observer-Observed Continuum

Relativity and quantum mechanics, each in their own way, involve a reassessment of human knowledge in terms of a most important relation: the relation of the observer to the observed. Einstein's theory of relativity, for example, established the importance of the relative motion between observer and observed when measuring length or duration. The frame of reference of the observer moving in relation to what is observed needs to be taken into account, especially as speeds approach the speed of light. According to special relativity, the maximum speed of light, approximately 186,000 miles per second, is considered a limit not to be exceeded. As a consequence, the dimensions of 'space' and 'time' can no longer be considered as absolutes, as they were in classical newtonian physics. Einstein's general theory of relativity later resulted in treating 'space' and 'time' as inseparable aspects of an undivided matter-space-time.

In quantum mechanics, Werner Heisenberg demonstrated the role of the observer in measuring sub-atomic processes. Calling his finding the "uncertainty principle," he showed that when the position of a subatomic particle is measured, the momentum cannot be known. When the momentum can be known, the position cannot be measured. Other quantum physicists, such as Niels Bohr, showed that electrons behave like particles under some experimental setups and like waves under other experimental setups. So what 'are' they—waves or particles? They 'are' neither and both—or rather, we can't say what they 'are' apart from their behavior within our experimental setups for observing and measuring them.

What we observe depends on the way we observe. The observer-dependent nature of quantum mechanical knowledge allows only probabilistic predictions. This breaks down the newtonian view of absolute certainty regarding causality/determinism. Scientists, philosophers and the rest of us are still assimilating the implications of the inherently observer-dependent condition of human knowledge.

The Evolution of Human Knowledge

We can use the relation of observer to observed to roughly characterize the evolution of human knowledge in three stages of development, one stage emerging out of the other. In the first "Pre-Scientific" stage of human knowledge, "the observer was everything, the observed did not matter." [2] In this period, humans projected their own reactions, 'thoughts', emotions, onto the rest of the world. This resulted in an animism in full force. Gods and spirits were seen to inhabit all things. If the river overflowed its banks, the spirits of the river were angry. A good crop meant the spirits of the earth were gracious. Since, in this view, 'everything is everything else',[3] magic and sacrifice could be used in attempts to control the spirit forces.

As human knowledge developed, a second, "Classical or Semi-Scientific," [4] stage began, one which emphasized observed phenomena and reduced the role of animistic forces. The Greek natural philosophers and later, those of the Scientific Revolution, sought out the 'laws' of nature. Researchers in this phase came to believe that they could attain a neutral, objective understanding of the way things 'really' work through some combination of observation and logic. This 'objective' knowledge did not, for the most part, seem to require taking the human observer into account. In this aristotelian view, 'everything is identical with itself'. [5] So the purpose of science was to classify each thing according to its nature and the laws that governed it.

According to Korzybski, humans had only just begun in the first half of the twentieth century to enter the third fully "Scientific" or "Non-Aristotelian" phase.[6] This transition involves more fully recognizing the role of the observer in the development of human knowledge. How we perceive, talk about and interact with the world, affects what we seek to understand.

Postulates of Science-at-a-Date

The assumptions which Korzybski took to underlie a scientific, relational worldview were not presented by him as articles of faith or as a priori absolute 'truths', to be accepted for all time without question or evidence. He emphasized the importance of putting one's undefined terms 'on the table' for examination, elaboration, and possible criticism and testing. Unlike the faith of traditional metaphysics or religion, general-semantics' scientific postulates (basic assumptions, undefined terms) may be subject to revision, no matter how firm they may seem at present.

Here I present a basic set of GS postulates which seem to me especially important and fruitful.

Structure as the Only Content of Knowledge

The universe, including each of us, necessarily involves structure, relation, and order, with asymmetrical relations of particular importance.

From this we derive the notion that structure constitutes the only content of knowledge, with the observer-observed relation as basic. This implies something I've already touched upon: human knowing constitutes a natural process, with 'thoughts', 'feelings', etc., able to be characterized in terms of 'physical' events. It thus becomes problematic if the study of knowledge (epistemology) is not consistent with up-to-date scientific understandings about 'physical', 'biological', and 'neurological' processes. (I place single quotes around these terms because it seems an error to view them as if they deal with entirely separable processes.)

This also means that science and mathematics (which includes logic) can be understood as forms of human behavior that we can study. Korzybski—whose work qualifies as a theory of scientific, applied epistemology—may be considered one of the forerunners of both "naturalized epistemology" and "evolutionary epistemology." The GS theory of human knowledge as a neurological process is further discussed in the next three chapters.

Non-Identity

No two individual objects, events, reactions, etc., no matter how similar, are identical in the sense of absolute or complete sameness in all aspects; each remains unique. Knowledge depends upon the similarity (not the exact sameness) of structure between our languages and the world. "Words are not the things spoken about." [7]

Robert P. Pula has commented on the radical nature of Korzybski's assumption of non-identity:

> "Whatever you say a thing *is*, it *is not*." This rejection of the 'law of identity' ('everything is identical with itself') may be Korzybski's most controversial formulation. After all, Korzybski's treatment directly challenges the 'Laws of Thought', revered for over two thousand years in the West and, differently expressed, in non-Western cultures. Korzybski's challenge is thus *planetary*. [8]

I discuss non-identity further in Chapter 12.

The Process Universe

Non-identity implies the process character of everything in the universe. Although we tend to view things as static and unchanging, change underlies everything we know. As Pula puts it, we might better think in terms "not of things changing but of change thinging." [9] No individual thing, situation, phenomenon, etc., remains absolutely the same in all aspects even to itself from one moment to the next. In such a process world, "a premise that 'everything is identical with itself' is *invariably false to facts*." [10]

This process character of the world, ourselves included, is corroborated by the unification of 'matter', 'space', and 'time' brought about in relativity theory, which considers the universe as a four-dimensional space-time continuum. Studies of the structure of 'matter' in quantum physics also corroborate it.

Non-identity (including this process view) does not mean that relations of similarity don't exist. Non-identity does, however, imply the primacy of asymmetrical relations of difference. There are different kinds of difference and these differences may or may not, in a given situation, make a difference for each of us.

Non-Elementalism

With our habitual language habits, we may tend to divide up the world into isolated elements which we then treat as if they exist as isolated and separate, thus neglecting important and necessary relations. This habitual mode of evaluating is called "elementalism." An important aspect of elementalism involves either/or, two-valued, 'black and white' evaluating which over-emphasizes the polar extremes of a continuum, i.e., 'all good'/'all bad', 'all right'/'all wrong', etc. and neglects the 'grayish' middle ground so common in actual life— the black in white, the white in black, etc.

If *to be is to be related*, then elements considered as separate such as 'space' and 'time', 'mind' and 'body', 'self' and 'society', 'human' and 'environment', etc., need to be connected again in order to talk about and deal with empirical structures more adequately. This more-connected mode of evaluating is called "non-elementalism." The use of non-elementalistic words and methods (which include getting to a 'higher' viewpoint by finding the 'good' in the 'bad', the 'wrong' in the 'right', the 'positive' in the 'negative', etc.) plays a central role in applied GS.

The General Principle of Uncertainty

Many scientists, philosophers and other formulators have acted and still seem to act as if rejecting two-valued 'certainty'/'uncertainty' provides a prescription for despair. Even Einstein could not accept that " 'God' played dice with the universe." Both the notions of non-elementalism and non-identity led

Korzybski to a *general principle of uncertainty* related to human knowledge that goes beyond Heisenberg's more limited principle.

The general principle of uncertainty involves forthrightly facing and embracing *the statistical or probabilistic nature of all statements about the non-verbal world*. This actually provides the best possibility we have for precision and understanding. "It should be noticed that the notions of probability are very flexible, and entirely cover our structural needs, the field of degrees of probability ranging from impossibility to certainty."[11]

Multi-Valued, Probabilistic Determinism

For human purposes, the universe does not need to obey a principle of completely uniform causality. Predictability in science does not require absolute determinism in the world. Rather, "maximum probability of predictability"[12] at-a-date can be obtained through the acceptance of multi-causal factors involving probabilities, not only where the Heisenberg uncertainty holds but in any situation under investigation.

However, accepting the generalized uncertainty of all statements does not require accepting 'indeterminism', which would involve a denial of structure or relations, an inherently contradictory viewpoint. Instead, we can accept that 'chance' and determinism are not opposites. However definite our knowledge-at-a-date may seem, more can be learned later about causal factors previously unspecified and labeled as 'chance'. Hence, a multi-valued, probabilistic determinism.

This view of probabilistic determinism accepts that the world *is not* 'governed' by scientific 'laws'. The world does what it does. Humans formulate scientific 'laws' which constitute generalizations formulated from observed regularities of nature. New factors may always intervene between what have previously been identified as 'cause' and 'effect'. Thus scientific 'laws' may change as new factors become known.

Non-Additivity

Multi-valued, probabilistic determinism further involves a conscious recognition of the importance of non-additivity, the notion that "the world around us does not happen to be an additive [linear] affair in its most fundamental structural aspects."[13] This early GS notion preceded the related viewpoints of "Chaos Theory" and "Complexity Theory."

Chaos Theory deals with complex and, to some degree, predictable order in apparently random processes. Such nonlinear, dynamic processes include smoke curling from a cigarette, water dripping from a faucet, the turbulent flow of heated fluids, branching patterns of a tree, stock market patterns, weather trends, etc. 'Chaotic' processes can change dramatically and non-additively (non-linearly) with only small changes in initial conditions, contributing factors, etc. 'Chaotic' order may be understood in terms of fractal geometry which studies similarities of structure among different size scales. For example, the view of a coastline seen from walking several yards alongside it may appear similar to the view seen from an airplane several miles above it. The similar shapes have a fractal structure.

Complexity Theory has grown out of Chaos Theory and Systems Theory. It focuses on emergent levels of organization in non-living and living systems. To understand these levels requires eliminating the "additive or plus tendency" from people's evaluating. This tendency is represented, for example, by the use of 'and' and 'plus', etc., by scientists and others which may misrepresent complex, non-additive, nonlinear processes, relationships, organizations, etc. "As a structural fact, the world around us is *not* a 'plus' affair, and requires a functional [relational] representation."[14] One mother and one father 'plus' one small baby leads to a whole new, complex set of relations in the life of a family.

A Science of Humanity

The implications of the above for the behavioral/social sciences seem considerable. The behavior of nature, including human nature, is indeed 'determined' by multiple, non-additive (non-linear), probabilistic factors which provide for some predictability but which also insure that the future is not absolutely set in stone.

Multi-valued, probabilistic determinism provides the means both for whatever freedom and whatever responsibility we can experience in our lives. Our knowledge of some of the factors that determine our own behavior may constitute one of the many, non-additive factors that can determine our ongoing behavior through spiral feedback mechanisms. In addition, our own behavior toward our children, friends, neighbors, etc., may have significant determining effects on their behavior, among other factors.

Korzybski's scientific, relational worldview was built on his consideration of structural, evaluational and methodological advances in a wide variety of disciplines of his time. His research led to a remarkable theory of human behavior which, though in some ways limited in scope, also has great generality. Having examined its foundations, let us go on to more explicitly explore this theory—*general semantics*.

Chapter 9
General Semantics

A General Theory of Evaluation

"Evaluation" implies both *'intellectual' and 'emotional' factors as inseparable aspects of human behavior*. Even mathematics and science, as forms of human behavior have 'emotional' content. (Want to see some passionate discussions?—go to a convention of mathematicians and scientists.) The practical study of human evaluation in science and in daily life defines the field of general semantics.

In *Manhood of Humanity* Korzybski called this field, with its basis in time-binding, "human engineering." Later, he called it "humanology."

However, due to his focus on evaluation, by the time of *Science and Sanity*'s publication in 1933 he had renamed his system of formulations "general semantics" —two words used as a unified term. He subtitled the book *An Introduction to Non-Aristotelian Systems and General Semantics*.

Supporters and critics alike have continually confused Korzybski's use of "semantic(s)" in "general semantics" with other uses of the word which refer to linguistic 'meaning', the history of words, etc. To say that "something is a matter of semantics" implies 'just a quibble' about words. Because of this confusion, labeling his system "general semantics" may constitute Korzybski's biggest error.

Even a quibble about 'words' involves much more than words, much more than isolated verbal consequences. The term 'semantic(s)' as used in "general semantics," "semantic reactions," etc., functions as a synonym for *evaluation(al)*. Thus general semantics constitutes a *general* theory of *evaluation*, such evaluation involving people's inseparable thinking-feelings in a particular context.

I find it useful to contrast "evaluation, evaluational" as used in GS with the current use of the terms "cognition, cognitive" in the field of Cognitive Science. The common, habitual interpretation of 'cognition' tends to separate 'intellectual' from 'emotional' factors. Such a separation is explicitly denied in GS.

GS constitutes an applied general theory of human evaluation and awareness. In ways that may seem odd to conventional views of mathematics and science, GS looks at the meeting point of scientific-mathematical methods and daily life. This provides ways for us humans to more fully develop our critical and creative potentialities and to cooperate to achieve optimal time-binding.

"The Astonishing Hypothesis"

Human evaluational (or semantic) reactions provide the basic unit of study for general semantics. Evaluational reactions involve *neurologically*-based responses of an organism-as-a-whole-in-an-environment (you, me, every living individual on the planet) to words, symbols and other events in terms of their 'meanings', significances, etc., to each of us.

'Meanings' or significances in this sense are *not merely verbal*. Words and symbols considered as products of human behavior inevitably occur in association with what J. S. Bois called *"happening-meanings"—organic, neural processes which correlate with language symbols but do not themselves qualify as what people normally refer to as 'language'.*[1] Rather, these happening-meanings consist of neurological reactions which include so-called 'intellectual', 'emotional', 'physiological', and 'physico-chemical' aspects, etc., inseparable from one another.

Read the following sentences slowly while imagining what the words describe. *Can you see, smell and touch a ripe, yellow, juicy lemon? I take a knife and cut through the skin, re-*

leasing the lemony smell. The juice drips onto my knife. I bite into the lemon and the sour juice makes me pucker... What physiological aspects of your evaluational reactions to these words (happening-meanings) do you notice?

I eschew the traditional division of 'mind' and 'body'. Can you show a 'mind' separate from a 'body'? What assumptions do you engage if you continue using those terms which can so easily imply separate entities? Korzybski had a seminar student who insisted that he had a 'mind' separate from his 'body'. "Give it to me!" Korzybski said. "I can," the student replied peevishly, "but I don't want to."[2]

Naturalistic humanists would do well to follow general semanticists here. Our so-called 'mental' life has a physiological or bodily basis in nervous system functioning. Korzybski proposed that it can be understood most accurately in terms of *neuro-evaluational* (neuro-semantic) reactions built upon electro-colloidal structures.

We now know much more about the structure of the nervous system than was known in Korzybski's time. Nowadays scientists acknowledge the colloidal behavior of cellular stuff while focusing in much more detail on the behavior of particular colloidal structures—macromolecules such as proteins, etc. Korzybski recognized the tentativeness of his discussion in these areas.[3]

Nonetheless, his basic assumptions regarding colloidal behavior and neurology still hold. We constitute living stuff—the stuff that dreams, 'life,' 'mentality', 'logic', etc., are made on. This stuff has 'material', physical-chemical structure. This implies that 'culture' and 'biology', 'nurture' and 'nature' don't exist in separate realms. What we think-feel (evaluate), say and do result from, indeed *constitute*, organic processes. What we and others do and say, in turn, *must* affect us, not through some 'immaterial' 'mental' processes, but neurologically, physiologically, physico-chemically, etc. (Korzybski

coined the non-elementalistic term "psycho-logic(s)" to emphasize the non-separation of 'logical' from neuropsychologi-
cal processes.)

Thus, very early in the century, he was already emphasizing what Francis Crick later called "the astonishing hypothesis" that:

> ...all feelings and thoughts are essentially the behavior of
> an enlarged set of nerve cells, neurons, and their associ-
> ated molecules and other cells in your brain. One has to
> say two things: It's really not astonishing to a lot of scien-
> tists, especially neuroscientists who work on the brain; its
> what they normally assume. On the other hand, if you take
> the ordinary citizen, in general, not only is it regarded as
> astonishing, he or she decides it is almost certainly *false*. [4]

In emphasizing the *neuro* aspect in how we talk about
evaluating, GS formulating does not require that all thinking-
feeling must be completely localized in the brain—that part
of the nervous system inside the skull—which could imply a
'brain'- rest-of-'body' dualism inconsistent with the facts of
neurobiology today.[5] Although "the pain in sprain is *mainly*
in the brain," events related to that experience may not be
solely located there. Such events are distributed throughout
the nervous structure of the organism and involve other physiological systems as well.[6]

This viewpoint also considers socio-cultural factors as
facts in their own right which affect individuals through neurological, organic means.

Korzybski saw "the astonishing hypothesis" as an intrinsic part of his work and made significant efforts to spread
knowledge of it as a basic aspect of his teaching. He contended
that if one wishes to act more sanely, each individual needs
to *understand and have a language for talking about the
mechanisms* of his or her reactions. Because of this he felt it
crucial for the sanity of the human race that ordinary citizens
as well as scientists, mathematicians and philosophers evalu-

ate and talk about themselves and what they do from a neuro-logical, neuro-evaluational standpoint.

To my knowledge, no one before or after Korzybski, ex-cept for some of his students, has stressed to a similar degree the importance of applying this neuro-evaluational, psycho-logical understanding to how we view *and talk about* all behavior: mathematics, science, and everyday life included.

The Structural Differential

Shortly after the publication of *Manhood of Humanity*, Korzybski devised a model of the neurological process of hu-man evaluation. He originally built this model out of metal, wood, strings, etc. He came to label it "the structural differ-ential" because it shows the different primary structural lev-els involved in human experience and knowledge (what he called the process of abstracting). The structural differential on the next page appears substantially like Korzybski's pic-torial representations. The labels for the different levels, al-though based on Korzybski's terminology, were chosen by me and my wife originally for *Drive Yourself Sane*. In Chapter 11, where I discuss the process of abstracting in greater de-tail, I present another visual model, based in part on the struc-tural differential. For now, I provide a brief description of the levels of the differential.

According to the best, current, scientifically-inferred knowl-edge, you and everyone and everything else constitute dynamic energy systems—fields within fields of activity within a larger cosmic process—built up from relationships of sub-microscopic events. We call this whirl of activity the *Event* or *Process Level*.

Out of this whirl, individuals perceive/create their sense of 'things', 'objects', phenomena, etc. From a given 'common' event, each of us abstracts differently and so constructs a differ-ent experience. Some particulars get included, some left out—indicated by the connected and unconnected strings. At this per-ceiving level, we sense but have no words for our experiences.

You have probably had the experience of "knowing" something and yet feeling unable to convey this to someone else adequately; you may say, "It's hard to put into words," at such times. We call this the silent, *Object Level*, or the level at which we non-verbally experience objects and other macroscopic phenomena inside, outside and on our skins. At this level we can see, touch, taste, smell or otherwise experience with more or less unaided senses. The circle on the left represents the animal object level.

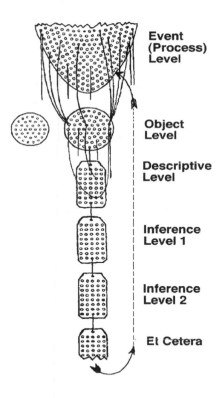

Event
(Process)
Level

Object
Level

Descriptive
Level

Inference
Level 1

Inference
Level 2

Et Cetera

Figure 4 Structural Differential [7]

We do put many things into words, and this ability represents a central difference between us and other forms of life. Other animals do not appear to have our elaborated symbolic-linguistic abilities. We humans can use language; we can operate at *Verbal Levels*.

As an example, let's talk about bananas. Imagine a banana on your kitchen counter. From childhood, we learn to label and describe what we perceive. We learn, for example, that this thing we can point to, touch and eat is *called* a banana. We can call this use of language the *Descriptive Level* or the level of statements of 'facts'. We also learn to make inferences about our experiences. For example, in learning that what we call a banana tastes good, we might infer that when we see something else that looks like what we call a banana, this something else will taste good too. Let's call this *Inference Level$_1$*. We might generalize that certain things shaped similarly but looking somewhat different are all called bananas. We can form "theories"; for example, the theory that anything we see which looks like what we've learned to call a banana will also taste good. Based on this questionable inference, we may take a bite out of a plastic 'banana' or a rotten one. Let's call this *Inference Level$_2$*. We can think or talk about each of these levels of experience, and then think or talk about our thinking and talking, make inferences about our inferences, etc. Theoretically, this process can go on unendingly. So we say *Et Cetera*.

When we function at our best, we use our ability to differentiate our evaluations in this way to lead us back to events and our silent-level experiences and observations of them (represented by the arrows going back toward the *Event*). This helps us to eat bananas we find delicious and avoid eating the plastic or rotten ones. These different levels occur together. However, we often are not aware of them or of how they affect our lives. Using GS we focus our attention on them. The Structural Differential provides a visual tool which can help to separate out the different levels of existence and experience in order to understand them better and function more effectively.

As Stuart Mayper showed, this model of the abstracting-evaluating process seems remarkably similar to that of Einstein's model of thinking, discussed in Chapter 7. As shown below, Mayper flipped the Structural Differential around, which makes it easier to see how the elements of Einstein's model of thinking map onto it. While Einstein's model emphasizes the scientist's process of making conjectural jumps from experience, applying 'logic', and then testing against experience, the Structural Differential emphasizes the structure of the underlying neuro-psycho-logical process of abstracting through which this takes place. The movement from E (experience), to J (the conjectural jump) to A (assumptions, axioms, theoretical models) to S (statements about experience deduced from A) and back to E again (testing against experience) is shown on the two diagrams side-by-side.

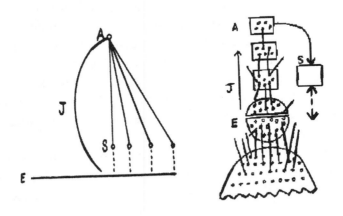

Figure 5
Einstein's Model of Thinking / Korzybski's Model of Abstracting [8]

Korzybski's Legacy

After publishing *Science and Sanity*, Korzybski worked intensively with individuals and seminar groups, seeking to find out to what extent his system worked. The importance of language as a neuro-evaluative 'lever' (discussed in detail in the following chapter), of having the courage of one's assumptions, and of questioning them, remained key to his teaching and writing. He founded the Institute of General Semantics in 1938 in Chicago—in 1946 moving it to Lime Rock, Connecticut, where he continued writing and teaching individuals and groups until his death on March 1, 1950.

In "A Memoir: Alfred Korzybski & his Work," Korzybski's close co-worker, M. Kendig, wrote:

> The circumstances of his death, it so happened, were symbolic of his life and work. In working with students, he exhibited a tremendous power of caring about any individual bit of humanity before him. He was continuously aware that some infantile evaluation he might be struggling to change in an individual mirrored a symptom from the social syndrome. He spent the last few hours of his life at his desk working on such a problem. In his non-elementalistic orientation, the individual *and* society were split verbally only for convenience. Empirically, they could no more be split in the world of facts than space *and* time, psyche *and* soma, heredity *and* environment, etc. To him, no human problems were 'insignificant' problems. Thus the intensity, the warmth of his social feelings, the lavish extravagant ways he spent himself. He died March first at three o'clock in the morning. He had lived for 70 years, 7 months and 29 days.[9]

In the remainder of Part II of *Dare to Inquire*, I provide a broad but detailed thematic overview of the legacy which Korzybski left us—the general theory/discipline of evaluation, which became known as "general semantics." The theory was already present in less-well-developed form in Korzybski's earlier writings. It is based upon the foundations of time-binding, logical fate, scientific-mathematical attitudes and worldview, the neuro-evaluational view, and the structural differential. In *Science and Sanity* and later writings, Korzybski developed a consciously integrated system of formulations, exploring their connections, implications and applications in more rigorous language and detail. The system has a kind-of fractal structure. Each formulation is related to others and has relations with the whole. I hope my discussion of the development, shape and implications of the GS system will stimulate you to explore Korzybski's legacy—and more importantly to apply it.

Chapter 10
What We Do With Language—What It Does With Us

Neuro-Linguistic Relativity

A particular view of language relates to the applied, evaluational approach I'm suggesting. Language is intertwined with behavior, consciousness, etc. It has a neurological base; that is, it doesn't exist entirely separately from nervous systems-persons using the words. By means of spiral feedback mechanisms, we create our language; our language affects us; we create our language; etc., ongoingly. This individual process is embedded in, influences and is influenced by, a particular culture and community of others.

This view, "linguistic relativity," has a history in western culture going back at least several hundred years to the work of Vico and von Humboldt and more recently to linguistic anthropologists Franz Boas, Edward Sapir and Benjamin Lee Whorf, among others.

For those who espouse linguistic relativity, what we call 'language' and 'culture', 'consciousness' and 'behavior' develop and operate together through individual and group experience. (Since they do not function in complete isolation from each other, although they can be considered separately, I put the terms in single quotes here.) Linguistic anthropologist Michael Agar has coined the term "languaculture" to label the joint phenomenon of language-culture. How do these factors work together?

Without denying cross-cultural similarities among humans, the principle of linguistic relativity implies that, as Whorf scholar Penny Lee wrote:

> ...although all observers may be confronted by the same physical evidence in the form of experiential data and although they may be capable of "externally similar acts of observation"... a person's 'picture of the universe' or 'view of the world' differs as a function of the particular language or languages that person knows.[1]

Korzybski and Keyser independently and earlier formulated similar notions in relation to undefined terms, logical fate, etc. As you may recall, they contended that the culturally-inherited structure of an individual's language, *including his or her terminology, grammar, logic, doctrines, etc.*, relates to assumptions, premises, implications about the structure of ourselves and the world.

In *Science and Sanity*, Korzybski hinted at the practical implications of this structure even within a particular, apparently 'unified' languaculture:

> We do not realize what tremendous power the structure of an habitual language has. It is not an exaggeration to say that it enslaves us through the mechanism of *s.r* [semantic or evaluational reactions] and that the structure which a language exhibits, and impresses upon us unconsciously, is *automatically projected* upon the world around us.[2]

Various distorted versions of this view have come to be known as the "Sapir-Whorf Hypothesis," an academic abstraction which does not label anything that Sapir or Whorf ever put forward as a hypothesis on their own. (The principle of linguistic relativity which they did put forward can be interpreted in various ways and may lead to many different hypotheses.) Some scholars have pursued their own distorted interpretations and made a straw-man rendering of Whorf's views.

As you might imagine, much controversy has been generated by the various versions and responses to them. I consider this controversy important to examine in some detail in *Dare to Inquire,* due to the centrality of linguistic relativity in general semantics. I discuss the general-semantics view in the course of going into various other versions.

Language and Thought

According to psychologist Steven Pinker, both Whorf and Korzybski presented linguistic relativity as a single-valued, absolutistic and uni-directional belief that "language determines thought."[3] This "strong version" (and 'weaker' ones as well) of the supposed Sapir-Whorf hypothesis is "wrong, all wrong"[4] claims Pinker (widely accepted as an expert in linguistics and psychology).

Actually, neither Whorf nor Korzybski posited a 'language' entirely isolated from human behavior-in-a-culture as the sole, one-directional, single-valued determinant of some separable entity called 'thought'. According to both men, 'language', 'thought' (more accurately, neuro-evaluational processes), 'behavior', and 'culture' do not function separately but rather as elements within a gestalt (a unified whole) where they mutually interact in multi-dimensional and probabilistic ways.

In saying that 'language' does not function separately from 'thought', I do not mean to imply, as Pinker does, that either formulator claimed that there is no 'thought' without 'language'. Whorf, at the very least, qualified this and Korzybski denied it.

Neither did they deny the possibility of inborn and 'universal' language-related processes, more or less impervious to cultural modification. Nevertheless, the thrust of their work suggests that language has important aspects modifiable through learning. Through *neuro-linguistic* (a term originated by Korzybski) processes, our language use helps create modifiable *neuro*-evaluational, *neuro*-linguistic environments, i.e., cultures, which can change and grow through time-binding. We not only do things with 'language', 'language' does things with us.

The general-semantics view of linguistic relativity appears unique among other versions of linguistic relativity for several reasons. First is its explicit *neurological emphasis*. Using general-semantics language, we can talk more accurately in terms of neuro-linguistic relativity:

> Even a gramophone record undergoes some physical changes before words or noises can be 'stored' and/or re-

produced. Is it so very difficult to understand that the extremely sensitive and highly complex human nervous system also undergoes some electro-colloidal changes before words, evaluations, etc., are stored, produced, or reproduced?"[5]

Before his untimely death, Whorf appeared to be struggling toward such an explicit neurological formulation as well.[6]

A second point which distinguishes general semantics from many other views of linguistic relativity is its focus on an individual's *language behavior or use* as it relates to his or her evaluative (roughly 'cognitive') processes. The term "language" as neurocognitive linguist Sydney Lamb has noted, does not necessarily stand for one thing. Using a device suggested by general semanticists, Lamb indexes language$_1$, language$_2$, and language$_3$.

> ...when we look closely we can see that it ["language"] is used for a number of quite distinct collections of phenomena selected from the kaleidoscopic flux, including especially these three: (1) language as a set of sentences (e.g. Chomsky) or utterances (Bloomfield); (2) language as the system that lies behind such productions; (3) language as linguistic processes, as in the title of Winograd's *Language as a Cognitive Process* (1980).[7]

A given general language$_1$ system such as English, French, German, etc., can have within it distinguishable dialects (regional variations) and registers (professional and group variations, such as the language of physicians, etc.). Individual speakers or writers of a given language$_1$ will have unique particular variations within the more general system—which may include their vocabulary, logic, metaphors, doctrines, etc. Language$_2$ includes the neuro-linguistic processes by which we generate language$_1$. A large part of human evaluative processes relates to language behavior or use, i.e., language$_3$. We learn how to do things with words in a social context in order to negotiate our lives with others—and with ourselves. Language$_3$ has become an area of increasing academic interest in recent years, as for example in discussions of "thinking for speaking" and "speech acts." General semantics especially focuses on language$_3$—how an individual's evaluative processes relate to their language$_1$ generated from the neurological processes involved in language production, language$_2$.

A third factor that distinguishes general semantics from other forms of linguistic relativity is its specific attention to *practical implications and applications*—even within the boundaries of a particular, apparently 'unified' languaculture. Whorf, who died in his forties, noted but was not able to elaborate much on the more practical implications of linguistic relativity. On the other hand, general semantics focuses on ways in which individuals can become more aware of the effects of their language and its implicatory structure for ill and for good.

"Sticks and stones can break my bones but words can never harm me," goes a saying from my childhood. On the contrary, neuro-linguistic factors, i.e., *words with the associated neuro-evaluative processes in each of us*, can play a harmful, sometimes quite toxic role in our lives—especially if we remain unconscious of their implications.

We have particularly good access to our linguistic behavior, which appears modifiable to some degree. This is not any form of word magic. We're interested in the underlying implications and orientation reflected in the structure of language. These involve our evaluational (semantic) reactions, including so-called verbal 'thinking', as well as non-verbal 'thinking', 'feeling', behaving, etc. By becoming more aware of our language and its implications, we can nudge our orientation to get closer in line with so-called 'facts'.

The Chomskyite Protest

The theory of Noam Chomsky has dominated linguistic studies in the United States for decades. Chomsky has consistently argued for the universal, innate and unlearned structure of human language. Building on Chomsky's work (focusing on language$_1$), Steven Pinker has proposed that the structure of language, i.e., grammar, etc., comes primarily by means of what he calls a "language instinct" determined by genes.

This chomskyite approach has now begun to show serious wear with little positive results for the claim that "language is an instinct." (This failure has serious implications for the more general program of "sociobiology" or "evolutionary psychology" as well.) Linguist Geoffrey Sampson has done an especially thorough job of analyzing the inadequacies of chomskyite views. Sampson has concluded that:

> ...there are some universal features in human languages, but what they mainly show is that human beings have to learn their mother tongues from scratch rather than having knowledge of language innate in their minds. Except for the properties that lead to that conclusion, languages are just different (except that they probably do all contain nouns and verbs)...[8]

It seems that Dante had more or less the right view when he wrote in his *Paradiso*:

> Tis nature's work that man should utter words,
> But whether thus or thus, 'tis left to you
> To do as seems most pleasing.[9]

Nonetheless, the great popularity of the chomskyite program has probably prevented many people from taking Whorf's and Korzybski's work more seriously. To those who believe that most of language structure gets determined genetically, the differences between different linguistic groups can in some sense be considered trivial. If one accepts Pinker's claim that in its most significant aspects "language is not a cultural artifact," [10] then attention to language use cannot be used to affect human perception and behavior in the way general semanticists and others claim it can.

I decided to closely examine Pinker's dismissal of linguistic relativity in his book *The Language Instinct*, to see if there was anything there that would require me to revise my own views. The lack of substance in his arguments surprised me. Pinker's presentation does not seem notable for its accuracy and fairness regarding opposing views. It illustrates how someone nominally functioning as a scientist can block the way of inquiry. As Lamb noted, "Those who doubt that language can influence thinking are unlikely to be vigilant for the effects of language on their own thinking." [11]

Non-Verbal 'Thinking'

Pinker states that "General Semantics lays the blame for human folly on insidious 'semantic damage' to thought perpetrated by the structure of language." [12] Pinker finds this something to scoff at. However, Korzybski did not talk or write in terms of 'blame' or of 'thought' and 'language' so elementalistically.

A more accurate rendering of a general-semantics view of 'language' and 'thought' states that the structure of a language, with its associated neuro-semantic (evaluative) reactions—in each of us, at a given time, among other factors—affects our ongoing behavior, perception, evaluating, etc., for good and ill. Pinker may be unable to understand the nuances of this view because, as a good chomskyite, he lacks the linguistic consciousness that would allow him to stop objectifying the abstract terms 'language' and 'thought' as if they represented isolated entities in the world.

Despite his inaccurate description of general semantics, Pinker does correctly conclude that general semanticists find some support for their views in Whorf's work. Unfortunately, Pinker also *in*correctly concludes that linguistic relativity must imply that "thought is the same thing as language" [13] and writes at great length to refute this. However, his efforts here have *no relevance whatsoever* to either Korzybski's or Whorf's actual views. Neither claimed that "thought is the same thing as language." In fact they both directly denied this while not eliminating the importance of what Penny Lee calls "linguistic thinking" (Lamb's language$_3$).

In Korzybski's case, as I have already emphasized, the term "semantic(s)" in general semantics implies "evaluation" and does not typically refer to "just words" despite the usage of those ill-informed about general semantics. Evaluation, as I've already noted, refers to happening-meanings, i.e., 'thinking', 'feeling', verbal and *non-verbal* organism-as-a-whole transactions within an environment. Indeed, Korzybski stressed the importance of non-verbal formulating within his understanding of neuro-linguistic behavior, noting that silent contemplating and visualization can allow us to take in and develop fresh information, relatively unbiased by verbal ruts.

Basic Color Terms

Pinker also makes much of the "basic color term" research of Berlin and Kay, and of Rosch, as disproof of whorfian-korzybskian views.[14] Even though different languacultures have differing numbers of color terms, there does seem to exist a rough, cross-cultural sequence of those colors which get labeled first, second, third, etc. In addition, people across different cultures may tend to pick particular focal colors as the best examples or prototypes for a particular category. Although at least some of this work has flaws in both its data collection and interpretation, it does lend support to the notion that some aspects of language may depend upon the biologically-based perceptual equipment of humans across cultures. This doesn't, by the way, prove that some gene or genes are directly responsible for specific, observable language behaviors. Trial-and-error empirical learning may still play a role even in the development of color terms, however biologically based. (Note that "based" does not equate with "solely determined by.")

Despite Pinker's and other chomskyite's attempts to make this an either-or issue, any research which shows the possibility of some cross-cultural, biological basis for some of the terms we use does not actually challenge the notion of linguistic relativity. Neuro-linguistic relativity held non-absolutely has no inherent conflict with some degree of non-absolutist neuro-linguistic universalism, which may have some more or less direct biological basis.

Hopi Concept of 'Time'

Unfortunately Pinker doesn't play fair when it comes to discussing these issues. His representations of linguistic relativity cannot be relied upon for accuracy. For example, he uses selective quotes to 'prove' that Whorf made "outlandish claims" that the Hopi Indians were "oblivious to time" and did not have tenses in their language.[15] Although Whorf's analysis of Hopi languaculture may not be entirely flawless, a comparison of Pinker's claims about it and what Whorf actually wrote results in very different pictures.

It seems clear from a full, non-selective reading of Whorf's work that he recognized the importance of how the Hopi languaculture clearly deals with durations and times. Whorf did not deny that the Hopi have used dating or calendars, counted the number of days or duration of events, etc. What he did claim was that the Hopi did not conceptualize "space or time as such" in the reified manner that we do in English and other Indo-European languages. This has been corroborated by others who have lived within and studied Hopi language and culture, such as anthropologist Edward Hall.

Eskimo Snow

In his crusade to show how linguistic relativity is wrong, Pinker doesn't seem to mind descending to personal attack either. A common "urban legend" claims that Eskimo language has hundreds of different words for snow. By connecting Whorf's work to this popular claim, Pinker suggests that Whorf was party to a hoax. According to Pinker, from a report of four Eskimo words for snow made by Boas in 1911 "...Whorf embellished the count to seven and implied that there were more. His article was widely reprinted, then cited in textbooks and popular books on language, which led to successively inflated estimates in other textbooks, articles and newspaper columns of Amazing Facts." [16]

Whorf actually wrote that English had one word for snow and Eskimo had three. Whorf used data that he had available at the time of this writing (1940) to emphasize that: "Languages classify items of experience differently. The class corresponding to one word and one thought in language A may be regarded by language B as two or more classes corresponding to two or more words and thoughts." [17] To say that Whorf embellished anything here distorts what he said. Whorf does not have responsibility in any way, as Pinker tries to suggest, for other people's exaggerations and misinterpretations. This constitutes pure name-calling and has no basis in fact. [18]

Experimental Evidence for Linguistic Relativity

Studies to deliberately test one or another interpretation of linguistic relativity have gone on for at least a half-century. This research remains an area of great contention and, despite the claims of chomskyites to some sort of victory, their efforts to declare linguistic relativity "bunk" don't stand up to analysis. Pinker and others have attempted to downplay the significance of tests that corroborate the notion that words can in some sense have an effect on memory or categorization. However, the evidence hardly seems "weak." The results of these tests have sometimes surprised researchers who didn't necessarily favor linguistic relativity.

In one set of classic studies, subjects were shown colored chips. The colors varied in their *codability*, how easily an individual could apply a color label or name from his or her language to a chip. The chips were then removed, mixed up and shown again to the experimental subjects, who were asked to pick out the chips they had been shown before. The more easily labeled, more codable chips, appeared *more available*. In other words, the subjects had a better memory for, and could pick out, the more easily labeled chips, even though they could also remember colored chips without names.[19]

Pinker briefly mentioned and pooh-poohed the significance of another study about which the experimenters concluded that that the habitual categories of speakers' languages could indeed influence their color-categorizing behavior.[20] One of the researchers, Willett Kempton, later wrote:

A simple experiment, clear data, and seeing the Whorfian effect with our own eyes: It was a powerful conversion experience unlike anything I've experienced in my scientific career. Perhaps this all just goes to affirm Seguin's earlier quote, as applying to us as both natives and as theorists: "We have met the natives whose language filters the world—and they are us."[21]

Neuro-Linguistic Revision

Do this simple experiment. Have a friend select a number of newspaper headlines of similar size. Find a distance at which the friend can hold the headlines so that you cannot make out what they say. At this distance, when your friend tells you what an unfamiliar headline reads, the headline will probably 'pop out' at you.

This experiment provides a literal demonstration of *neuro-linguistic revision*. It illustrates how your linguistic maps may have a visible effect on what you 'perceive', respond to, etc. Indeed, to a great extent we react to what goes on around us as a function of the linguistic maps that we hold. In other words, we often appear to react to our neuro-linguistic reactions.

To the extent that the structure of our language fails to adequately map the non-verbal territory, we may ignore important 'facts' or respond to fictitious entities created by our way of talking. We do well to become aware of and, when necessary, change the structure of our language in order to create more adequate linguistic maps. The languages of science and mathematics not only provide another worldview but also serve as models for the kind of linguistic behavior that can help us improve our evaluative abilities. They provide especially powerful means for helping us to fit our language to the non-verbal world.

This doesn't mean that we can create a language that perfectly matches the world. Quite the reverse: our representations remain that; never exactly the same as what we're representing. Does it follow from this that we waste our time when we try to tidy up language, to make it more structurally in keeping with the structure of the non-verbal world? Surely not!

On the contrary, if our representations have properties not shared by the thing represented, or vice versa, we need to look at that. It indicates a lack of fit or structural similarity between our mode of representation and what we wish to represent. This lack of fit can lead to problems and should be put right to the degree possible. We can study other languages and linguistically expressed viewpoints, including the language of science and mathematics, to expand our 'perceptions' and 'conceptions' of the world.

Neuro-linguistic relativity provides another way of understanding logical fate. Its significance relates not only to different 'languages' as conventionally understood, i.e., English, Hopi, Tarahumara, etc. (language$_1$), but also and perhaps even more importantly to the "linguistic" behavior of each individual (language$_3$). The words we use, the sentences we say, the logic we apply, the doctrines we espouse, insofar as they are done in language, must be produced and affect us through neuro-linguistic (language$_2$) mechanisms.

If we do not understand these mechanisms, we are more likely to misuse them and/or to become misused by means of them. The faith-based mass-murderers of September 11, 2001 probably screamed "Allahu Akbar" (Arabic for "God is Great" as they killed themselves and thousands of others. They could not have done what they did without their particular language-based evaluations. Their actions inevitably required neuro-semantic, neuro-linguistic mechanisms and influences in order to occur.

Training in the system of GS provides an explicit language of evaluation. This language and its associated evaluative (semantic) reactions make our own neuro-evaluative, neuro-linguistic mechanisms more codable and thus more available for each one of us to consciously control. Semiotics pioneer Charles Morris wrote:

> The work of A. Korzybski and his followers, psycho-biological in orientation, has largely been devoted to the therapy of the individual, aiming to protect the individual against exploitation by others and by himself.[22]

In the next chapter, "Mapping Our Experience," I illustrate the basic mechanism through which this neuro-evaluative, neuro-linguistic control occurs. The suggestions for practice which follow provide many neuro-linguistic devices which, if used, can influence perception and behavior in less unsane/insane and more positive, inquiry-oriented directions.

Chapter 11
Mapping Our Experience

Extensional Orientation

A more positive, inquiry-oriented direction for human evaluating consists of giving primary importance to non-verbal 'facts'. We call this an *extensional orientation*, in contrast to an intensional orientation based on words and definitions.

It seems generally the case that any given languaculture, unless it provides for ways to do otherwise, will tend to encourage an intensional orientation, i.e., accepting the categories it establishes verbally as the way the world actually 'is'. This seems as true of various scientific-mathematical 'tribes' (seen as languacultures) as it does for those in New Guinea, and elsewhere.

This distinction between intensional and extensional orientations is derived from the more limited distinction in logic between intensional and extensional definitions.

An intensional definition defines a term by relating it to other words, categories, etc. For example, I can define the word "horse" as "a large solid-hoofed herbivorous mammal...domesticated by man since a prehistoric period and used as a beast of burden, a draft animal, or for riding."[1] An intensional definition places the term we define within a broader set or class.

An extensional definition defines a term by pointing to a non-verbal referent or fact. Thus, I define "horse" by pointing to an actual horse. I broaden this somewhat to include pointing to pictures as well as providing examples in words. Extensional definitions also encompass operational definitions which give instructions for experiencing what we are defining or talking about. With extensional definitions we enumerate individuals considered within a classification.

Both intensional and extensional definitions seem useful and necessary. We need both the ability to define words with other words and to point to what we are talking about. Ultimately, however, we use words to help us deal with non-verbal facts. In GS, we extend the notions of intensional/extensional definitions to talk about general orientations toward life.

An intensionally-oriented person orients him or herself primarily in relation to the intensional, verbal definitions of a particular languaculture (neuro-evaluative environment). He or she knows 'all' about someone upon learning that they 'are' Jewish, gay or Republican.

Extensionally-oriented people may have certain biases based on how someone or something gets classified in their languaculture. However, they practice seeing every individual as a unique member of that class, different from any other member. A particular Jew, gay or Republican differs from any other. Thus an extensionally-oriented person investigates the non-verbal 'facts' beyond words.

Developing an extensional orientation includes acquiring or maintaining an ability to use intensional definitions without getting caught in a web of words. Since different languages 'slice' the world in different ways, learning a new language (a languaculture) with its associated neuro-evaluational reactions can often help us to break out of that web. Even in the 'same' language, we can help ourselves break out by finding out how someone else defines and uses a term. Gather together with several other people and play a game of "Twenty Definitions." How might "democracy," "red," "work," for example, be defined? This extensional game can provide many revelations.

GS provides a system for learning how to function more extensionally. It was designed to help individuals gain deeper insight into how we variously map the world with our 'perceptions' and 'concepts', our images and words, and how we can improve the process.

Maps and Territories

A useful way of understanding an extensional orientation consists in viewing our 'perceptions', symbols, languages, etc., as systems of representation or maps. In mathematics, mapping involves "...establishing correspondences between points in one region and points in another. The corresponding points in the second region are said to be *images* of the points in the first region."[2] Once we understand the principles of correspondence being used, the 'images' of our map can be said to have, in Korzybski's words, some "similarity of structure" to whatever is getting mapped.

A road map, insofar as it is accurate and useful, has such a similarity of structure to the territory it represents. The map establishes correspondences with a territory, the actual roads of city or town, which can then usefully guide travelers on their journeys. Does it require so much of a stretch, then, to also view our perceptual, symbolic and verbal representations as maps?

Not really. The centrality of the notion of mapping to general semantics appears to have a solid footing in more recent work on the centrality of mapping to nervous systems. What we each perceive depends upon what our nervous systems filter and select from the patterns of relations (the structure) of the happenings around and within us. Relations among our nerve cells literally map certain aspects of these patterns. Basing their work on that of Hughlings Jackson and others, neuroscientists like John Allman have found intricate multi-level mappings within the visual cortex, sensory-motor cortex, etc., which correspond to areas in the visual field, areas of the body, etc.[3] These mappings are not entirely 'hard-wired' genetically, but have some plasticity or ability to change size and connectivity based on experience.

Our nervous systems, in turn, create higher-level mappings of these basic sensory-perceptual mappings by means of additional patterns of relations among neurons, which ultimately correspond to the symbols and words we use. These higher-level mappings in turn are connected to and can influence lower-level mappings, motor processes, etc.

So, the world—which includes us—has a structure: complex, dynamic, and multi-dimensional. The structures of our 'perceptual' and 'conceptual' maps more or less fit the structure of the world. The greater the similarity of structure of our neural mappings to the world, the better the fit. Our maps become more useful, providing better predictability. We are less likely to wander in an apparent wilderness, more likely to reach our destination.

Structure, as noted previously, provides the sole content of knowledge. And greater similarity of structure provides the criterion for moving in a more extensional direction. By connecting epistemology with neurology in this way, Korzybski was an early proponent of "naturalized epistemology." Logician W. V. Quine, one of Korzybski's early seminar students, later labeled and promulgated this notion.

Korzybski formulated the following premises regarding maps. First, "a map *is not* the territory." Our perceptions, symbols, words, statements, etc., are not the same as what they represent. Second, "a map covers *not all* the territory." Aspects of what we represent inevitably get filtered out in the process of mapping, representing, symbolizing. Third , "a map is *self-reflexive*." We can map our maps, represent our representations, symbolize our symbols, talk about our talking, etc.[4]

These three premises of mapping provide a way to consider intensionally- and extensionally-oriented behavior. Intensionally, I may formulate in words that "gay people are no good," based on my limited (or non-existent) experience. If I self-reflexively apply the three premises to this statement, I may begin to extensionalize my words and reorient them toward facts.

I realize first that my map of gay people is not the same as the 'territory' of gay people as a whole or of any particular gay person. Second, the statement has an implied allness to it, i.e., 'all' gay people are no good. How do I know? Have I met and observed all of them? Could I be wrong? Do I know everything about any individual gay person? Insofar as I have begun to analyze my statement, I am applying the third premise, making statements about my statements, thinking about my thinking, etc.

Becoming more extensional involves internalizing the GS premises about mapping. This may sound 'simple'. But it is not necessarily easy since prejudices and outworn beliefs, no matter how false, often feel safe and comfortable. Extensional self-challenge requires a certain willingness to discomfort oneself, a willingness to question one's familiar maps that goes to the core of what I mean by daring to inquire.[5]

The Process of Abstracting

In GS, we have a special interest in the function of language as a mediated mapping, a mapping of non-verbal 'perceptions', 'thinking', 'feelings', etc., that in turn constitute mappings derived from the processing of sensory inputs. The activity of nervous system mapping is referred to as *the process of abstracting.*

The process of abstracting qualifies as one of the most central formulations in GS. As a general-semantics term, *abstracting* includes the mapping of our non-verbal experiences from the energetic processes inside and outside our skins as well as the further representing of it symbolically and linguistically. A product of this process, at any level—whether a non-verbal perception or a mathematical formula—is referred to as an *abstraction* (at a given level).

On the next page is a model of the neurological abstracting process that incorporates the main components of GS. This model combines aspects of the Structural Differential (SD) with a later diagram on the process of abstracting which Korzybski used.[6] My wife and I have modified Korzybski's original models in order to emphasize interactivity and feedback loops. As you read, contemplate how the following components relate to your life.

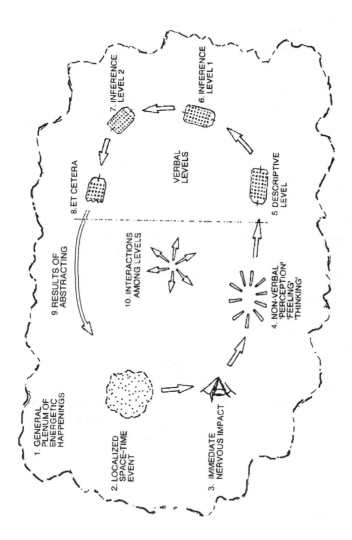

Figure 6 Abstracting Process

1. GENERAL PLENUM OF ENERGETIC HAPPENINGS

2. LOCALIZED SPACE-TIME EVENT

3. IMMEDIATE NERVOUS IMPACT

4. NON-VERBAL 'PERCEPTION' 'FEELING' 'THINKING'

5. DESCRIPTIVE LEVEL

6. INFERENCE LEVEL 1

7. INFERENCE LEVEL 2

8. ET CETERA

9. RESULTS OF ABSTRACTING

10. INTERACTIONS AMONG LEVELS

VERBAL LEVELS

1. A general plenum (fullness) of ever-changing events; an energetic field of space-time happenings which comprise "all" by definition; the broken outer line indicates that the plenum goes on indefinitely.

2. Within this plenum, a localized space-time event which comprises the happening of interest at a particular moment. On the structural differential (SD) the plenum and localized event are represented by the event-level parabola.

3. The immediate nervous impact of the event, as experienced through each individual's senses. At this level, we enter the realm of abstracting, the nervous-system process of representation of sub-microscopic, energetic events into internal non-verbal and verbal experiences. On the SD this corresponds to the connected and hanging strings from the event to the object level.

Abstracting occurs on different levels or orders. Each subsequent 'higher' order involves further abstracting from previous 'lower' orders. At each level, some particulars get left out, while others get included. Categories are created and details can be overlooked. In this way, similarities may tend to get overemphasized.

Although this discussion of abstracting begins, by convention, with an 'initial' nervous impact, I want to make clear that I *do not* accept a linear causal, stimulus-response view of behavior, with an 'initial' stimulus from the environment 'setting off' behavior. In this GS view, abstracting involves an ongoing, circularly causal, organism-environment transaction guided by the internal processes (including higher-level abstractions such as beliefs, etc.) of an individual adapting the environment to her/himself.

When the notion of negative feedback began to be discussed in the 1940s as part of the new science of cybernetics, Korzybski quickly saw that this provided a framework for talking about the cyclic or spiral processes of abstracting and time-binding that he had previously described. In recent years, feedback control mechanisms have been most comprehensively applied to human behavior in the Perceptual Control Theory (PCT) of William T. Powers and associates. This important work supports the approach developed by Korzybski by providing an explicit and exact theory which shows "...behavior [as] the process by which we act on the world to control perceptions that matter to us."[7]

4. Our individual non-verbal 'perception', 'feeling', 'thinking' (including assumptions, expectations), etc. This corresponds to the object-level circle in the SD, what Korzybski called the "unspeakable objective level." It is at this non-verbal level that we experience what we call 'objects', which we abstract from the inferred space-time plenum of events. This level remains inseparable from so-called 'subjective' factors.

Philosopher F. S. C. Northrop referred to this non-verbal level as the "immediately apprehendable...differentiated aesthetic continuum" which involves "the aesthetic, intuitive, purely empirically given component in man and nature."[8] At this level we may read instruments, make observations and take measurements as well as enjoy art, make love and feel at 'one' with nature. (The process of abstracting and an attitude of inquiry encompasses 'all' human activities, including the 'arts'; vital but not the focus of this book.) Korzybski strongly advised practice in "silence on the un-speakable objective level" in order to adequately internalize general semantics (he wasn't, however, advising the total abandonment of speech).

5. The verbal levels start here with our individual first-order languaging (use of language) in relation to the un-speakable. Indicated by the picture of a label, first-order languaging includes naming of objects and description of observations made at the non-verbal level. It can be called the level of statements of 'fact' or the descriptive level, the first verbal level of the SD. The general distinction between non-verbal and verbal levels is indicated in the model by the vertical, dotted line.

6. Inference Level$_1$ represents our individual second-order language use in relation to the previous levels. Represented similarly on the SD, this can be thought of as the first level of stating inferences, making assessments and judgements about what we've abstracted so far.

7. Inference Level$_2$, both here and on the SD, represents our individual inferences about our prior inferences and other abstracting; in part this can include generalizations as well as further reacting to reactions.

8. As on the SD, the "Et Cetera" level indicates that we can continue to abstract from our abstractions, theoretically unendingly. The higher orders of abstracting include scientific theories at a date; i.e., our 'knowledge' about the workings of the universe—tested through laboratory experiments and field observations—which comprise what we know about the plenum of sub-microscopic happenings.

9. An arrow returning to the plenum, indicating that the results of our abstracting at a particular time become part of the plenum from which we and others further abstract.

10. Arrows in several directions moving out from the center of the model, indicating that the various levels of abstracting occur simultaneously and interactively. When we speak about them as if they are completely separate (elementalism), we introduce an artifact of language.

Everything we know gets mediated through the nervous system, through the process of abstracting. As far as I know, there is no way out. Rather, as Robert Anton Wilson wrote, "We cannot make meaningful statements about some assumed…'true reality', etc. apart *from ourselves and our nervous systems and other instruments.*" [9]

Knowledge consists of the similarity of structure (isomorphism) between the presumed 'reality' outside of our nervous systems (which we never 'experience directly') and our nervous system abstractions or mappings.

By viewing abstracting in terms of a mapping process, we can understand anew the basic principles of general semantics: *A map is not the territory. A map is not all of the territory. A map is self-reflexive.* These non-aristotelian premises (going beyond but incorporating aristotelian logic and viewpoints) represent a non-absolutistic, process orientation which recognizes the individuality of particular conditions and purposes, etc., in daily life. With it we adopt an attitude of generalized uncertainty while still allowing for a limited definiteness open to revision.

Now, let's consider further the map-territory premises. Immersed in, and comprised of a sub-microscopic, energetic process of ongoing flux and change, we use our senses to abstract what becomes our individual experience of 'reality'. So even at a non-verbal, sensory level—what Korzybski called the "unspeakable"—we have created perceptual maps that are not the presumed 'sub-microscopic' territory. Thus general semantics falls within the realm of constructivist theories:

> Modern constructivism examines those processes of perception, behavior, and communication which we human beings use to *create* our individual, social, scientific, and ideological realities, instead of *finding* them ready-made in the outside world, as we all naively assume."[10]

Our perceptual maps inevitably are not identical to the presumed territory they represent and necessarily leave out aspects of it, due to human biological limitations and our personal physical limitations and histories. Our perceptions form our non-verbal worlds.

On the verbal levels, we then can talk about our non-verbal experiences. However, our words cannot capture all of those perceptual experiences, and cannot fully express the non-separable, un-speakable aspects of non-verbal sensing, feeling, thinking and behaving. We can learn how to make our language more closely fit our non-verbal reality, but our word maps *are not* the non-verbal 'reality' they represent, nor can we ever completely map it with words. Language, despite the limitations of the abstracting process, enables us to use our human ability to communicate among ourselves and across generations and to build testable theories that may improve life. We do well, however, to remain conscious of these limitations.

Further, nervous-system processes allow us to self-reflexively create verbal maps of our verbal maps, potentially unendingly. We can spin ever-more-general categories, hypotheses, etc., for better and worse. These higher-level verbalizations influence our perceptions and non-verbal experiences in an ongoing way. In addition, our maps can be seen as mappings of our own nervous system processes along with those of whatever else we're mapping.

Lack of consciousness of the mechanisms of abstracting (which can occur in varying degrees) generally involves confusing or identifying the results of our abstracting processes at different levels with what they represent (their respective territories). It corresponds to an intensional orientation. Definitions and higher-order verbalizations become the prime 'reality'. Nigh all of us have probably had experience with people who prefer to talk abstractly, grandly, endlessly in lieu of getting down to the nitty-gritty of what's going on, or of practicing new and different behaviors.

Consciousness of the mechanisms of abstracting allows us to remember that our abstractions at various levels (nervous system mappings) are not the territories they represent. Such *consciousness of abstracting* as Korzybski called it, gives us a greater possibility of revising our maps when we bump our noses against 'reality' and find that our maps are not as similar to the presumed territory as we would like. This corresponds to an extensional orientation. With consciousness of abstracting, we can consciously abstract. We can use higher-order categories, generalizations and hypotheses to our benefit, while extensionally orientating ourselves primarily to 'facts' and behavior, i.e., to our non-verbal experiences. This enables us both to develop sound theories and live our daily lives on a sound factual basis.

Abstracting in Philosophy, Science and Everyday Life

The central GS notion of abstracting resonates with the work of Kant, Schopenhauer and other philosophers who had previously explored this epistemological territory. For example, Schopenhauer, who built upon Kant's work, very much seemed to be talking about abstracting when he wrote:

'The world is my idea' [This has also been translated as 'The world is my representation']: this is a truth which holds good for everything that lives and knows, though only man can bring it into reflected, abstract consciousness. If he really does this, philosophical discretion has evolved in him. It then becomes clear to him, and certain, that he knows not a sun, and not an earth, but only an eye that sees a sun, a hand that feels an earth; that the world which surrounds him exists only as an idea – that is, only in relation to something else, the one who conceives the idea, which is himself.[11]

What, then, makes GS special?

The GS model of abstracting brings previous philosophical discussion about epistemology into a scientific, naturalistic framework, one that is workable both for further research and application in everyday life. My general-semantics transformation of the passage from Schopenhauer reads:

Anything I experience or know about the 'world' consists of my abstractions: this truth, as far as I know, holds good for everything that lives and knows, though only a human can bring it into reflected consciousness. If one really does know this, philosophical-scientific-mathematical discretion (consciousness of abstracting) has evolved. It then becomes clear, and as 'certain' as anything, that one knows not a 'sun', and not an 'earth', but only the result of one's eye-brain-nervous-system transactions with a 'sun' and hand-brain-nervous-system transactions with an 'earth'. Each one of us participates in the 'world' as an integral part of it. The 'world' (which includes what is called "the body") exists—*as each of us experiences and knows it*— only in terms of abstractions at various levels. These abstractions exist only in relation to something else, the one who abstracts, oneself.

The notion of abstracting provides a key for Korzybski's critique of aristotelianism in philosophy, science and everyday life.

Chapter 12
De-Worming the Apples of Knowledge

Non-Aristotelian, Not Anti-Aristotelian

In the Introduction, I wrote that aristotelian 'worms' within 'the apples of human knowledge' have blocked the advancement of up-to-date scientific viewpoints and attitudes. Basic aristotelian assumptions about how the world works have become embedded and embodied in the structure of language and logic. Many scientists, philosophers, humanists and others have long taken these assumptions for granted. Korzybski's boldness in questioning them has led some people to consider him a maverick at the fringes of scientific-philosophical acceptability. In this chapter, I indicate the main features and applications, as I see them, of Korzybski's important critique of aristotelianism. This will lead us into methods for daring to inquire in different and more useful ways.

More than 2000 years ago, Aristotle and his followers created a system of logical rules for deriving valid propositions from starting premises. The "laws of thought" formulated by them are still considered by many people to provide the basis for sound reasoning. While he explored the limitations of aristotelian logic, Korzybski did not believe that it should be completely discredited or overturned. Rather the non-aristotelian revision that he outlined included the aristotelian system as a limited, special case.

Others have pointed out the limitations of aristotelian formulating. John Dewey, for example, wrote on problems within aristotelian logic and the need for a theory of inquiry which would include modern scientific understandings and methods.[1] Bertrand Russell, who was far from agreeing with Dewey's approach to philosophy, had also strongly criticized aristotelian logic, although he appeared to backslide in his later years. Korzybski, like these other formulators, attempted to show the underlying unity of scientific methods, as he interpreted it. Indeed, he shared this aim with Aristotle.

Non-Identity

The aristotelian 'law' of 'identity' was implied although not directly mentioned in Aristotle's works.[2] It constitutes one of the so-called laws of thought of traditional philosophy, along with the laws of contradiction and the excluded middle, which Aristotle did explictly advance.[3]

The law of identity, "A is A," often gets interpreted as a metaphysical statement that "everything is what it is and not something else."[4] In other words, everything is identical with or the same in all respects with itself.[5] In the view of Aristotle and his followers, when anything changes, some underlying "substance" of that which undergoes the change must remain permanent.[6] Knowledge consists of finding the 'essence' of this underlying nature or substance, which can be expressed in a definition.[7] We can call this an "essentialist" approach.

In contrast, GS is based on the process view formulated much earlier by Heraclitus, one of the most famous of the pre-Socratic philosophers of Greece who said, "Everything is flux."[8] In such a process universe, supported by current scientific understanding, nothing is 'identical' from moment to moment in all respects either with itself or anything else. Rather, the presumed 'identity' constitutes a verbalistic confusion: "...whatever we may *say* an object *'is'*, *it is not*, because the statement is verbal and the facts are not."[9]

A non-aristotelian denial of identity thus involves a divergence in basic assumptions from Aristotle's metaphysical views. Although we may treat them as equivalent, A is not A. Even as written on a piece of paper, the second "A" differs in space-time coordinates and 'physical' makeup from the first "A."[10]

The heraclitean flux of non-verbal facts does not, however, preclude observed regularities, which do occur within it. Similarity (not exact 'sameness') of structure exists and knowledge consists of finding such similarities through empirical research. This appears consistent with what Popper called "methodological nominalism" which aims to understand how things act in particular circumstances and looks for regularities in nature rather than for 'essences'.[11] We can call this a non-essentialist approach.

How can we explain the recognizable aspects of any particular individual if it is not even 'identical' with itself from one moment to the next? With Korzybski, we can postulate that the similarity of some 'thing' from moment to moment involves *varying degrees* of difference, from highly different to highly similar. But absolutely the same? Never! You can join with general semanticists in boldly going where Russell, Popper and others did not go by following through with the full implications of this position.

Logic and Empiricism

Formal logic and pure mathematics work when their rules are followed consistently to the logical conclusion. Useful in certain circumstances, but how about in daily life? When logic and mathematics are applied to the empirical world, our deductions no longer work absolutely and we are justified in comparing these symbolic structures to empirical facts. We can do this in regard to the so-called laws of thought. Thus in denying "identity":

> If we start, for instance, with a statement that 'a word is *not* the object spoken about', and some one tries to deny that, he would have to produce an actual physical object which would *be the word*,—impossible of performance, even in asylums for the 'mentally' ill.[12]

From an empirical standpoint, "identity" (absolute sameness in all aspects of any two things, events, formulations, etc.) cannot be shown non-verbally. Thus "identity" (so defined)[13] appears false to facts.

Symbolic Equivalence

In order to communicate, however imperfectly, we need to retain some similarity of 'meaning' for words and phrases used in discussion. Even given this, we do well to recognize that we had better work at agreement, rather than assume it. We do well to accept this agreement as approximate at best. We can label this similarity of 'meaning', "symbolic equivalence" or "symbolic univalence." [14] We can thus reject identity—sameness in all respects—and still avoid rejecting "A=A" or "1=1" as illusions. The "=" can be used to indicate equivalence, a function of an agreement by some humans to ignore differences.

From a neuro-linguistic viewpoint, 'meanings' constitute space-time happenings within human nervous systems (happening-meanings). 'Identity' of 'meaning' would involve an 'identity' of neurological processes between two or more people or even within a particular person from one time to another—not demonstrable. We must satisfy ourselves with getting as much similarity as possible, never perfect 'sameness', in a given context.

We must therefore take care when anyone begins to talk about their definition of a term as 'identical' or the 'same', even partially, with someone else's. Caution also seems warranted when we say that two things 'are' "identical with respect to their inclusion in the same class or in respect to the same property." [15]

Perhaps such limited uses of 'same' and 'identical' do not violate the GS principle of non-identity. Perhaps I may harmlessly say that you and I have the 'same' or 'identical' brand of raincoat if we both own a "London Fog" coat. Nonetheless, such usage can easily veer into overemphasizing the similarities and underemphasizing the extensional differences between the individual objects, persons, etc., under discussion. This became clear to me when a 6' 4" friend, seeing a raincoat the 'same' as his, went home with a 5' 4" man's coat draped over his arm.

Identification

The process of abstracting, as described in the last chapter, consists of the nervous system process of constructing or mapping our experience from the non-verbal process world and representing it in words and other symbols. The abstracting process is stratified on different levels: First comes some aspect of the un-speakable process world; then our non-verbal, aesthetic experience abstracted from it; then our lower-level labeling and descriptions of our experience; then our higher-level inferences and inferences about inferences, etc.

Each one of the levels of the abstracting model maps the previous level which serves as its immediate 'territory'. However, each abstracting-level map *is not* the territory it represents. Identification consists of confusing the different levels or orders of abstraction, ignoring the differences among them. Thus a map on one level is treated as if it is the same as the territory on a lower level that it represents. If we identify, we mistakenly attribute identity, creating disturbances of the abstracting process.

What kinds of disturbances? Identifying 'objects' with the non-verbal process world of events, qualifies as a kind of ignorance. Identifying our beliefs with the order of nature, characterizes delusions, illusions or hallucinations. Identifying our assumptions with the way things must be, often results in unnecessary arguments. How can we avoid or at least minimize such disturbances?

The Ises of Identity and Predication

In English and other Indo-European languages, using the "ises" of identity and predication can facilitate identification or confusion of orders of abstraction. With the "is of identity," e.g., when I say "Dewey is a philosopher," I take a lower level label for a particular man, "Dewey," and relate it by means of the word "is" to a higher level noun classification, "philosopher."[16] Statements such as "Business is business" and "Boys will be boys" also involve this usage—this particular business deal 'is' as business deals 'are', ruthless, dishonest, clever, or however else I habitually categorize business deals in general.

With the "is of predication," e.g., when I say "water is wet," "grass is green," etc., I relate the subject of the sentence to a quality. This suggests that "wetness" and "greenness" exist as properties inherent in the water or grass. This can lead to pernicious results, e.g., a teacher saying a child 'is' "bad" or "stupid" when the child cannot hear instructions and thus "ignores" the teacher.

In each case, the classification or quality does not exist 'out there' somewhere. It results from my *relation* with something 'out there'. I have constructed the classification or quality through my abstracting processes. In these cases, using the verb "to be" may contribute to hiding my role in this transaction. Aristotle's formulation of logic and the laws of thought accentuates this use of "to be" and thus encourages treating the classifications and qualities we ascribe to the world as self-evident givens rather than *abstractions we create.*

Such uses of "is" may occur in conjunction with identifying or confusing individuals at one level of abstraction with our generalizations and categories at higher levels of abstraction. In this way we may overemphasize similarities and underemphasize or ignore differences among individuals we're describing or among those doing the describing.

To the extent that our language habits 'nudge' our ongoing neuro-evaluational processes, avoiding habitual use of the "ises" of identity and predication can help us to avoid identifying individuals with the linguistic categories and qualities in our heads. We can acknowledge our responsibility in the abstracting process. Thus we might more accurately say: "I classify Dewey as a philosopher," "This business deal fits my standard of how business deals operate," "The grass looks green to me." Some students of GS use the term "rewording" to describe the practice of making these sorts of changes.

In recent years, GS scholar D. David Bourland advocated a rewording method called E-Prime (E'), a restructuring of English (E) by leaving out all forms of the verb "to be." He argued that eliminating from use all forms of the verb "to be" provided the best way he knew to eliminate the "ises" of predication and identity.

Other GS writers, myself included, agree with Allen Walker Read that using E-Prime as a constant practice would eliminate useful forms of the verb "to be." [17] Furthermore, neither eliminating just the "ises" of identity and predication, nor using E-Prime or any other device or rewording technique *guarantees* eliminating all identifications. Identification can occur in any languaculture whether or not it has a verb like "to be." Since language involves orders of abstraction, any statement, no matter how structurally correct, could potentially be confused with a lower or higher order of abstraction.

We can, with Korzybski, feel "amazed at the power of structurally correct terminology," and thus feel "full of sympathy toward the primitive interpretation as the 'magic of words'!" [18] Nonetheless, while recognizing the power of neuro-linguistic mechanisms, we ought to also recognize that consciousness of abstracting entails not word magic but rather *an orientation*: *a habit of ongoing vigilance in not confusing our linguistic-symbolic productions with their presumed referents*. The goal of general semantics 'is' consciousness of abstracting, not changing the language per se. A given instance of the 'is' of identity or predication is not in itself sure evidence of identification. Indeed, some students of general semantics rather freely use the "ises" of identity and predication, preferring to concentrate on *awareness* of language use and the orders of abstraction. Even this group, however, tends to use the "ises" of identity and predication with much less frequency than others in the general population.

A Multi-Valued Orientation

How about the two other aristotelian laws of thought? The law of the excluded middle (or "excluded third") sharply defines two-valued logic with its statement that everything must be either A or not A. In other words, an "attribute either does or does not belong to a subject (x either is y or not y); or a proposition is either true or it is false. Any middle ground between truth and falsity is excluded." [19]

The law of non-contradiction states that nothing can both be A and not-A. In other words, "the same attribute cannot both belong and not belong to the same subject at the same time and in the same respect (x is not both y and not-y); or, a proposition cannot be both true and false." [20] Together with the law of identity these two "laws of thought," constitute the basic premises of aristotelian "two-valued" logic.

In his book *The Labyrinth of Language*, philosopher Max Black reproached Korzybski for his "unnecessary...rejection of 'two-valued' conventional logic." [21] Black's misreading of Korzybski's work here, repeated by Martin Gardner and other detractors, exemplifies the transmission of error that has surrounded many critiques of general semantics. The applied humanistic approach of GS does not reject but rather allows for a limited use of two-valued logic.

However, a GS approach does require rejecting a dogmatic, inflexible two-valued *orientation* to which two-valued aristotelian logic can lead if viewed as *'the'* logic rather than *a* logic. Instead, GS appears consistent with the work of Lukasiewicz and others who formulated multi-valued logics. (Korzybski was familiar with and gave acknowledgement to the Polish tradition of analytical philosophy to which Lukasiewicz belonged.)

GS goes beyond pure 'logic' to involve a multi-valued orientation— evaluating in terms of degrees, continua, infinite-valued probabilities, etc., in which two-valued aristotelian 'logic' has a place.

While condemning Korzybski for saying what he in fact didn't say, Black basically admitted to a GS view :

...It seems at least plausible that if we have been forced to recognize 'non-Euclidean' geometries, belief in a single and unmodifiable logic might also be merely a hangover from earlier dogmatisms. [22]

Uh-huh.

More recent corroboration of the GS, multi-valued focus can be found in the field of "fuzzy logic" which has been successfully applied to machine control systems, especially by the Japanese. This field was started by electrical engineering professor Lotfi Zadeh, who reformulated set theory in light of Lukasiewicz's multi-valued logic. In fuzzy logic, sharp exclusion or inclusion in a set is replaced with graded membership. Sharp, two-valued distinctions are formulated as special cases of multi-valued or fuzzy sets. Fuzzy logic shows in an exact manner how something can be considered both A and not-A. Either/or language may indicate an oversimplified approach to non-verbal complexities. "Either you like your job or you don't." Well, many people both like and dislike their jobs to some degree. This degree orientation captures 'reality' with more exactness than a two-valued approach.

Aristotle's Non-Aristotelianism

The emphasis on definitions and 'essences' and a rigid insistence on the 'laws of thought' characterize what I have called aristotelianism or essentialism. Despite the essentialism which he got from Plato, Aristotle himself went beyond it in several ways that show he was not strictly an aristotelian. For example, although Aristotle systematized the search for essences in his logic, the focus of this search seems somewhat different from that of Plato.

Plato had clearly emphasized the secondary importance of the visible world compared to the more important world of ideal forms or essences that he postulated. Aristotle, on the other hand, emphasized the importance of the world we live in, with the forms or essences existing within the objects around us which we see and touch. This 'realistic' bent of Aristotle makes his philosophy in some ways congenial to a naturalistic, empirical and humanist perspective despite the essentialist drift of his logic. Indeed, Aristotle was noted for his extensive collections of plants and animals and is considered the founder of biological science.

There are also places in his writings on logic where Aristotle indicates some non-aristotelian-sounding leeway in the laws of thought. For example, in *Metaphysics*, he wrote, " ...however much all things may be 'so and not so', still there is a more and a less in the nature of things." [23] In *De Interpretatione* he noted that certain statements may have an "undecided" or indeterminate value, neither "true" nor "false." For example, take the statements "A sea-fight will take place tomorrow," and "A sea-fight will not take place tomorrow."

One may indeed be more likely to be true than the other, but it cannot be either actually true or actually false. It is therefore plain that it is not necessary that of an affirmation and a denial one should be true and the other false." [24]

Aristotle also moved to some degree beyond the two-valued approach of his logic in his work on ethics and politics. In *Nichomachean Ethics*, he emphasized the doctrine of the "golden mean," which involves each individual finding the best intermediate third value between two extremes. So courage provides a mean between excessive fear and over-confidence, and temperance lies between the extremes of self-indulgence and 'insensibility'. [25]

In his *Politics*, he emphasized that the individual and society did not have to exist in opposition to each other: "Man is a political animal" who develops his excellence in the company of others, while the State can function to aid the individual in his self-development. [26]

Despite these exceptions, Aristotle and the aristotelians put into place a system that, when carried into the orientation of everyday evaluating and science, became rigidified. This aristotelian orientation has outlived its usefulness as an overarching approach. Korzybski emphasized his admiration for Aristotle even as he criticized and sought to go beyond aristotelianism:

> To avoid misunderstandings I wish to acknowledge explicitly my profound admiration for the extraordinary genius of Aristotle, particularly in consideration of the period in which he lived. Nevertheless, the twisting of his system and the imposed immobility of this twisted system, as enforced for nearly two thousand years by the controlling groups, often under threats of torture and death, have led and can only lead to more disasters. From what we know about Aristotle, there is little doubt that, if alive, he would not tolerate such twistings and artificial immobility of the system usually ascribed to him.[27]

In summary, aristotelian logic still has an important though no longer exclusive role to play in useful formulating. The main emphasis of general semantics, however, is not on 'logic' as such but on psycho-logic, i.e., understanding and enhancing the entire scope of human evaluating including thinking-feeling-perceiving-doing-etc.; our evaluational reactions.

GS objections to Aristotle's views and those of his followers are directed toward the orientation or system of evaluation which they represent. An overemphasis on aristotelian logic as 'the' logic encourages an essentialist, intensional orientation in science and life. This involves identification or confusion of orders of abstraction. A non-aristotelian, non-essentialist, extensional orientation encourages non-identification or consciousness of abstraction. How can we develop this orientation in our everyday evaluating?

Chapter 13
Living Extensionally

Controlling Phantom Worlds

The aim of living extensionally lies at the heart of general semantics. Living extensionally involves remembering that your abstractions (representations, perceptions, conceptions, symbols, words, maps, etc.) are not what they represent. As long as you remember this, you can remain free of entrapment by your abstractions. As long as you remember that your abstractions do not represent 'all' of what exists to represent—and that you can always make new, possibly more useful representations—you can free yourself from the tyranny of your representations.

This involves much more than superficial, intellectual agreement. Novelist Robert Heinlein invented the word "grok" to refer to the deep, internalized understanding of something or someone. Getting extensional involves grokking important aspects of a non-aristotelian, non-essentialist worldview. If you think you have grokked (fully understood and can easily carry out) what the last paragraph implies, you might be fooling yourself. For whatever we say, most humans (probably also you) appear to do exactly the opposite, much of the time.

Most likely, you often take your perceptions for 'realities'. Probably, at least some of the time, you take words for the things of experience, the menu for the meal. You likely, at least sometimes, confuse inferences with descriptions. The habit of identifying our experience of the world with the world, and our words with our experience, leads humans into an ever-expanding maze of unresolvable conflicts and difficulties.

This habit of identification involves confusing levels of abstraction, treating similarity as identity (sameness in all aspects), and acting as if the differences between things that we consider the 'same' don't exist. In this way, by identifying we make our higher-order abstractions more important than what they represent. Our words and symbols get in our eyes and we reverse the "natural order of abstracting."

This 'natural' order of abstracting lays out the relative values (for living) of the different levels represented in the Abstracting Model in Chapter 11. So the 'natural' order places the process world first in importance for survival; non-verbal experience second; verbal description third; inference fourth; etc. Since confusing and reversing this order, i.e., identifying, seems in some ways more 'natural' to humans (more people reverse the order than not), I like to call it, as did Stuart Mayper, "the appropriate order of abstracting" or what Robert Pula refers to as "the preferred order of abstracting."[1]

Korzybski emphasized that when humans identify (lose consciousness that they abstract), they *copy animals* in their nervous reactions. This may be true in a certain sense, since animals have limited levels of abstracting and presumably don't have the ability to understand *that* they abstract.

On the other hand, animals do not create elaborate symbolic forms with which to confuse themselves. Lacking the obscuring veil of symbolism, they cannot help but live within and as a part of the flowing, process world. So animal consciousness functions naturally in an extensional manner with the lower order of non-verbal experience primary. In that sense, we would all do well to learn to copy animals more. I have learned a great deal about constructive silence from my cat. (Of course, cats don't have *to choose* to stop a constant stream of verbal chatter in their heads in order to bring their consciousness to the silent, un-speakable level of experience. Since they don't have speech to begin with, they're already there. They have no choice. We do.)

Humans, as a symbolic class of life, need to develop controls over the phantom worlds that they create with their symbol systems. Identification may exist as an inevitable first stage of symbolic development in the infancy and childhood of both in-dividuals and societies. Identification now gets unnecessarily and undesirably reinforced and carried into chronological adulthood by powerful social forces and institutional factors—not the least of which includes the unexamined and unrevised assumptions built into the structure of our common aristotelian language and 'logic'.

As far as I know, there is no way of knowing anything unmediated by your and others' organism-nervous systems—*no way*. You cannot know 'reality' apart from the means you have for knowing it. Living extensionally requires not identi-fying your perceptions, descriptions, judgements, values and beliefs with "reality," "the thing in itself," "the naked it." It also requires not identifying *yourself* with your perceptions, your descriptions, your judgements, values or beliefs.

I am not advocating solipsism here, the belief that only I exist and that you and the world don't. (Would ultra-solipsism mean that even I don't exist?) For those who find solipsism appealing, I offer this limerick:

There was a faith-healer of Deal
Who said, "Although pain isn't real,
If I sit on a pin
And it punctures my skin,
I dislike what I fancy I feel." (Author Unknown)

If you are alive, you cannot not abstract. If you accept with William James that "anything is real of which we find our-selves obliged to take account in any way,"[2] then there exist better and worse ways to take account—to abstract. What ex-tensional tools for better abstracting does GS offer?

Extensional Techniques

GS formulators have derived from GS theory, and incor-porated from other approaches, many ways to move toward an extensional orientation. These methods involve a con-tinuum of non-verbal and verbal techniques. In this chapter, I review some of the techniques that emphasize the non-verbal side of evaluating and behaving in the world (although talking, I must emphasize, is definitely involved). In the next chapter I focus on more-verbal techniques or devices (which definitely have non-verbal aspects as well).

Understanding Perception

Some aspects of the nature of perception—how we construct what becomes our 'reality'—seem of particular concern for functioning extensionally. We each perceive differently, as previously noted, influenced by our individual and species characteristics. Relevant individual differences can be such factors as height and acuity of senses, as well as basic assumptions and premises. When understood and accepted, this notion promotes a *"to-me-ness"* attitude that can improve relationships—reduce arguments, encourage openness to the views of others, etc. It can also contribute to a celebration of uniqueness and appropriate (though surely *not unconditional*) self-and-other acceptance.

In groups, I often use experiments which demonstrate how we each see differently, such as how we each see different colors in a spinning disc, which, when the spinning stops, appears black and white. Even with one person, this can be used to demonstrate the construction of multiple colors from a seemingly black and white figure.[3] Even more simply, note the way you create a "disc" when viewing a fan in motion, which, when still, appears as individual blades. In an analogous way, you create 'objects' from the sub-microscopic plenum of events.

Another approach is to study so-called "optical illusions." These demonstrate how our 'perception', as a form of non-verbal abstracting, does not involve passively reflecting what our 'senses' receive. Rather, our perception consists of our active attempts to construct a world out of cues we receive. These attempts are based on past abstracting, which includes assumptions, inferences and expectations, both verbal and non-verbal.[4]

In a sense, we make 'bets' about what is going on. These perceptual 'bets', hypotheses or inferences, are made unconsciously in fractions of seconds and give us some predictability in dealing with the incomplete information that our senses provide. An awareness of this process can help you reduce absolutistic reliance on what you perceive; hence can help you to reduce error and argument.

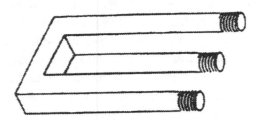

Figure 7
Draw this! Go to a carpentry shop and try to make one!

Look at Figure 7 above. If you start from the side with the three rounded ends, past experience probably leads you to bet, or guess, that they are extending out from three prongs. The figure is drawn so that from the other end you probably bet, or guess, that two extensions with squared edges extend from either side of a rectangular base. These two 'perceptual bets' are not compatible if you unconsciously assume that someone could build a 'real' figure using the drawing as a blueprint. Somewhere in the middle, you somehow realize that the spaces between the prongs also serve as sides of the squared off extensions. The result—a visual 'paradox' which comes from entertaining two rival hypotheses. The 'paradox' does not exist in the drawing. It exists in you.

Un-Speakable Awareness

Each of us live and experience life on the silent (non-verbal), un-speakable level of existence, although it seems that we are endlessly talking to ourselves. (For the moment I'm putting aside the 'fact' that our words also exist in some sense on the silent level.) This self-talk, if intensional, can prevent us from functioning well. If we talk to ourselves extensionally, we can help ourselves to get in better touch with what is happening within and around us.

Eventually, however, a large part of living extensionally involves learning to turn down and turn off the volume of the words inside your head. So an important part of general semantics training involves practice looking, listening, tasting, 'feeling', etc., at the silent, un-speakable level.

Most of us are concerned with building better ways of evaluating, with improving the quality of our lives. We often recognize that this quality involves some sense of a vast 'something' that we cannot put into words but that somehow connects us with our environments.

By learning how to contemplate non-verbally—creating inner silence—you can prepare yourself to behave extensionally. As Yogi Berra said, "You can observe a lot by watching." Freeing yourself as much as possible from your beliefs about what you 'should' see, you can become a better observer as you test your higher-order abstractions.

In GS, we seek to encourage contemplation and so greater creativity, aesthetic appreciation, sense of well-being, communication, etc. We also seek to connect such contemplation with our higher-order verbal evaluating, in recognition of the inevitable connections between silent-level and verbal-level functioning. We seek, as expressed by Charlotte Schuchardt Read, "To <u>feel</u> ourselves as time-binders, considering 'time-binding' not just intellectually but as participating in the human experience of millenniums..."[5]

Many disciplines and philosophies touch on this. For example, Zen practices and other forms of meditation, hypnosis, "healing" practices, etc., can point people toward experiencing such connections. I have found the discipline of sensory awareness particularly useful in developing skill in "silence on the un-speakable level."

As part of silent level practice, Korzybski also emphasized
the organism-as-a-whole interconnectedness of 'psyche' and
'soma', 'mind' and 'body'—not separate, and functioning
within a particular environment. This focus on the organic basis of evaluating and the rhythmicity of our organic processes
led Korzybski to devise his own approach, which he called
"neuro-semantic relaxation," a method of learning self-relax-
ation to eliminate excessive muscular effort related to 'emotional' tension and "defensiveness which is no defense."[6]

Neuro-semantic relaxation has connections to various
forms of posture-movement work such as the Alexander Technique and the work of Wilhelm Reich. However, elaborate study
is not necessary to start with. For example, momentarily bringing attention to your breathing throughout the day can begin
to bring some useful organismic awareness into your life.

Visualization

Visual imagery, either remembered or imagined, constitutes an important aspect of 'object' level experience which
merges into higher levels of abstraction. Visualization often
forms a more or less unconscious background to our fore-
ground verbalizing. We can benefit from doing it more consciously. Visualization works at a lower order of abstracting
than verbalization. As Korzybski pointed out, it provides a
direct link to structure and can show possible non-verbal relations, order, etc. By means of conscious visualizing (formulating, planning, etc.) you can move yourself in a more extensional direction—as long as you remember that your visual maps are not the territory either. So practice drawing,
diagramming, making visual models, etc. (however crudely)
of what you see, plan and formulate.[7]

A Calculus Approach

GS writer/teacher Milton Dawes, building upon Korzybski's work, refers to differential/integral calculus as an approach to living. Beyond doing calculations, getting a feel for the 'logic' or underlying structure of evaluating in calculus can have importance in evaluating more extensionally in everyday life.

Let's consider the value of calculus as a metaphor for living. The calculus is based on the mathematical notion of a function—a more-or-less exact relation between variables. Thinking-feeling in terms of functional relations can have usefulness in itself. If I feel tired, for example, I can 'step back' and consider some of the variables that my tiredness may exist as a function of: perhaps the amount of sleep I've had; the time of day; when, what and how much I last ate; how much coffee I've had; what medications I may have taken; etc. Considering some of these functional relations may have some bearing on what I decide to do next and what I decide not to do. Perhaps it's not a good time for operating heavy machinery or crossing a busy street.

The calculus was developed to better understand and describe 'instantaneous' change and rates of change involving distance, speed, acceleration, etc., in moving objects. Extended further, it provides a way for talking about rates of change, flow, etc., involving any kind of functional relation (often functions of time), e.g., the rate of cooling of a hot liquid, the rate of growth of compound interest, etc.

Calculus provides an especially good way of taking a dynamic, flowing process (a "continuous function") and stopping it (so to speak) for purposes of analysis. A dynamic process can be translated into a moment-to-moment series of indefinitely small static steps. Somewhat like the still frames which make up a motion picture, these static steps can be examined, studied, etc., more closely and carefully. The static pictures, when summed together, can be translated again into a moving picture, a dynamic process. This translation, from dynamic to static and back again, resembles the structure of human nervous system abstracting processes—with lower-order abstractions providing the more dynamic aspects, the higher-order abstractions the more static.

Dawes notes:

...if the continuous function we study is our own behavior with respect to time, one can easily get a feel that the calculus is more than a mathematical device. Since we live in a world of changing relationships, the calculus can also be used as a 'psycho-logical tool'. We can apply it to help us study factors related to personal development, improving communication, problem solving, conflict management, time management, stress management, and much more. The method of the calculus can be applied to help us understand and improve almost anything we do. It's mainly a matter of paying very, very close attention to what we are doing - how we are doing what we are doing - and what happens when we do whatever we happen to be doing.[8]

In his teaching, Dawes has used the example of attempting to park a car by pulling into a tight space. Making small enough movements of the car while gathering moment-to-moment feedback—paying very, very close attention to the results of what we are doing—will more likely lead to success than large and abrupt movements with less frequent checking on results. The latter will more likely lead to frustration and perhaps to scraped paint and dented fenders.

As in the parking example, I can apply the calculus metaphor by viewing the cycle of action-awareness in terms of a series of variably-sized steps. When I have a problem, a goal, want to change a habit, etc., I can divide it into a larger number of smaller steps. Any one of these steps can serve as a "wedge of awareness or consciousness," as Dawes has called it, which allows me to 'break up' the situation into manageable pieces.

Thus, when clients want to change their posture-movement habits, I help them to become more aware of what and how they are doing what they do from moment-to-moment. They learn that they can change their posture-movement habits, for example, by starting modestly with small areas of attention and brief moments (wedges of awareness) rather than trying to tackle all of their habits at once.

The metaphor of calculus can help you view your action-awareness in terms of variable increments or steps. Your degree of knowledge in a situation depends upon the number and size of steps you take to map, observe, assess, etc., what is going on. Your understanding-at-a-given-date will then depend on whether you have taken a "gross macro-mapping" approach with a few large steps, a finely-grained "micro-mapping" approach, or something in between.[9]

Awareness is key—awareness of what you are doing and then choosing what kind of mapping seems most appropriate in a particular situation. This calculus approach to knowledge and understanding can help you to consciously abstract, i.e., to become aware of your awareness and to manage your awareness better. You can apply the calculus (or wedge of awareness) approach to practicing non-verbal awareness and the other extensional techniques discussed in this chapter and the next.

Seven Steps of Personal Inquiry

GS, as an applied theory of knowledge (epistemology), provides an approach for helping people to become personal scientists. GS 'fellow traveler', psychologist George A. Kelly, wrote:

Might not the individual man each in his own personal way, assume more of the stature of a scientist, ever seeking to predict and control the course of events with which he is involved? Would he not have his theories, test his hypotheses, and weigh his experimental evidence? And, if so, might not the differences between personal viewpoints of different men correspond to the differences between the theoretical points of view of different scientists? [10]

We don't need to have laboratories or degrees in scientific studies to improve how we observe, form hypotheses, and, most especially, check them out; in other words, *how we challenge our beliefs with evidence*.

As a personal scientist, you can follow these seven steps of inquiry:

1. Formulate your assumptions, theories, etc.
2. Clarify them by defining your terms as extensionally as possible. What do your assumptions imply?
3. Frame them in the form of clear answerable questions that you can ask in order to make observations that will help you test them.
4. Make your observations in a calm, 'unprejudiced' manner.
5. Report your observations as accurately as possible and in such a way as to answer the questions that you asked to begin with.
6. Revise/reformulate any assumptions, theories, etc., held before the observations were made, in light of the observations made and the answers obtained.
7. Begin again, and again, and again...

Implications of this approach include:
• Formulating/reformulating your assumptions, theories, etc., involves imagination as much as 'logic'. Asking "How is this like that?" can open up new perspectives as long as you also remember to ask "How is this different from that?"

• Our 'knowledge' evolves in a circular or spiral manner. You can 'begin' at any one of these steps. However, the decision to ask questions and make observations usually seems to arise when you encounter something unexpected, have some problem, due to some questionable assumption(s) you hold.

• At any step, "we can know more than we can tell."[11] As a personal psycho-logical process, inquiry/discovery un- avoidably involves layers of tacit assumptions, habits, and skills which at a given date will remain more or less in the background of consciousness. You, inquirer, can learn how to cultivate this "tacit dimension" of knowing, as Polanyi called it, by allowing time for silent level contemplating, exploring, playing with, becoming acquainted with, etc., the object(s) of study.

• As fallible abstractors, our conclusions are more or less supported or refuted; nothing is finally 'proven'. Therefore, you had best hold your views tentatively, subject to further revision.

The steps of inquiry can be summarized by the following questions, which we do well to ask when we want to use in- quiry as an approach for everyday life.

What do I (and you) mean? (Steps 1 and 2 and 3)

How do I (and you) know? (Steps 3, 4 and 5)

What then? (Steps 6 and 7)[12]

What then? Elaborate on these steps with problems you ex- perience and find out how they work for you.

Personal Time-Binding

We talk to ourselves a lot. We can use this internal chatter for worse and better. When we label ourselves "stupid" or with similar negative higher-order abstractions, we create a nega- tive time-binding environment for ourselves. When we make perfectionistic demands on ourselves, unconditionally and absolutistically telling ourselves what we "must" do, we diminish our chances of fully realizing our potentialities. Instead, as Albert Ellis has emphasized throughout his writings, we can extensionalize our internal chatter, just as we extensionalize our talk with others. Ellis' books provide valuable material for learning how to talk to yourself in this way.

For example, I can change absolutistic demands, such as "I must have good relationships" into probabilistic preferences, such as "I prefer to have good relationships but I don't absolutely have to have them." Rather than absolutistically 'shoulding on myself', I can use conditional or non-absolutistic shoulds instead. So I can tell myself that "If I want good relationships, I probably should accept other people and take responsibility for how I act. However, it is not absolutely guaranteed that people will accept me just because I accept them and act responsibly. Moreover, I am not a total 'shit' if I fail to do this perfectly all of the time even if it might seem more preferable."

In learning how to talk to yourself this way, you not only take greater responsibility for your behavior, but take responsibility for treating yourself well. Thus, you can learn how to use your time-binding capacities most effectively by cooperating with yourself—enhancing your realistic self-acceptance.

Part of time-binding involves each of us learning from ourselves, learning how to make the most of our individual experiences. My wife has referred to this as *personal time-binding*. With personal time-binding, you can recognize that you communicate with yourself as well as with others. Your personal time-binding includes both the environment you create for yourself and others as well as the personal legacy you leave for future generations. As you act in such a way as to bring your legacy to fruition, you also contribute to your own and others' daily well-being: Inquirers—Go for it!

The Abstracting Model

The abstracting model derived from Korzybski's structural differential provides a hands-on technique for becoming more conscious of abstracting and thus more extensional. Looking at, manipulating, explaining and applying a visual and tactile model of the abstracting process in relation to actual problems (analyzing different aspects of the problem in terms of the different orders or levels) can help you to grok GS increasingly deeply on both non-verbal and verbal levels.[13]

The verbal world remains a smaller, in some ways less important, 'outgrowth' of the larger, more inclusive un-speakable level—the non-verbal, extensional world. In this chapter, I have sought to emphasize the non-verbal aspects of general semantics as an extensional practice. James D. French, present Editor-in-Chief of the *General Semantics Bulletin*, describes the interplay of the non-verbal and verbal aspects of general semantics:

> As a field of study, general semantics is not predominantly about language but (one might say) about neuro-evaluating; and yet language and how we use it play a prominent role in apprehending and using the discipline.[14]

Let us further explore that role.

Chapter 14
Extensional Languaging

Linguistic Revision

Mathematics advanced considerably when Arabic numerals with positional notation replaced Roman numerals. This structural, linguistic change permitted people to calculate with greater ease. Similarly, structural, linguistic changes in our everyday language can lead to improvements in other ways that we evaluate.

Korzybski developed a number of extensional devices which provide such notations for our everyday language. These devices provide a method of linguistic revision by changing the structure of our languaging (our language behavior and associated evaluations) in a way that codifies some of the basic assumptions of a relational worldview. Since Korzybski's time, additional linguistic revision methods have been developed.

Rewording: Language Minus Absolutisms

I've already discussed E-Prime, English minus the use of the verb "to be," and reasons for not embracing it uncritically (despite its usefulness as an exercise to develop linguistic awareness).

I do advocate avoiding possible "ises of identity" (He is a nurse.) and "ises of predication" (She is bothersome.) at times when feasible. Instead, you can increase clarity and reduce disagreement by wording your speech in ways which make conscious your own and others' roles as abstractors. This practice, advocated by James D. French, was labeled "rewording" by Charlotte Read. The term can be broadened to cover any sort of everyday language re-structuring done for GS purposes.[1] Rewording helps us to avoid identifying individuals with the linguistic categories and qualities we ascribe to them. Changing "It is blue" to "It looks blue to me" is a rewording example. Thus avoiding the 'is' of predication is a rewording practice, and so is avoiding the 'is' of identity. E-Prime is one rewording method.

A rewording method that I especially favor is an approach to language use that Allen Walker Read formulated and labeled EMA, short for English Minus Absolutisms. EMA applies the general principle of uncertainty to our linguistic behavior. As Read pointed out, "It is clear to many of us that we live in a process world, in which our judgments can only be probabilistic. Therefore we would do well to avoid finalistic, absolutistic terms. Can we ever find 'perfection' or 'certainty' or 'truth'? No! Then let us stop using such words in our formulations." [2]

Even while we remain aware that the 'meanings' of words are in us, certain words seem to carry an absolutistic baggage and we would do well to employ them with care. According to Read, "When we find ourselves using the very common absolutisms such as *always, never, forever, eternity, pure, final, ultimate*, and so on, we could say to ourselves, was that term necessary? Could we frame our sentence in some other way?" [3]

Using the whole system of general semantics will tend to de-absolutize your language use, whatever language you speak. By explicitly rewording your language to avoid absolutisms, you can gradually nudge yourself, including your non-verbal behavior, to function less dogmatically and more tentatively, as befits a fallible human being. You don't necessarily have to always slash every term that may have absolutistic 'baggage'. Remember, non-absolutism remains a matter of orientation. The absolutism is not in the words.

Rewording your language to reduce absolutisms can have very positive effects on your relationships. My wife finds that one of the most powerful things she has done in her psychotherapy and personal coaching work is to introduce EMA to clients and encourage them to use it. Dramatic positive improvements in relationships are often reported at the next session.

Indexing

Denial of identity leads to non-identity as a basic assumption: no two individuals are identical in all aspects. Even a particular individual is *not exactly the same in all respects* from one moment to the next. Non-identity implies that our words *are not* the things we are talking about and our maps *are not* the actual territory. Since, in spite of this, our word categories lead us to focus on similarities, we need some method to help us represent and remember differences as well—indexing.

The use of indexing comes from mathematics, where variables are given numbered subscripts to specify them, for example x_1, x_2, x_3, etc. In our everyday language, the variables we're concerned with consist of the words we use. We consider any statement at least somewhat indeterminate or 'meaningless' in an extensional sense until we specify or index our terms.

Religionist$_1$ is not religionist$_2$. Humanist$_1$ is not humanist$_2$. Unless you explicitly specify the differences, you may tend to ignore them. Over-emphasizing similarities, you may identify one individual with another, and thereby with the verbal category that you have in your head. By using indexes, you can remind yourself of the important differences among individual people, 'objects', events, etc. Almost automatically, you can avoid identifying your categorical maps with the individuals you are categorizing. This helps you to avoid identifying your words with your non-verbal experiences and the non-verbal territory. While maintaining links to other individuals in a category, indexing gives each individual a unique separate sub-category.

How will we respond to individual humans if we continually index to remind ourselves that, for example, atheist$_1$ is not atheist$_2$, Muslim$_1$ is not Muslim$_2$? Discriminating among individuals by noticing how they differ encourages less discrimination against individuals because of the categories we put them in.

You can also use indexes to help you to evaluate in terms of degrees along a continuum. Without indexes it seems easy to say, "I either feel pain, anxiety, etc., or I don't." Placing "pain" or "anxiety" on a continuum, you can index it, say with 0 indicating no pain or anxiety and 10 indicating the maximum imaginable. In this way, you can more realistically note the degree nature of these variables. You can begin to notice and encourage degrees of improvement in yourself and others rather than expect instantaneous, all-or-nothing results.

In addition, you can use indexes to enhance how you deal with second-order problems. You can talk about $anxiety_2$ about $anxiety_1$, $fear_2$ of $fear_1$, $enjoyment_2$ of $enjoyment_1$, $hate_2$ of $hate_1$, etc. I discuss this further in the multiordinality section below.

You don't need to always use index numbers in order to get the benefits of indexing. In *Drive Yourself Sane*, we define indexing as "making our terms and statements as descriptive as possible by emphasizing individual differences as well as similarities."[4] In this broader sense, anytime you become more specific in your evaluating and emphasize individuality and differences, you practice a form of indexing. For example, people who say, with despair that, "I'm just like my mother," can be helped by being led to consider the differences between them.

Dating

Accepting that we live in a dynamic, process universe, with change as fundamental has implications for daily living. Physicists talk about a constantly changing sub-microscopic whir of activities, events, energies, etc. Einstein's theory of relativity views the world in terms of four-dimensional space-time events. Our nervous-system abstractions from these events can be considered as events themselves. As noted before, they represent "not things changing, but change thinging." We may get a glimmer of this when we look in the mirror.

Yet, although we live in a process world of 'change', we can intensionally evaluate and talk about it, ourselves included, as if time differences don't matter. We may often fail to take change and time differences into account in our relationships, work situations, etc., leading to inadequate adjustments to changing circumstances.

We can remedy this by indexing differences over time: applying dates to our terms and statements so that our everyday evaluating can better incorporate space-time considerations. This can encourage us to make our words and statements—and related evaluations—more extensional in regard to the time factor. For example, I can help myself get "unstuck" from old patterns by recognizing that I (2003) am not exactly the same in all aspects as I 'was' in 1970 or 2002.

Dating can help you to differentiate a particular individual at a given date from that individual at another date. It can help you to realize that no particular individual 'is' exactly the 'same' from moment to moment. You today are not you 10 years ago. In what ways have you changed? Some individuals, like a good tailor, seem 'naturally' more extensional and seem more likely to take the time factor into account. Most of us need the reminding that dating our terms and statements gives us.

Non-Allness

Here I discuss several aspects of rewording to support a multi-valued, rather than an either/or orientation. How can we take into account that our maps do not represent all of the territory, our maps do not necessarily match the maps of others? How can we help ourselves to open up to a variety of alternatives when solving problems?

An extension of language minus absolutisms involves moving away from such phrases as " 'the' best way" and toward "*a* better way" or "*some* better ways" to do something.

Talking about " 'the' solution" rather than "*a* solution" or "*some* solutions" may contain a hidden assumption of absolutism or allness—that this is the only way, period! Using *plurals* rather than singular forms, and *a*, *an*, or *some* rather than 'the', can keep you from looking for 'the cause' and for single factors rather than causes and multiple factors.

Qualifying and quantifying phrases that specify the situation under which you are making a statement, and that acknowledge your role as evaluator, allow you to make quite definite statements extensionally. Such phrases as "*as far as I know*," "*under these circumstances*" and "*to me*" can help you to qualify and limit what might otherwise sound like overgeneralizations. Using phrases such as "*up to a point*," "*to some extent*," and "*to a degree*"can help nudge you away from either-or evaluating. Answering even approximately such questions as "*how many?*" "*how much?*" "*how big?*" "*what proportion?*" "*at what rate?*" "*with what probability?*" etc., can help you map situations more usefully.

As noted previously, Zadeh's "fuzzy logic" involves a multi-valued approach within applied mathematics which has relations to general semantics. According to Pula: "Both approaches seem examples of what I call *gradient evaluating* or, in formalisms, *approximatics*, that is evaluating ('thinking,' measuring, sizing things up, etc.) and *formulating* from a plenum, process, degree, continuum, etc., *orientation.*"[5]

How can such gradient evaluating help us to deal with a whole range of possibilities in between all or nothing, either/or choices? First by recognizing that they exist; then by delineating what can be found in the shades of gray between black and white. In this way, we give up false expectations for precision and certainty and gain greater relevance, accuracy and reliability. We recognize that we can have degrees of knowledge, of information, of success.

Problems often can be ameliorated by viewing such areas of life as ethnicity, conception, dying, sexual orientation, disability, etc., as matters of degree. People can move beyond either/or and toward 'both-and evaluating' through an understanding of fuzzy logic. You're not either totally in control or not responsible; totally well or disabled, etc. Using the formulations and techniques of general semantics presented in this chapter and elsewhere can help you to deal with the complex, fuzzy middle ground in your life.[6]

Et cetera (*etc.*) has a prominent place in general semantics. The term comes from the Latin "and other things." Looking for and enumerating examples when we speak and write can help us get extensional about our higher-order abstractions. Explicitly using "etc." and other similar phrases helps us to remember that, even after we've done this, we haven't said it all. When we thus have an et cetera or non-allness attitude, we ask ourselves: What might I have left out? What else? What other effects does this have, etc.? It seems useful to remember "etc." whenever you see a period. You can thus encourage yourself to move from a "period and stop" attitude toward a "comma and more" attitude.

Non-Elementalistic Terms, Hyphens and Quotes

As a basic premise, general semanticists accept that nothing exists in complete isolation, unrelated to anything else. Yet we may speak in ways that imply the contrary. For example, we talk about 'space', 'time', 'body', 'mind', etc. Because we use these as separate terms we can evaluate them as if each of them stands for a separate, isolated element.

As we know from the theory of relativity, 'space' and 'time' do not exist separately. Rather, we accept space-time as fundamental. Since no one ever has found a 'mind' separate from a 'body', we may do well to eschew the term 'mind' altogether and talk about neuro-semantic processes of an organism, organism-as-a-whole-in-an-environment, evaluative reactions, etc.

When we verbally treat as separate what does not exist separately in the non-verbal world, we use "elementalistic" language. If we then confuse our verbal maps with the territory, we end up with misevaluations. Non-elementalism involves recognizing and remedying elementalisms in various ways.

For example, we can use *non-elementalistic terms*, such as "evaluation" (which implies both 'intellect' and 'emotion') and "abstracting" and "abstractions of different orders or levels" (which bridge 'mind' and 'body'). We can also use *hyphens* to create non-elementalistic terms like thinking-feeling, organism-as-a-whole-in-an-environment, psycho-somatic, etc. If we continue to use elementalistic terms with potentially false-to-fact implications, like 'mind', 'body', etc., we can at least use *single quotes* around them to help us remember their possibly problematic baggage.

Multiordinality

I have already touched upon the unavoidable self-reflexive quality of the human nervous system and nervous system representations or mappings. We can make maps of our maps and react to our reactions. Mapping our maps is represented in the abstracting model by the different levels of abstraction. First we have the generalized field and within it the more localized event or presumed process we're mapping. Next we have our silent-level mapping or 'perceptual' experiences. Then come our descriptions and labels of our silent-level mapping; then our inferences and other verbal reactions based on descriptions, our higher-order inferences (generalizations, theories) based on lower-order inferences and reactions, etc., with this process theoretically unending.

This multi-leveled, self-reflexive process of human abstracting is based on the multi-leveled, self-reflexive structure of the nervous system. We call such a multi-leveled, self-reflexive process "multiordinal"; this relates to a characteristic of language referred to as "the multiordinality of terms."

Many, if not most, of our important words can be assigned definite 'meanings' only when we can specify the level of abstraction at which they function. This includes such words as 'mean', 'love', 'hate', 'fear', 'prejudice', 'fault', 'effect', 'abstraction', 'evaluate', 'question', etc. We cannot know what a multiordinal term 'means' apart from the context of its level or order of abstraction.

A rough test for multiordinality consists of checking whether a term can be applied to itself. For example, do you love someone? Do you love being in love? Do you have a prejudice against prejudice? Do you believe in believing? What facts can you learn about facts? What inferences can you make about inferences? What do you know about knowing? What do you assume about assumptions? How can you question your questions? Do you hate hating someone? Indexing can be used to specify the level of a multiordinal term—for example, $love_2$ of $love_1$, which amplifies love, or $hate_2$ of $hate_1$, which reverses $hate_1$.

Even terms for common everyday objects have a multiordinal aspect in relation to the level of abstraction we refer to. For example, we can use the word 'apple' to refer to an event or process level apple ($apple_1$), that particular apple you perceive non-verbally ($apple_2$), the label "apple" of that particular non-verbal apple ($apple_3$), the general class term "apple" ($apple_4$), etc. When you can get beyond the common feeling that 'this is just silly word play', you may find that awareness of multiordinality can give you greater flexibility in referring to the multi-leveled, self-reflexive aspects of living-evaluating.

Multi-'Meanings'

A familiar statement in general semantics is that "Words do not 'mean', people 'mean'." Because I accept this literally, I often put quotes around the terms 'mean', 'meaning(s)', etc., as in the phrase the " 'meaning' of this word or phrase." It sometimes seems convenient to talk *as if* a word, phrase, sentence, etc. has *a* 'meaning'. Nonetheless, whatever sense that anyone 'takes' from words, phrases, etc., (indeed any symbol or event) remains the sense that she or he gives to it.

The principle of non-identity implies the *multi-'meanings' of words*. No two 'meanings' given to a word or combination of words can be exactly the same in all respects. A simple illustration of this involves giving two or more people a word, say "rhythm," and asking each person to generate a list of 10 other words or phrases that they associate with it. Although reactions may be similar, no two individuals will come up with exactly the same associations in the same order.

What makes communication with language possible is that language as a social behavior gets learned in relation to some sort of shared experience among individuals in a culture. This increases the possibility that the 'meanings' you make while reading this book, for example, have some similarity to the 'meanings' I intend to convey as I write it. Given the degree or gradient nature of understanding/misunderstanding, there are no guarantees that they will.[7]

Remember Murphy's Law: "If something *can* go wrong, it *will* go wrong"? General-semantics teacher Kenneth G. Johnson taught me what I have come to call Johnson's Communication Corollary of Murphy's Law: "To communicate is to be misunderstood."

What's in this for you? You will nigh guarantee unneeded misunderstandings and conflicts in your life, if you do not habitually assume that *how you interpret what other people say is not exactly in all respects (perhaps important ones) what they intend when they say it*. Read the previous sentence again. You will also do well to assume that *how other people interpret what you say is not exactly in all respects (perhaps important ones) what you intend when you say it*.

Ambiguity and Specificity

Multi-'meaning' implies that just about every word we use can have many possible 'meanings' assigned to it. We can think of the words of our everyday statements as variables much like the terms of a mathematical function. Therefore, statements can be considered neither 'true' nor 'false' but rather ambiguous, indeterminate, or even 'meaningless' until we come to adequate agreement on specific 'meanings' for the relevant words of a discussion. Until we *do* so—a matter of degree—we might better call our statements "propositional functions" (as Bertrand Russell suggested), rather than propositions. Problems arise when participants in a discussion treat their ambiguous propositional functions as propositions—as if they had greater specificity than they in fact do.

"Government interferes/doesn't interfere with free enterprise." "Science can/cannot save us." "Religion does/doesn't fulfill people's needs." Consider the words "government," "free enterprise," "science," and "religion" in the previous three sentences. These terms, without specification, seem to imply the existence of *some actual things* called 'government', 'science', 'free enterprise', and 'religion' which do something to someone. If we assume we know what those words 'mean', then the sentences above may mostly provide grounds for fruitless arguments. However, when further specified in terms of what, for example, particular government *workers* do at specific times in particular locations, there might exist some possibility of useful agreement.

How can we bring our ambiguous overgeneralizations (propositional functions treated as propositions) down-to-earth? How can we turn them into something closer to useful propositions? We can do this by getting as specific as we can about the particular human activities, extensional events, etc., that we refer to. Indexing and dating, qualifying and quantifying, specifying the level of abstraction of our multiordinal terms, etc., provide simple structural means to give our words extensional space-time coordinates. (Extensional statements also include those that refer to internal psycho-logical events in one's experience.)

Please don't assume that I consider literature (poetry and fiction) and statements in mathematics as just 'meaningless' because of their mainly symbolic, intensionally-defined, ambiguous content. In their own particular ways, fiction, poetry, and math do show important extensional aspects and can be given valid 'meanings' within their own 'intensional' realms. Korzybski said that "poetry often conveys in a few sentences more of lasting values than a whole volume of scientific analysis."[8] I can enjoy and use art, poetry, fiction, etc., and still function within a broadly extensional orientation. However, when I begin believing enough in stories about unicorns to start looking for them in the forest, and when I begin seriously trying to make 'square circles', I will have shifted into an unsane —or perhaps even insane—intensional orientation.

Propositional functions should not be considered as 'bad' or simply 'nonsense'. Their elaboration has important implications for understanding the higher-order abstractions of 'ideas' and theories. A set or system of related propositional functions—a doctrinal function—underlies any particular scientific theory, philosophy, belief system, ideology, etc. A system-function, such as aristotelianism or non-aristotelianism, constitutes a higher-order doctrinal function of lower-order doctrinal functions.

A doctrinal function or a system-function specifies certain relationships and constraints and variables for the doctrines that 'embody' it (it cannot just 'mean' anything). However, until the variables are specified the doctrinal or system-function does not have specific content.

Thus, theories or viewpoints such as psychoanalysis, evolutionary psychology, Islam, etc., unless further specified and described, may be better understood as doctrinal functions rather than doctrines. A particular doctrine (a specific belief, for example) depends upon the specific 'meanings' allocated by someone to the variables within its particular doctrinal function. Thus, if 'Islam' as such constitutes a doctrinal function then to talk about which kind of Islam is the 'true' Islam qualifies as nonsense. Idries Shah's 'Islam' and Osama bin Laden's 'Islam' may share some commonalities in terms of a doctrinal function, yet the particular doctrines each man espoused could not work out more differently.

At a higher level, the aristotelian and non-aristotelian viewpoints qualify as system-functions embodied in different ways and degrees by different doctrines. Specifying the doctrinal functions and system-functions underlying specific doctrines constitutes important theoretical work, equivalent to unveiling the root assumptions or "structural unconscious" of a point of view or language.[9] The notions of the *doctrinal function*, the *system-function*, and the *structural unconscious* remain among the most important, though neglected, GS formulations. They provide a potentially fruitful approach for talking about the history, relations and developments (the logical fate) of 'ideas' and theories—*including your own*.

Extensional Bargain

Successful communication using language involves a continuing effort by senders and receivers—talkers and listeners, writers and readers— to specify and thus to calibrate their various ambiguous 'meanings'. We don't need a perfect match of our individual 'meanings' to acquire an adequate fit among different 'meanings' for a given situation. The question "What do you mean?" asked in a tone of genuine inquiry, not as a hostile challenge, can become a working tool for extensional functioning, operating by means of a scientific attitude. By accepting the possibility of approximate agreement adequate for a situation (moderate postmodernism?) we can avoid getting stuck in an extreme postmodernist web of "any interpretation goes."

Asking "What do you mean?" in the way described above is not the same as the traditional request to "define your terms." The request to define terms often gets used as an intensional invitation for detached verbalism and may lead to consulting a dictionary (useful at times) rather than finding out what the speaker intends. An ultimately fruitless effort to pin down all 'meanings' of all the words in a discussion—impossible to achieve—may ensue.

Applying an extensional approach does not require that you "…talk too much and get increasingly involved in increasingly fine distinctions, as if language could be made n-dimensional." [10] Rather "What do you mean?" used as a working tool of extensional languaging can lead, with the other extensional techniques and linguistic devices, to what Wendell Johnson called an "extensional bargain." [11]

An extensional bargain amounts to an agreement to carry forth a discussion once terms have been pinned down adequately enough extensionally. Making such a bargain leads to not having to define every term in a definition or to explicitly use every extensional language device whenever we participate in a discussion. If communication breakdown does occur, as it inevitably will, further work can then be done to re-calibrate terms and 'meanings' toward useful agreement.

Breakdown is not in itself a sign of failure. Successful communicating doesn't equal no disagreement. If we assume that "to communicate is to be misunderstood," we will be better prepared to negotiate 'meanings' extensionally when necessary. This will tend to result in taking greater responsibility when communicating. If you are not getting the results you want when you communicate with someone, you can do something differently.

The Dynamics of Insult

Richard Bandler and John Grinder, the originators of "Neuro-Linguistic Programming" (which they derived, in part, from their study of GS) wrote: *"The meaning of your communication is the response that you get.* If you can notice that you are not getting what you want, *change what you're doing."* [12] This way of stating a potentially useful point leads to some problems relevant to issues of extensional communicating and responsibility. If people feel insulted by what I say they can claim, according to the statement above, that their feeling of insult 'is' the 'meaning' of my communication, for which I—the speaker—am totally responsible.

This is indeed what fundamentalist Muslims (unfortunately not just a vocal minority in the Muslim world) claimed about novelist Salman Rushdie and his book, *The Satanic Verses.* In what may be the ultimate expression of 'political correctness', the Ayatollah Khomeini, the combined 'spiritual' leader of Shiite Muslims and secular ruler of Iran, issued a fatwa (a formal pronouncement of Islamic law by a religious authority) on February 1989. The fatwa called for Rushdie's death and a generous bounty was offered to any Muslim who would kill him. Rushdie, a British citizen, went into hiding under heavy security for a number of years. He has survived— so far (2003). Some of the translators of *The Satanic Verses* did not.

Many Muslims approved of the fatwa. Some who did not nonetheless argued that the book 'insulted' their religion and that at the very least it should be banned or taken out of circulation. Was the 'insult' in the book? Did Rushdie have responsibility for the 'insult' that many Muslims experienced?

No one has ultimate responsibility for the 'meanings' another person makes. The 'meanings' of your (the sender's) communication at a given date—*that your listener derives*— consist of the listener's interpretation of your communication. The 'meanings' that you (the receiver) give to what someone else has communicated consist of your interpretation—which may or may not have much similarity to what the sender intended. Both senders and receivers have responsibilities in the communication process if they want to find agreement (even agreement to disagree).

Both senders and receivers can change what they're doing if they're not getting what they want. For receivers, this can include asking "What do you mean?", other methods for seeking further information, choosing to interpret the messages they receive differently, etc. For senders, this can include speaking/writing as clearly as possible and being graciously willing to rephrase their messages until adequate communication occurs.

This has important implications for the dynamics of insult, issues related to "political correctness," etc. For example, although I do intend to challenge absolutist evaluating, I don't intend to insult anyone, and work toward avoiding this. However, I cannot guarantee that some individuals will not feel upset, even insulted, by some of the things that I say in this book. I take responsibility for communicating as clearly as I can to get my intended 'meanings' across. Beyond that, I deny having the responsibility for anyone else's interpretations, including their feeling insulted.

Even if someone intends to insult you with something they say or do, *you do not have to get insulted.* As Eleanor Roosevelt once said: "No one can insult you without your consent." Milton Dawes, who lives in Montreal, was once standing and waiting on a streetcorner there. Milton, born in Jamaica, has dark brown, chocolate-colored skin. A young 'white' man came up to him and asked him: "Are you a nigger?" Milton looked at him calmly and asked, "What do you mean?" The young man looked perplexed and asked: "How come you don't get upset like the others?" Milton replied: "I don't think like that. I live on a higher plane." The young man walked away, still looking perplexed.[13]

IFD Disease

People frequently get caught in what Wendell Johnson called *IFD Disease*: *Idealization*, which leads to *Frustration*, which leads to *Demoralization* or *Depression*.[14] Idealization can be viewed as synonymous with intensionally-oriented perfectionism. Using general semantics we can focus specifically on the IFD sequence as part of helping ourselves and others move from action-stopping idealization to change-promoting extensionalized goals, etc.

For example, many people often set goals phrased as higher-order abstractions, such as "I want to be a success," or "I want to be happy." Phrased in this way as absolutes, these goals appear unattainable; how would you know where to begin and how would you know when you got 'there'? As phrased, they function as terms which suggest opposites, in an either/or way. Either I'm a 'success' or a I'm a 'failure'; either I'm 'happy' or I'm 'unhappy'.

People can help themselves by applying various extensional techniques to how they express their goals. Thus, you can visualize in detail the results you want, find less absolutistic terms to describe your wishes, eliminate the "ises"of identity and predication, index and date 'success', acknowledge that individuals create their own definitions of goals and can re-evaluate them, etc.

Instead of "I want to be a 'success'" you might say, "I want to achieve such-and-such a result; I will follow these steps, starting on these dates, re-evaluating on this date," etc. With specific, non-absolutistic goals, you can evaluate each step as you take it, applying a calculus approach. At any point, then, you need not evaluate yourself as a 'failure'. Rather, you can say, "I'm not doing as well at step four as I'd like—what can I do differently?"

Workable Humanism

Extensional languaging leads to an emphasis on present actualities rather than untestable essences; on using and evaluating what you know, not just collecting information. This change in emphasis, combined with an orientation which encourages silence and contemplation of the "un-speakable," can lead to much improvement in our daily lives.

Humanists, skeptics and professional scientists, among others, can learn to evaluate better with general semantics training. For example, they can benefit from using the Haney Uncritical Inference Test, based on William V. Haney's doctoral research in general semantics. This test, or versions of it, has been used for years in GS seminars to help teach the critical evaluating skill of distinguishing among the orders of abstraction—particularly in separating the levels of observation statements (descriptions, reports, statements of fact) from inferential statements, which may appear quite similar.

In a paper that Korzybski delivered at an annual meeting of the American Psychiatric Association, and which was later published in *The American Journal of Psychiatry*, he noted:

Ordering of human reactions, for which we need a special technique, and which is the main neurological mechanism of general semantics and of the non-aristotelian system, automatically introduces delayed reactions. These are predominantly cortical functions in contrast to the predominantly reflex, undelayed subcortical (animalistic) functions. The stress on delayed reactions is not new 'wisdom.' There is an age-old saying, 'When mad count to ten.' Practically all human maladjustments, including most neuroses and psychoses, involve undelayed reactions; hence the *preventive* and even therapeutic value of the introduction of permanent automatic delayed reactions, for a fraction of a second, which prevents 'emotional' outbursts.[15]

We can apply GS to extend human potentialities in science, religion, ethics/social policy, etc. In Part III, I explore some implications and applications of general semantics in these areas. In Section A, I explore issues related to applying a scientific attitude to science (which unfortunately is not as paradoxical a statement as it may seem). In Section B, I outline an extensional approach to religion. Section C focuses on the possibilities of a time-binding approach to ethics.

Come, let's inquire together.

Part III
Implications and Applications

**Anyone who has begun to think places
some part of the world in jeopardy.[1]
—JOHN DEWEY**

Section A
Applying a Scientific Attitude to Science

It is a mistake to believe that a science consists in nothing but conclusively proved propositions, and it is unjust to demand that it should. It is a demand only made by those who feel a craving for authority in some form and a need to replace the religious catechism by something else, even if it be a scientific one.[1]

— SIGMUND FREUD

Chapter 15
Limited Maps of Unlimited Territories

A naturalistic humanist worldview is based on understanding ourselves, others, and the world as effectively as possible at a given date. This includes awareness of the fallibility and incompleteness of our necessarily limited maps. With this understanding, we can promote positive time-binding as effectively as possible at that date. Approaching this goal requires an understanding, also, of how to apply a scientific attitude to our formulating about many basic life issues, including science itself.

Individuals identified as 'scientists' or 'scientific skeptics' do not necessarily always do a very good job with this. With insufficient consciousness of their own abstracting processes, scientists may identify their maps with the actualities they supposedly represent.

An underlying need for comfort and security may lie behind the view held by some scientists and philosophers that 'linguistic issues are trivial'. Insufficient attention to their language use and its evaluative implications can thus make it easier for scientific and naturalistic formulators to maintain familiar but potentially misleading terminology and attendant assumptions. Unnecessary roadblocks and wasteful detours along the path of scientific inquiry result. Creative problem-solving gets blocked. The fragmentation of human knowledge continues. These, in turn, work against the application of a generalized scientific attitude to human affairs.

In this chapter, I discuss some specific examples of current scientific formulating which illustrate this. These include discussions about the beginning of the universe, controversy about the end of science, and some current problems in the human sciences. I give particularly detailed treatment to evaluational problems related to the scientific study of consciousness. The following chapter treats issues related to attempts to unify the sciences. Let's start at the beginning.

The Beginning of the Universe

Serious misevaluating may complicate some of the current discussions about the "big bang" and the beginning of our presently known universe. Cosmologists (physicists who study the large scale structures of the universe) generally agree that some momentous event called "the big bang" occurred some 12 to 15 billion years ago. This began the presently expanding universe that we live in. However, there is much speculation involved with this theory and more than one version of it. Some top-notch scientists have created confusion by implying that the 'beginning' of the known universe is the same as the 'beginning' of 'everything' including 'time', therefore placing off-limits any discussion about the pre-conditions of the 'big bang', etc. After all, nothing can come before the beginning of everything—can it?

There are serious reasons for questioning the legitimacy of attempts to close discussion by possibly confusing 'the big bang' with the beginning of 'everything'. For one thing, such an interpretation conflicts with the traditional naturalistic-'materialistic' assumption that "nothing comes out of nothing" and that the existence of something depends upon previous existences. This basic assumption should not be abandoned lightly by naturalistic formulators.

It has by no means been definitely established that the 'big bang' beginning of the known universe, even if it did occur, is equivalent to the beginning of 'everything'. Alternative scenarios which elaborate on possible preconditions to the 'big bang' and even multiple 'universes' with different 'laws', have been developed by some physicists.

There seems to be more room for scientific discussion and disagreement here than many people think. Blithe talk about 'the beginning of the universe' can easily result in finalistic, absolutistic formulating. How might a change from "the" universe to "a" universe affect current cosmology?

Discussion about the beginning of 'time' lends itself to catchy verbal play which, however much fun, may represent a confusion of orders of abstraction—objectifying 'time' as a 'thing' which can have a 'beginning'. If 'time' is not an object, but a word to label a dimension of observation and experience, how can it have a defined 'beginning' and 'end'? How might we re-view cosmology if we spoke of an indefinitely continuable process?

The End of Science

Formulating about the beginning of 'the universe' and of 'time' provides one of the 'legs' for science journalist John Horgan's argument that humans are approaching or have already reached the end (as in "stopping") of science.

In *The End of Science*, Horgan surveys the natural and social sciences and attempts to build a case for the view that scientists have either 'sewn-up' their fields with firmly established theories, such as quantum mechanics and relativity, or have reached the limits of knowability in particular areas such as cosmology and superstring theory. In either case, we may know now pretty much what can be known. The so-called social sciences, according to Horgan, may better be considered as story-telling rather than scientific inquiry. Meanwhile, philosophers of science cannot agree on the nature of science or on what we can conclude from the scientific enterprise.

The main problem with Horgan's view remains that of the self-fulfilling prophecy. To the extent that people accept his argument, scientific inquiry *will* indeed have reached an end. Yet there exist ample reasons for doubting the end of science. The three basic non-aristotelian premises (*map is not the territory, map represents not all the territory, maps can be made of maps*) provide a rather firm foundation of knowledge about human knowledge. Given these premises and the history of science, it seems rather presumptuous to assume that our present maps provide all we will ever know or can know. 'Ever' seems like a very long time.

In fact, the expansion of human knowledge has been accompanied by the expansion of the boundaries of what we don't know. With new answers, new questions occur. There remains much that we don't know and nigh undoubtedly much we don't know that we don't know.

But the existence of the unknown is not by any means equivalent to the existence of 'the unknowable', which, upon analysis, appears self-contradictory and therefore 'meaningless'. If I can declare something 'unknowable' then I appear to 'know' something about it (its 'unknowability') and if I 'know' at least that, I can't call it 'unknowable'. The 'unknowable' thus represents nonsense talk which can only lead to confusion if we indulge in it. (Some things may remain unknown by us—like Jupiter to an ant—because of our structures, brains, etc. This is not a scientific hypothesis because there is no way to test it.)

The existence of fairly solid knowledge in some areas, such as relativity and quantum physics, does not indicate that there is nothing much else to learn. In a universe of structure consisting of a complex of relations based upon multi-dimensional order, many levels of order can exist. As David Bohm pointed out, new kinds of order can be discovered which will require further explanation, etc. I think that Bohm and Korzybski both had it right in claiming that, in Korzybski's words, "human knowledge is inexhaustible." [1]

Deadends and Detours in the Study of Humans

The possibility of extending human knowledge to knowledge about humans has enticed humans for years. Different disciplines devoted to the study of human behavior remain diverse and to some extent divided. Humans and human behavior have many dimensions. It seems unlikely that one specific model or one particular method will unravel all of these aspects. Nonetheless, attempts to unify various approaches might give us broader vistas, provided that researchers do not achieve premature closure based on overly-limited viewpoints. The dangers of what Robert Anton Wilson called "model-theism" and what Abraham Maslow called "means-centering" ('methodolatry' or method-idolatry) are based on researchers taking their limited maps for the unlimited territory.

We are living in an exciting time when biological studies and psychology are beginning to get bridged. Along with some promising approaches for a deeper, more unified understanding of 'what makes us tick', some discouraging trends indicate some of the deadends and detours—formulational obstacles—that epistemologically-innocent scientists may place in the path of inquiry.

Attempts to build a human sociobiology (now renamed 'evolutionary psychology') have so far demonstrated much more evaluational rigidity than knowledge of either evolution or human psychology. Speculations based on flimsy data have often been presented with unwarranted definiteness and insufficient consideration of alternative explanations.

For example, Steven Pinker—who has zealously joined the sociobiology/evolutionary psychology camp—crusades against what he calls the "Standard Social Science Model." This model, according to Pinker, considers the human brain as an infinitely malleable "blank slate" to be written on by environmental stimuli. Very few social and behavioral scientists advocate anything approaching this stereotype. Nonetheless, Pinker's extreme model-theistic version of genetic determinism seems to require a 'devil'—an equally extreme environmental determinism—which he may have found 'under the rocks' in some corners of academia. Neither extreme merits serious consideration.

Early in the 20th century Korzybski and his friends, geneticist C. B. Bridges and zoologist H. S. Jennings, among others, warned against what Jennings described as, "The fallacy that the characteristics of organisms are divisible into two distinct classes; one due to heredity, the other to environment..."[2] Despite intellectual acknowledgement of this, many so-called 'evolutionary psychologists' do not actually talk and write as if they know it. Instead, they dichotomize human behavior into environmental and genetic factors in the most simplistic, additive way. What could have become a promising part of expanding human knowledge threatens to become a pseudo-science with university tenure.

The over-simplification of genetic and evolutionary knowledge by Pinker and some of his fellow 'evolutionary psychologists', their smug dismissiveness of other viewpoints and their undue dependence upon inadequate views of language and other aspects of human behavior may encourage the widespread dismissal of important alternative models of behavior. Human behavioral plasticity/responsiveness to cultural learning—our time-binding potential—remains overwhelmingly important in understanding what we do and is a product of complex enviro-genetic factors. (The non-elementalistic term "enviro-genetic" was coined by C. B. Bridges.)

Despite pretensions to knowledge by some 'evolutionary psychologists', no one has yet found (2003) a *completely isolated* module in the brain or a *completely separate* gene/gene complex *specific only* for language, or any other complex form of human behavior. The links and interactions among genes, environment and behavior are only beginning to yield to understanding in terms of non-elementalistic developmental models. However, lack of evidence doesn't seem to have given Pinker or his fellow enthusiasts pause to consider the grounds for their elementalistic but definite-sounding claims about 'how the mind works' in terms of 'language instincts', 'innate mental modules', 'grammar genes', 'gay genes', etc. And they call this cognitive science?[3]

The study of consciousness provides another area in the human sciences where evaluational confusion may have resulted in slowing down, halting, or even reversing the growth of knowledge. The rest of this chapter focuses on some of the formulational problems related to the scientific study of consciousness.

The 'Mind' / 'Body' Problem

Scientific interest in the relations among brain, consciousness, and human activity is increasing. For those developing a scientific, naturalistic perspective toward human life, some resolution of the so-called "mind/body" problem therefore seems not only timely, but also desirable and necessary.

Yet, some philosophers and scientists, among others, have declared the 'mind'/'body' problem "insoluble." This seems true, *if* one expects universal agreement among those with different metaphysical viewpoints. In a related vein, some philosophical formulators seem to actually prefer the insolubility of this and related problems:

Myself when young did eagerly frequent
Doctor and Saint, and heard great argument,
About it and about: but evermore
Came out by the same door where in I went.[4]

The apparent failure of traditional philosophical approaches in resolving the 'mind'/'body' problem does not mean that scientists can avoid dealing with the consequences related to basic assumptions in this area (although they may try). Scientific study can benefit from clarifying the underlying assumptions in 'brain'/'mind' research. I propose that naturalistic formulators *can* come to some agreement about what assumptions are necessary to best account for consciousness in terms of current knowledge, and do it in a way which will further continuing investigations.

Some terms and related structural assumptions don't appear adequate from a naturalistic, humanist, general-evaluational perspective. Others work better. In order to follow scientific, naturalistic standards we need to criticize and select our terms and assumptions according to the most up-to-date-knowledge that we have. In this way naturalistic inquirers can move forward, not with blind faith but rather with the courage of their consciously chosen assumptions.

In light of this concern for consistent, naturalistic formulating, I present in what follows a 'solution' to the 'mind'/'body' problem. First, I look at the formulating of Karl Popper and John Eccles, whose work on brain and consciousness demonstrates some of the failures of traditional approaches. I then look at other more recent and similarly failed attempts by philosophers and scientists to understand the "explanatory gap" between brain and consciousness. This 'gap' results from the ongoing failure of most formulators in this area to seriously and systematically contend with their own neuro-evaluational, neuro-linguistic 'baggage'. Finally I present a general-semantics approach to a solution which provides consistent naturalistic ground for attempts to build a science of consciousness.

Popper's 'Mind'

Supernatural belief in a human 'mind' existing apart from a human brain-body remains common in our culture. This belief relates to the common linguistic separation of 'mind' and 'body' (Remember—human 'language' and 'culture' cannot be entirely separated except verbally.) Referring to 'the mind' or 'the body' uncritically without comment—say, without the safety device of single quotes—can feed into this supernaturalistic belief system, reinforcing it and making it easy to identify higher-order abstractions with non-verbal, object-level 'things'. Individuals within the so-called 'scientific' and philosophical academic communities also participate in this supernaturalism, even many of those supposedly sympathetic to a naturalistic outlook.

Consider the case of Karl Popper, whom I mention here as a non-religious, humanistically-oriented philosopher. Popper said, "I think that I was always a Cartesian dualist."[5] In his theory of human consciousness, he gave separate autonomous existence to *World 1*, the 'physical' world; *World 2*, the 'mind'; and *World 3*, the world of the products of the 'mind', e.g., 'ideas', theories, problems, stories, etc.[6]

Popper, considered one of the foremost philosophers of science in the twentieth century, made quite clear that he did not consider 'the mind' or the world of 'ideas' as part of the physical world. Popper's three worlds interact with each other but constitute separate metaphysical realms.

In *The Self and Its Brain*, Popper and his neuroscientist colleague, Nobel Prize winner John Eccles, elaborated this viewpoint. A passage by Eccles that appears to reflect both men's viewpoints seems worth quoting at length for its extraordinary conclusions:

> If as conjectured the self-conscious mind is not a special part of World 1, that is of the physical and biological worlds, it is likely to have different fundamental properties. Though it is in liaison with special zones of the neocortex, it need not itself have the property of spatial extension. Apparently it integrates instantaneously what it reads out from diverse scattered elements of the active neocortex, largely of the dominant hemisphere, but probably also from the minor hemisphere of the normal brain...but the question: where is the self-conscious mind located? is unanswerable in principle. This can be appreciated when we consider some components of the self-conscious mind. It makes no sense to ask where are located the feelings of love or hate, or of joy or fear, or of such values as truth, goodness and beauty which apply to mental appraisals. These are experienced. Abstract concepts such as in mathematics [World 3 'objects'] have no location per se, but can be materialized, as it were, in specific examples or demonstrations. Similarly a location of the self-conscious mind appears when its actions become materialized in its interactions with the liaison brain. It is otherwise with the question: does the self-conscious mind have some specific temporal properties?...for practical purposes experienced time and clock time are closely locked together. We can thus envisage that World 2 has a temporal property, but not a spatial property. However, much more investigation is needed into these deep questions.[7]

As admitted by Eccles, the question of where 'the mind' exists remains unanswerable. The postulate of the non-spatial character of 'the mind'—'the mind' exists but has no location anywhere—appears untestable in principle, i.e., non-verifiable and non-falsifiable. (How could it, if it doesn't make any sense?) Popper strongly advocated that scientific notions must lead to tests by which we conceivably can falsify them. Accordingly, can we count the non-spatial character of 'the mind' as a scientific notion? No.

Although Eccles admitted that 'the mind' has some temporal qualities, he postulated that it "integrates instantaneously" what it selects from the brain. This introduces an infinite velocity to 'thought': the interaction of 'the mind' with the brain happens in 'no time'. How does this fit in with anything testable? It doesn't. Korzybski noted:

> ...structure involves relations and orders, and order could not exist in a world where 'infinite velocities' were possible....Any one who treats 'mind' in 'isolation' makes a structurally false assumption, and, by necessity, unconsciously ascribes some meaningless 'infinite velocity' to the nerve currents.[8]

Therefore, using Popper's and Eccles' scheme, a science relating consciousness to the brain-nervous system actually becomes impossible. Rather than lead the way to further investigation of 'deep' issues, Popper's and Eccles' work places insurmountable blockages to understanding the relation of the nervous system to consciousness in the brains of those who accept their theory.

As an agnostic, Popper did not appear to have any religious 'ax to grind' in propounding this theory.[9] However, from the age of fifteen, he accepted the following exhortation: "Never let yourself be goaded into taking seriously problems about words and their meanings. What must be taken seriously are questions of fact, and assertions about facts: theories and hypotheses; the problems they solve; and the problems they raise."[10]

With this dictum Popper created a barrier between questions of verbal interpretation and questions of 'fact'. In other of his writings Popper seemed to recognize that the barrier between verbal and factual problems was not impermeable.[11] Unfortunately, this understanding didn't seem to affect his formulating about Worlds 1, 2, and 3. Too bad, since taking seriously problems about words and their possible associated evaluations (semantic reactions) could have allowed Popper to avoid getting himself stuck in the shoals of 'supernaturalistic naturalism'.

A concern with clarifying and analyzing the words we use does not mean, as Popper implied elsewhere, that we need follow an infinite regress of definitions, seeking absolute precision before we deal with 'real' problems.[12] As noted earlier, we cannot define all of our terms. However, any discussion implicitly or explicitly starts with undefined terms. In GS, getting to this level has greater importance than it did for Popper.

It seems likely that Popper's failure to take problems of words seriously led him to contend that the "choice of undefined terms is largely arbitrary."[13] He ignored the structural implications of his undefined terms: 'physical', 'mind', 'ideas', etc. This leads to a supernaturalism that I presume he would have rejected if it had been made clear to him—well…maybe not.

Students of Popper's work might find it interesting to filter out these aspects of his formulating and map the useful remnants onto the model of abstracting. Popper's three worlds seem like elementalistic shadows of the three main levels represented in the model. World 1 could be related roughly to the event level, World 2 to the 'object' level (the level at which we experience the nervous system constructs of phenomenal 'objects', whether apples or toothaches), and World 3 to the verbal levels.

These do not correspond to different metaphysical realities. In a view where structure, relation and order are considered basic, Popper's three worlds represent different major categories of sub-structures within the process universe or general world of events. This world includes human nervous systems and what they do. As the model of abstracting in Chapter 11 shows, any given process of abstracting and its products at various levels of abstraction constitute—in themselves—events within a larger plenum or fullness of events. In other words, they constitute parts of nature to which we can ascribe 'material' or 'physical' characteristics. In this sense, a general-semantics view has one world, not three—the plenum and all in (of) it.

With Eccles, an admitted "believer in God and the supernatural,"[14] the supernaturalistic view implicit in Popper's formulating became explicit. With Daniel N. Robinson, a psychologist, Eccles later wrote: "Since materialist solutions fail to account for our experienced uniqueness, we are constrained to attribute the uniqueness of the psyche or soul to a supernatural spiritual creation...It is the certainty of the inner core of the unique individuality that necessitates the 'Divine creation.' We submit that no other explanation is tenable..."[15]

This passage shows the constraints not of naturalistic solutions but of the authors' imaginations. Antonio Damasio, Gerald Edelman, Patricia and Paul Churchland, Francis Crick, J. Allan Hobson, Oliver Sacks and others have provided alternative naturalistic formulations in terms of nervous system functioning to begin to account for the individual sense of uniqueness that each of us experiences.

Eccles and Robinson consider their theorizing, unlike that of their critics, to represent "a true scientific attitude as described by Popper..."[16] However, their resorting to "Divine creation" leaves scientific formulating behind. Given their premises of an immaterial 'mind', the conclusions of faith follow, based on religious revelation and authority. Can this provide any useful basis for claims to scientific knowledge?

As I see it—no. For if faith, revelation, etc., derive from a non-physical realm, some inner 'essence' of mystic insight can always be described as untouchable by 'normal' means of physical measurement or observation. Popper's and Eccles' claim of an immaterial realm of 'mind' and 'ideas' provides the basis for a closed, self-sealing system of belief. For those who espouse a naturalistic view, there seems no way out, except by finding the courage of their assumptions and shifting to a naturalistic view—a naturalistic naturalism.

The Explanatory Gap and 'Mind' / 'Body' Dualism

John Horgan has promoted the notion of an "explanatory gap" in the human sciences. First labeled in a 1983 paper by philosopher Joseph Levine, an "explanatory gap" is posited to exist between our experience of consciousness and theories of neuroscience. With apparent glee, Horgan has argued that this gap will never be bridged and makes impossible a comprehensive science relating neural events to consciousness. This continues the theme of Horgan's earlier writings on "the end of science" in general: Apparently, as in other scientific fields, brain researchers can expect only ever-diminishing returns for their efforts. The subtitle of Horgan's book on neuroscience, *The Undiscovered Mind*, reads: "How the Brain Defies Replication, Medication and Explanation."

Although I consider Horgan's views here mistaken he has unintentionally done a potential service to naturalistic inquiry into consciousness. Horgan's discussion of the "explanatory gap" brings to the surface a belief shared by many philosophers and neuroscientists who don't necessarily realize its science-stopping consequences.

The explanatory gap has been described as follows by Antonio Damasio:

There is a gap between our knowledge of neural events, at molecular, cellular, and system levels, on the one hand, and the mental image whose mechanisms of appearance we wish to understand on the other. There is a gap to be filled by not yet identified but presumably identifiable physical phenomena. The size of the gap and the degree to which it is more or less likely to be bridged in the future is a matter of debate, of course. Be that as it may, I wish to make clear that I regard neural patterns as forerunners of the biological entities I call images.[17]

This seems related to what philosopher David Chalmers has called the "hard problem" of consciousness, " the question of how physical processes in the brain give rise to subjective experience."[18] Given the rigorous efforts of so many thinkers, I risk seeming presumptuous here by declaring that belief in the existence of an explanatory gap or hard problem constitutes a serious explanatory gaff. Let me risk it. *Belief in an explanatory gap results from a mistaken view of the nature of explanation.*

Although we may have gaps in our explanations, there is no 'explanatory gap' in neuroscience (as characterized by Damasio) any more than there is an explanatory gap in physics, biology or any other science. An explanation (a higher-order abstraction involving inferences, and inferences about inferences) about lower-order abstractions is never identical with those lower-order abstractions, can never be complete and remains open to potential revision at any time.

The belief that there does exist an explanatory gap shows an expectation for an explanation to do what no explanation can ever do, i.e., *to be identical with* what it attempts to explain, *an impossibility to accomplish.* Our non-verbal experience can already partially be verbally explained by existing *incomplete and revisable* neuroscientific theories. We can expect these *necessarily* partial verbal explanations to improve. However, our partial explanations are not and never will *be* what they explain—no matter how much more we learn about the brain and consciousness.

Philosophers and scientists who accept the existence of "the explanatory gap" may claim to avoid Cartesian 'mind'/'body' dualism (a form of elementalism which verbally separates what appears connected in the non-verbal world). Nonetheless, in GS terms, their acceptance results from a serious, elementalistic (dualism-promoting) confusion of orders of abstracting.

In a consistent naturalistic way of formulating, 'mind' and 'body' need to be treated as modes of talking about *one multi-leveled process* from different points of view and orders of abstracting which must always involve so-called 'subjective' (introspective, phenomenological) factors.

What we call an "I" 'having' thoughts, images, etc., ('mind') may be verbally formulated as completely separated from 'bodily' sensations. However, this separation is one step removed from the unitary but multi-dimensional nature of non-verbal, aesthetic experience.

Used as lower-order, verbal abstractions, the terms 'mind' and 'body' label different aspects of this immediate, unitary, non-verbal level. When used in this way, the terms 'mind' and 'body' qualify as "concepts by intuition," what F. S. C. Northrop called those terms which label the unitary realm of immediate, un-speakable, non-verbal experience. I have already referred to this immediately-given, non-verbal realm as the object level.

As concepts by intuition, the terms 'mind' and 'body' may be used as readily available, though potentially confusing, descriptive labels for aspects of directly felt, object-level, experience. At this level, 'mind' or 'mind'-like events might include something like picturing an elephant with your eyes closed. 'Body' or 'body'-like events might include a process like the movement of your chest when you breath. 'Matter' or 'physical'/ 'material' events might include parts of nature that you experience 'directly' like the patterns of gray and white you call a "cloud." These various, non-verbally experienced events do not exist in different metaphysical realms.

At a different, higher order of abstraction, 'body' and 'mind' are used differently and typically refer to more abstract entities defined in terms of a particular set of theoretical postulates. Northrop called such higher-order abstractions, "concepts by postulation." As a concept by postulation, 'body' usually refers to various theories regarding physiological processes developed in biology, neuroscience, etc. As a concept by postulation, 'mind' usually refers to the theory of 'mental substance' of Descartes, Popper, Eccles and other philosophers, metaphysicians, etc.

Northrop pointed out that "no one has been able to formulate clearly, within a single deductive theory, how the postulated mental substance is related to the postulated material substances of physiology and physics." He concluded that,

> ...although 'mind' in the sense of a mental substance given by a concept by postulation must be thrown away, 'mind' in the sense of a concept by intuition ["what is immediately apprehended when one introspects"] or some other word meaning the same thing denotatively, must be retained. [19]

The distinction between lower-order-of-abstraction "concepts by intuition" and higher-order-of-abstraction "concepts by postulation" can clarify the problem behind talking about an 'explanatory gap' or 'hard problem'. Much of the confusion stems from failure to index the terms 'mind' and 'body' to indicate whether we are using them as concepts by intuition or concepts by postulation. Thus confusion reigns.

From a consistent and clear naturalistic viewpoint, what each of us may apprehend directly in our awareness—what philosophers call "qualia" or "subjective experiences"—do not need to be located in a different metaphysical realm from the postulated neural states which are used to explain them.

They can be understood simply in terms of different orders of abstraction.

A famous problem among philosophers is the puzzler about whether a neuroscientist kept in a black-and-white environment from birth would 'know' what red looks like if she had a 'complete explanation' (whatever that might 'mean') of the nervous system mechanism for seeing red and other colors. From a GS perspective, 'knowing' what a red tomato looks like in terms of the high-order symbolic abstractions of neuroscience (concepts by postulation) would not allow her to 'know' in terms of sensation (concept by intuition) what a red tomato looks like. To know what it is like to see red in the latter sense, she would have to actually see or to have seen what we call a "red tomato."

It goes without saying—and even better with saying—that even 'knowing' something abstractly in terms of concepts by postulation will involve some related "qualia" (immediately-apprehended, non-verbal experiences). Accept for the moment that any such experiences that you have correlate with some postulated neural state. The "qualia"-neural states related to verbally explaining red tomatoes, yellow bananas, etc., are not the same as the "qualia"-neural states related to the un-speakable, non-verbal seeing, tasting, etc., of a red tomato, a yellow banana, etc.

Spinoza indicated the equivalence of 'mental' ('subjective') experiences to postulated organismic-neural states explained in 'physical' or 'material' terms. He wrote that "Mind and body are one and the same thing, conceived first under the attribute of thought ['mind', 'qualia', 'subjective' experiences], secondly, under the attribute of extension ['matter','physical' measurements]." [20]

This unitary view has major methodological significance for the human sciences: If 'mind' and 'body' are considered equivalent, then neither psycho-logical language nor physiological language has absolute precedence. Accordingly, observables that some researchers designate as 'bodily' (physiological) factors may just as likely be treated as functions of 'mental' (psycho-logical) factors, as the other way around.

Korzybski's Never 'Mind'

Spinoza's radical denial of 'mind'/'body' dualism appears basic to the GS system. The theory of abstracting takes as basic an assumption shared by many other naturalistic formulators: consciousness remains inseparable from certain brain-centered patterns of activity in a given organism-as-a-whole-in-an-environment. This view is also called "psycho-physical monism" by philosopher of science Mario Bunge.

GS psycho-physical monism qualifies as 'holistic' or "emergentist" to use Bunge's term. The structure of the world, ourselves included, constitutes a complex of relations of multi-dimensional order. This involves non-linear, non-additive factors in the emergence of characteristics, including consciousness, not found within the individual elements of a relationship.

Psycho-physical monism assumes less than Eccles' and Popper's dualism. (Given their three worlds, should we call it triadism?) Psycho-physical monism posits one world called "nature" rather than two or three separate 'worlds'. It appears simpler as well, in the sense that it does not have to bring in entities that exist nowhere and operate in no 'time', according to unknown rules. It carries farther than dualism since it provides an explanation of each individual's unique experience as well as accounting for widely observed effects of heredity, disease, trauma, chemicals, nutrition, learning, beliefs and other evaluative factors, etc., on conscious functioning. It also carries farther because it leads to testable hypotheses with no recourse to faith, revelation or religious authority.

In *The Mind-Body Problem,* Bunge presented an admirable critique of 'mind'/'body' dualism. He acknowledged that,

> Dualism is enshrined in ordinary language...Scientific theories, on the other hand, involve technical concepts and statements that call for expressions going beyond, and often against, ordinary language. (Think of any mathematical model in psychobiology.)[21]

This division between 'ordinary' and 'scientific' language doesn't need to remain an unbridgeable chasm. Indeed, we can and ought to change the structure of our 'ordinary' language to become more in keeping with scientific understandings. Unlike many subsequent naturalistic philosophers and scientists who have professed to follow Spinoza's call, Korzybski went farther by showing the importance of fully carrying through this understanding into linguistic usage. Otherwise not only 'ordinary' people but also, as we have seen, scientists and philosophers will remain prone to the effects of obsolete assumptions based on unexamined, undefined terms.

Logical fate works through neuro-evaluational, neuro-linguistic mechanisms. Although he has gone a lot farther than many other philosophers and scientists, Bunge, in his book, doesn't seem to have quite gotten to the personal application of this. There he persists in talking of 'the mind' when referring to conscious neural functions, while explaining that no independent 'mind' exists.[22] How unfortunate. As I have attempted to show, we can assume the 'innocence' of our language and related assumptions/evaluations only at our peril. Given naturalistic premises, if a 'mind' independent of a 'body' has no non-verbal referent, then it constitutes a map *without* a territory. Thus, retaining the traditional language may help perpetuate the old assumption that humans are a union of two substances, one 'mental' and one 'physical'.

What effects could increased awareness of neuro-evaluational, neuro-linguistic issues have on a scientific understanding of consciousness? To find out, such awareness needs to be applied.

To apply this understanding, you can work at putting the words 'mind' or 'body' in single quotes to indicate their possible elementalistic, false-to-fact implications. Specify the level of abstraction of these terms whenever you use them. Better yet, avoid these terms when possible. Work at reporting your experience descriptively. Work at keeping your language actional, behavioral, etc. Remember the implied to-meness of any statement by anyone. Talk about the conscious processes of the brain-nervous system of yourself and others in non-elementalistic terms such as "awareness," "organism-as-a-whole-in-an-environment," "abstracting," "evaluations," "evaluational reactions," etc.

Remember that I can directly describe my feelings of hunger, pain, etc.—object-level experiences to me—although they remain inferential to anyone else. In turn, your hungers and pains remain inferential to me although they appear as object-level experiences to you. This last point suggests the incoherence of the traditional dichotomy of 'subjective' and 'objective'—terms that you should use with care, if at all, if you want to avoid confusion of orders of abstracting.

Useful formulating about the nervous system and consciousness obviously does not absolutely require the explicit application of these general-semantics techniques.[23] However their use may remove some obstacles toward getting the full benefit of a naturalistic perspective.

Talking sense sometimes seems difficult. By ignoring or underestimating the 'undertow' effects of our habitual language and related evaluations/assumptions, even esteemed philosophers and neuroscientists can confuse orders of abstracting. In this way, they may promote unintended supernaturalism and create unbridgable gaps, impenetrably hard problems and impassable blockages for themselves and other inquirers.

Chapter 16
Unifying Human Knowledge

Basic to a naturalistic worldview is the premise of an underlying unity to nature. This unity implies, for one thing, that nature is understandable. Despite different specific scientific methods for studying different specific problems in various fields, a general scientific attitude combining 'reason' and 'observation' appears to provide the best means for increasing our understanding of nature, ourselves included.

This naturalistic view has led various philosophers, scientists, philosophers of science, etc., to attempt to define the possibilities and limits of science. Their efforts have involved a joint description-prescription of the activities of scientists. In doing this, these students of science have often classified the various existing fields of study, explored their relations and suggested new distinctions, unities and arrangements among them. Various journalists, philosophers, historians, physicists, etc., have weighed in with their observations and analyses.

At present (2003), science in general remains fragmented. Deep divisions appear to exist within and between the 'physical', 'biological', and 'social' sciences. Arguments range between defenders of scientific 'objectivity' and advocates of "postmodern" viewpoints. Different models and/or methods are proposed as unifying factors. Some formulators seem to accept the impossibility of any kind of unification. Is it possible to defragment science? I believe so. In this chapter I explore some of the issues and possibilities.

Beyond the 'Objective'/'Subjective' Split

Some of the efforts to describe and prescribe the fields of existing and possible scientific study have been handicapped by a common failure to get beyond the elementalisms (verbally-implied splits) of 'mind' and 'body', 'mind' and 'matter', observation disconnected from observer, etc. These splits have fragmented philosophical and scientific formulating for centuries.

Behind these elementalisms appears a presumed split in nature represented by the terms 'objective' and 'subjective'. 'Objective' is used to imply the 'truth' or 'reality' filtered out from and unsullied by 'subjective' human viewpoints and opinions. 'Subjective' here refers to human cognition/evaluation and implies someone's particular personal, 'emotional' point of view which is not 'objective'.

This division can be seen in the elementalistic distinction that some philosophers have made between so-called 'objective' "primary qualities" like length, width, etc., and "subjective qualities" such as taste and color, which implies that 'primary qualities' exist independently of observers.

Attitudes toward 'science' get affected by the elementalistic separation of 'objective' from 'subjective' factors. Science may be seen as some pure form of 'objective' truth uncontaminated by 'unscientific', 'subjective' opinion.

Nonetheless, within a naturalistic framework, human knowledge is necessarily based on human cognition/evaluation involving so-called 'subjective' factors. Each one of us can experience/know nothing outside of our nervous system abstractions.

As indicated in the last chapter, the so-called 'mental', 'bodily' and 'physical' aspects of non-verbal experience all exist within an un-speakable, phenomenological continuum. This 'object' level—as it's called in general semantics —can include imaginary pink elephants, toothaches, your breath, apples, clouds, etc. This continuum does not represent some ultimate 'truth' or 'reality' separate from human cognition. It includes anything you can experience, whether labeled 'objective' or 'subjective'; 'primary' or 'secondary' qualities.

Understanding experience in this way requires using the terms 'objective' and 'subjective' cautiously, if at all, e.g. with liberal use of single quotes. I choose to avoid these terms when I can. However, for many people, doing so requires transcending their habitual, fragmented view of human knowledge.

A Pragmatic Philosophy of Science

From a naturalistic perspective, *human knowledge involves the fallible nervous system process of abstracting*. No one can transcend this process to somehow otherwise 'know' 'ultimate reality' (the 'naked it'). 'Subjectivity', in this sense, is at the root of all knowledge. Our best understandings of the world beyond our observations depend solely on the cooperative time-binding process of scientific inquiry. This involves a social process of knowledge-construction within cultures (neuro-semantic, neuro-linguistic environments).

This social process includes what has been called "inter-subjective testing" among individually-abstracting human 'nervous systems'. Scientific advancement, in the sense of gaining more accurate 'maps' with greater predictivity, may actually result from the continual recognition of this kind of radical and fallible 'subjectivity' in all human formulating—consciousness of abstracting. This view is called a moderate or "liberal postmodernist" one by Albert Ellis. To avoid getting lumped in with the views of Rorty, Derrida, Foucault, Lyotard, and others; I prefer calling it a pragmatic philosophy of science.[1]

A general-semantics oriented, pragmatic philosophy of science seems more in line with the tradition of Peirce, James, Schiller, Dewey, and others. It accepts the social contexts of scientific formulating. It takes as given the notion of the impossibility of stepping outside our nervous systems to see and say 'how things really are'. It takes "constructivism" as a given: through the nervous system process of abstracting we construct 'realities' as we experience them. Undoubtedly, some of this construction is related to structural factors of our organism affected by our genes and developed though the process of evolution. The 'realities' we construct remain complex, non-additive functions of our genetic, cultural and personal histories. My apparent emphasis on the social, cultural and personal learning factors that contribute to 'reality' construction does not deny the organic aspect (by no means entirely genetic) of all of these factors.

The moderate, pragmatic view that I espouse accepts that in a particular area of inquiry a number of alternative viewpoints may vie at any one time without any one necessarily taking precedence. It acknowledges that there may exist a number of so-called 'scientific' areas of study where politics, prestige, the dead hand of habit and the thoughtless transmission of error may have had more to do than anything else with establishing accepted views. It acknowledges that we cannot absolutely and definitively prove many of our most basic working assumptions. Nonetheless it denies that 'any formulation goes'. Some abstractions do serve us better than others in terms of simplicity, explanatory reach, predictivity, etc.

There are those in the sciences who find even this moderate view unacceptable. They demand one or another kind of absolute in human knowledge. In regard to mathematics and logic, such people may still accept a platonic view that the formulations of mathematics have some timeless and independent-of-humans existence. They may also consider 'silly' the linguistic carefulness and qualifications about formulating which I advocate. (Do these people qualify as "pre-modern-science fundamentalists" ?)

I have also met a few people who did seem to express a "fundamentalist postmodernist," "anything goes" attitude toward science that some seem to think so prevalent. I once had a conversation about science with one such person who argued that 'science' constituted one narrative among many—

not necessarily a better one. 'Gravity', she claimed, was just another story. I replied that if she thought that the belief in 'gravity' was equivalent to the belief that she could fly if she jumped from the top floor of a high-rise building—without a parachute or bungee-cord— the story of her life would probably be a short one.

The traditional 'objective'/'subjective' split provides a shared, underlying, tacit assumption of both pre-modern-science fundamentalists and fundamentalist postmodernists. In the "science wars" that have gone on between these camps, participants on both sides might be surprised to learn that they were using the same brand of 'ammunition' for their dualistic dueling.

Other more moderate formulators, interested in developing a broad view of the sciences/human knowledge may acknowledge what I have said above. Nonetheless they have often failed to heed the evaluational, linguistic measures advanced in this book. Thus they have failed to avoid the confusions of formulating in terms of the elementalistic, dualistic split of 'subjective' and 'objective'.

An Elementalistic Attempt to 'Unify' Knowledge

Geologist/philosopher of science Arthur Strahler has written an excellent survey of the philosophy of science entitled *Understanding Science*. In it he has detailed a unifying model for the various fields of human knowledge, a streamlined version of one which Mario Bunge developed in his multi-volume *Treatise on Basic Philosophy*.

Although I admire both men's work, their model of the sciences maintains the sort of fragmentation already discussed and works against the naturalistic humanist viewpoint which they each have so resolutely promoted. Their schema illustrates the problems that can occur from failing to adequately deal with the neuro-evaluational implications of one's own language use.

Bunge and Strahler have demarcated science and history from other so-called knowledge fields. They have done this by labeling science and history as *Perceptional Knowledge*, which deals with the empirical realm of *"percepts,"* i.e., "perceived or perceivable" objects. Science and history are defined as "inquiry" or "research fields" because they study this empirical realm.[2]

Perceptional knowledge is distinguished, in this scheme, from *Ideational Knowledge*, which deals with the "transempirical," "transnatural" realm of "imaged or imagined" *concepts*. Ideational knowledge results from the process of "ideation...characterized by being *autonomous*, requiring no perception of or direct reference to things outside the brain."[3] The fields which study these areas are considered "belief fields" and include logic, mathematics, religion, ethics, socio-political ideologies and pseudoscience. [4]

Strahler and Bunge take the division of *percept* and *concept* as fundamental. Their continued dependence upon the old terminology— for talking about what we in GS call "levels of the process of abstracting"—brings in the old metaphysical implications of 'mind' separated from 'matter' ('body'), 'subject' separated from 'object', etc.

Putting logic and mathematics in a 'transempirical' realm of 'concepts' or 'ideational' knowledge makes them appear protected from inquiry or research. Yet how can we know that a particular 'ideation' or higher-order abstraction in logic, mathematics, etc., has had absolutely no source in 'perception'?

It doesn't seem warranted to create two realms of knowledge—one built on inquiry and one on belief. The division between perceptional (empirical) and ideational (transempirical) knowledge mirrors the dualism separating 'objective' from 'subjective' factors. Acceptance of this division may prematurely block the path of inquiry in areas that desperately need research and investigation. Because of this, despite their acknowledgement of the neural basis of human knowledge, Strahler's and Bunge's analysis does not serve adequately as a unifier.

A GS Model for Defragmenting Knowledge

If we accept that nature forms some kind of unity and continuity, then it makes sense that knowledge has unity and continuity too. Therefore, it seems more useful to postulate one multi-leveled realm of existence knowable by multiple abstractors (Smith 1, Smith 2, etc.) using multiple perspectives at multiple levels of abstracting.

Knowledge involves having a similarity of structure between our maps and *whatever* we are mapping. Indeed, structure constitutes the sole content of knowledge *in any field*. To improve our knowledge, we inquire (do research). In doing so we seek increasing similarity of structure between our knowledge structures or mappings and the other structures of the world that we wish to represent.

As depicted in the model of abstracting, our knowledge structures—or mappings—are ordered as non-verbal observations, symbolic and verbal descriptions, inferences about descriptions, inferences about inferences, etc. Extensionally, we seek predictivity by testing our inferences in relation to non-verbal observations. We create/discover converging inferences which point to similar conclusions about observable events. We can thereby increase the accuracy and generality of our conclusions.

Areas like pure mathematics and logic involve the formal elaboration of linguistic-symbolic structures. In these areas an extensional approach amounts to judging the validity of results according to standards of argument and proof agreed upon by the community of mathematicians/logicians.

Although it has been especially elaborated within the so-called 'sciences', an extensional orientation or scientific attitude toward our observations and inferences is not exclusively the property of the limited institutional areas that up to now have been identified as 'science'. Science in this broadened, attitudinal sense can start with the 'subjective' personal knowledge of an individual.

As chemist-philosopher Michael Polanyi pointed out, personal knowledge involves "the *personal participation* of the knower in all acts of understanding." [5] It consists of our individualized abstractings, both non-verbal and verbal, that include 'intuitions', 'perceptions', 'commitments', etc. Our daily activities constantly involve some sort of personal knowledge process of this sort. In this realm of personal knowledge, we can endeavor to behave as personal scientists by applying an extensional approach to our everyday problem-solving.

Institutionalized science makes this personal knowledge available to us all. Scientific inquiry expands into a social activity that builds upon our individualized, personal knowledge. A group of individuals can extensionally examine, cross-check and test knowledge claims on various levels of abstracting from observation to description to theory. In this way they can inter-subjectively establish broad agreement. This social or public character of science can provide more highly probable, general results than we can gain through our individualized abstractions alone.

A generalized scientific attitude—described in general semantics as an extensional orientation—provides an expanded view of science that includes both personal and public knowledge interacting in the process of time-binding. General semanticists and other naturalistic humanists share the goal of extending this orientation of inquiry into areas that have traditionally been considered outside the boundaries of science. Some people believe that such an extension qualifies as "scientism," an unquestioning faith in science. However, insofar as any field (science, religion, ethics, etc.) involves knowledge claims, it seems unreasonable to exempt these claims from the kind of extensional standards and approach that I've discussed.

What predictive value do our claims of factual significance have in religion, ethics, politics and other areas? Do those making these claims follow a more-or-less extensional approach with consciousness of their own abstracting processes? Or do they reverse the appropriate order of abstracting, by identifying and thus confusing levels? Do their claims remain testable and open to revision?

Those who call themselves 'scientists' should surely be held to the same extensional standards that I am suggesting for others. This hardly involves unquestioning faith in the practices and formulations of 'science'. Indeed it requires an exceptional openness to questioning that we need much more of in the so-called sciences and elsewhere.

The proposal for defragmenting science presented here has some similarity in aim to evolutionary biologist E. O. Wilson's vision for unifying the sciences presented in his book *Consilience*. What I propose differs, however, from Wilson's suggested means for achieving consilience, what he calls the cross-linking synthesis of theories and disciplines. Consilience is unlikely to happen either by just expressing the need for it (however eloquently) or by extending oversimplified 'biological' models and methods as favored by some sociobiologists and evolutionary psychologists.

The GS path I propose for unifying and extending human knowledge does not depend upon model-theism or methodolotry. Rather it is founded upon something more basic—the importance of up-to-date knowledge about knowledge (epistemology) *when actually applied.*

Sufficient attention to neuro-semantic, neuro-linguistic factors in their own and others' formulating will not, I predict, lead 'scientific' formulators to do away with the pluralism and variety necessary for the successful evolution of knowledge.

Rather, the evolving evaluative system of GS allows for a diversity of methods and viewpoints within a general scientific approach. It provides consilient tools for teasing out relationships among different areas of knowledge while remaining critical of premature and presumptuous closures around oversimplified viewpoints. Adequately-trained GS formulators can function as *clinical epistemologists* for individual problem-solving and as *consulting epistemologists* within interdisciplinary, basic and applied research teams in scientific, medical, organizational and governmental settings.[6]

Inquiry and the Extensional-Intensional Continuum

A non-elementalistic view of knowledge based on the abstracting model will focus on the continuum of extensional to intensional orientations and on the priority of an extensional one for any scientific methodology.

As you may recall, an extensional attitude or orientation involves following the order of abstracting most appropriate for long-term benefit and survival. In this appropriate order of abstracting, the event level is valued as most important, then the 'object' level, then description, then inference, then inference about inference, etc., leading back to the event level. On the other hand, an intensional attitude or orientation involves confusing or reversing the appropriate order of abstracting, identifying a map with the territory it represents.

No one, not even the greatest 'scientist' evaluates one hundred percent extensionally all of the time. It is the nature of an intensional orientation to involve deep belief that "I've got it!" Therefore, recognizing fallability, and concurrent self-criticism and self-evaluation, seem vital to promote oneself further along the continuum toward greater extensionality.

There exists an indefinitely great deal that we don't know. An extensional attitude also requires openness to new ways of looking at the world. This involves allowing free play of ideas, space to entertain and elaborate creative connections and new distinctions. This implies that a general extensional orientation requires the conscious use of limited intensional definitions, speculations, metaphors, stories, symbols, art works, mathematical 'objects', etc.

Thus, for example, enjoying stories about unicorns, collecting unicorn statues and art, etc., is not a problem in itself. As long as one allocates unicorns to the very important realm of the imagination, one still may function in a generally extensional manner. However, one who allocates unicorns to the realm of actual biology and goes hunting for 'real' ones, appears to have turned limited, possibly useful intensional formulations in the direction of a generally intensional orientation. Medication may be needed. Imaginative human nervous systems create unicorns, gods, square roots, etc. We need to keep such creatures well-fenced.

In this way, an extensional orientation (scientific attitude) requires both creative play and critical awareness. Creative and critical thinking are not elementalistically opposed. To acknowledge this creative-critical non-elementalism, GS teacher Stuart Mayper coined the term "creatical" (pronounced *creātical*) to label thinking or evaluating that consciously combines both.

Creatical openness seems essential to a naturalistic, scientific attitude. If someone makes a claim which opposes scientifically accepted (at-a-date) views or that 'science' has not yet established, we can apply a creatical, extensional approach. This includes seeing a claim as a possible means for extending knowledge and therefore giving it adequate consideration rather than immediately legislating against it.

Yogi Berra once gave a friend the following directions to his house: "When you come to the fork in the road, take it!" As I have already attempted to show, the innocent or willful neglect of neuro-evaluative, neuro-linguistic issues results in naturalistic formulators unknowingly advancing viewpoints laced with varying amounts of supernaturalism or other forms of misevaluation. While choosing a naturalistic path on the road to knowledge, they may still continue to move in opposing directions—not a good way to get to where they say they want to go. I contend that applying a non-aristotelian, general evaluational approach to these issues makes a consistently naturalistic approach to human knowledge more likely. Who knows where it might lead when, coming to a fork in the road, you face the naturalistic path and steadfastly take it?

Applying a consistent naturalism to science—a consistent naturalistic humanism—implies that an extensional orientation (a generalized scientific attitude) can be further applied to areas already accepted as 'sciences'. It also implies that a scientific attitude can be applied to areas traditionally considered outside the boundaries of science and scientific examination. Religious experience, ethical issues, socio-economic-political issues, etc., can be addressed in this way. What results from approaching these other areas in a consistently naturalistic way?

Section B
Religion: An Extensional Approach

Nothing is so firmly believed as that which is least known.[1]
— MICHEL DE MONTAIGNE

Chapter 17
When Religion and Science Collide

Religious Abstractions

The abstracting process provides us with maps—abstractions at-a-date made by human nervous systems. We can evaluate these maps according to extensional criteria. What happens when extensional standards are applied to religious maps?

If our maps have some similarity of structure with what they purport to represent, they necessarily possess some degree of predictivity. In other words, they necessarily predict or imply some observable, measurable consequences by which we can test them. Highly predictive maps give us the maximum probability of predictability (at-a-date). Less useful maps do not. But in either case, taking an extensional approach requires that we be willing to revise our maps based upon new evidence.

In this chapter, I discuss how this view of knowledge collides with non-tentative religious belief, as I define religion. (Indeed it collides with any non-tentative belief system.) In the next chapter, entitled "Probabilistic Atheism," I argue that the common notion of a personal 'God' seems to me most likely to consist of a map without a territory other than in the brain consciousness of religious believers. In the following chapter, "Beyond Belief in Belief," I discuss how fundamentalist religious and other belief systems can entrap people within dysfunctional, authoritarian worldviews. In the final chapter in this section, "The 'Meanings' of Life," I discuss some ways that humans can find/create 'meanings' on which to ground their lives—without the need for groundless beliefs.

Religion and Other Life-Stances

This chapter's title suggests possible conflict between religion and 'science'. What do I mean here by 'religion'? As I noted in Chapter 2, the term can be defined in a number of different ways. The functionalist approach to religion defines it as any overall guiding view of the cosmos and our place in it. It further defines religion as the main means (way) by which people derive psychological, moral, group, aesthetic and existential 'meanings' for their lives.

This definition could include any philosophy, practice, ritual or even hobby that people devote themselves to and by which they gain life-meaning and purpose. I've known people who use golf and gambling as metaphors for life. Seriously now—except in a playful, metaphorical sense, does it make sense to consider a devoted golfer or poker-player 'religious'?

Maybe. However, defining religion this way could also lead to confusion since it conflates all kinds of views and practices—which many people do not consider religious—with the commonly-held definition of religion. This common usage defines religion as belief in a supernatural realm which usually includes a personal 'God' or 'Gods'. Belief in a personal 'God' or 'Gods' is also called "theism." Religion—more narrowly viewed as theistic belief— includes the various ritualized individual and group practices by which believers relate themselves to the supernatural world of their 'God(s)'.

Naturalistic humanism, general semantics and other practical philosophies are not religions, according to this latter definition of religion. Instead, I consider these practical philosophies as non-religious life-stances or eupraxsophies. The terms "life-stance" and "eupraxsophy" can be used to include religious as well as non-religious views, rituals, ceremonies and practices. These terms can suggest a broader, more neutral viewpoint than "religion" that doesn't necessarily favor either theists or non-theists.

Other people are free to define things differently. And they do. For example, various kinds of Buddhists, Taoists, Pantheists, religious humanists, humanistic religionists, etc., may be called or call themselves 'religious'. Advocates of these life-stances may actually have little or no theistic belief. In that sense, their views may qualify as *more or less* non-religious.

Little or no theistic belief? More or less non-religious? Some people may find these references to *degrees of theistic belief* puzzling. But theistic belief not only "ain't necessarily so;" it also "ain't necessarily" an all-or-nothing affair. One's degree of belief may depend upon both elaborateness of for-mulation (a simple versus complex belief system) and inten-sity of emotional involvement.

In addition, both theists and non-theists may entertain vary-ing degrees of not-strictly-theistic superstition and/or super-naturalism. Particular religions or religious interpretations may also allow more or less humanistic free play in the forms of questioning, reasoned discussion, and even dissent. The extent to which religious claims conflict with 'science', as I define it below, depends on the extent to which these factors are allowed.

Further complicating things, some behavior that appears 'theistic' to outside observers may actually be interpreted symbolically— not literally— by individual 'religious' prac-titioners. People may go through apparently religious motions ('lip service' and 'hip service') for any number of reasons other than theistic belief. Not only are there non-theists in fox-holes[1]—they may also be found in churches, mosques, syna-gogues and temples.

Using the word "religion" to cover both theistic and non-theistic views of life-meaning and purpose may lead to con-fusion. Restricting the term "religion" to theistic belief and using terms such as "eupraxsophy," "life-stance," "personal philosophy," etc., to cover both religious (theistic) and non-religious (non-theistic) philosophies of life, may lead to greater clarity in discussions of religion and 'God'.

Religion and a Scientific Attitude

A basic conflict exists between religion, relatively narrowly defined in terms of theistic belief systems (especially dogmatically-held ones), and science. What do I mean by 'science'? Obviously, I do not equate science with particular scientists. Indeed, some scientists and scientific workers such as engineers, physicians, etc., may accept some sort of theistic belief system. In an article entitled "Can a Scientist Believe in God?" mathematician Warren Weaver, a founder of information theory, affirmed,

> I think that God has revealed Himself to many at many times and places. I think, indeed, that he keeps continuously revealing Himself to man today. Every new discovery of science is a further "revelation" of the order which God has built into His universe. [2]

Quite clearly, then, scientists *can* believe in 'God'.[3] However, despite Weaver's apparent assurance, new scientific discoveries do not in themselves reveal the order of 'God' to anyone who doesn't already question-beggingly assume it.[4] An awareness and sense of awe at the apparent order of the universe, does not necessarily require scientists or others to postulate a personal 'God' or 'Gods' to explain it. At least some respond as Einstein did: "The more a man is imbued with the ordered regularity of all events the firmer becomes his conviction that there is no room left by the side of this ordered regularity for causes of a different nature."[5]

Furthermore, scientific discoveries may falsify certain religiously-motivated claims. For example, Bishop James Ussher (1581-1656) calculated the age of the universe based on assumptions he derived from the Bible. According to Ussher, the universe started on October 23, 4004 BCE at 9:00 a.m.[6] Ussher's conclusion has since been refuted by radiocarbon dating and other geological and paleontological evidence regarding the age of the Earth. This has not stopped so-called 'scientific' creationists from reviving claims similar to his.

Nonetheless, despite the possibility of factually refuting particular religious claims, it doesn't seem likely that anyone will be able to definitely disprove the existence of 'God', 'angels', 'demons' and other 'supernatural' entities. To quote Einstein again, "...the doctrine of a personal God interfering with natural events could never be *refuted*, in the real sense, by science, for this doctrine can always take refuge in those domains in which scientific knowledge has not yet been able to set foot." [7]

Since neither particular individual scientists nor scientifically discovered facts *necessarily* conflict with theistic claims, the conflict between religion and science exists at a deeper level. Theistic beliefs—*other than those held in the most minimal and tentative manner*—clash with a scientific, extensional orientation or attitude.

Establishing a claim of 'fact' requires applying an extensional approach. No other method exists for establishing 'facts' except testing our maps against the territories we presume they represent. Those who, with great certainty, affirm the existence of 'God', Allah, prophecy, 'heaven', 'hell', etc., in elaborately structured detail want their claims to be accepted as unerring 'facts'. If so, they have "the burden of proof" to extensionally provide evidence adequate enough to warrant their definitive-sounding claims.

As far as I know, no one who has claimed to have definitively proved the existence of 'God' or Allah, the truth of prophecy, the literal truth of the 'miracles' in the Bible or the Koran, etc.—no one, I repeat, has succeeded in doing so. The 'evidence' appears flimsy, ambiguous, and ultimately insubstantial, according to the majority of philosophers and others who have studied the subject without a religious axe to grind. As philosopher J. L. Mackie concluded in his book, *The Miracle of Theism*, "The arguments against theism outweigh those in its favor."

In this light, claims for the existence of a personal 'God', 'Allah', etc., do not merit the level of certainty with which many if not most sincere believers appear to make them. Rather, theistic beliefs, if held at all, merit the most modest level of tentativeness imaginable. According to this analysis, *the certainty with which ardent theists hold their beliefs, argue for them, and often push them on others, involves either a loosening or abandonment of scientific standards of evaluation (an extensional orientation).*

An example of the loosening of scientific standards can be seen in Warren Weaver's discussion of 'God'. He noted that scientists accept the existence of unobservable entities like electrons even though they cannot directly observe them. Similarly, he contended, scientists can accept the abstraction 'God' because it too "works."[8] With this argument, Weaver muddled the scientific criteria which Korzybski and others had delineated for determining how high-order abstractions (concepts by postulation) in science work, i.e., predictivity.

Electrons, protons, quarks, etc., differ from 'Allah', 'devils', 'angels', etc., because assuming the existence of electrons, etc., involves risky (potentially falsifiable) predictions concerning specific observations and measurements. So far these predictions have been extensively corroborated. Corroboration of potentially falsifiable predictions remains key here because many individual theists also claim predictability, e.g., answered prayers, but the unanswered prayers are simply discarded.

If replacing electrons with other inferential entities eventually provides better predictivity, then scientists will abandon the notion of electrons. In other words, because of their predictivity we can accept these theoretical entities as highly reliable but potentially replaceable maps for dealing with the territories of cloud chambers, particle accelerators, chemistry experiments, etc.

If we follow scientific standards (2003), our continued acceptance of such entities will rest on how well they explain and predict what we or others can observe. In other words, following extensional standards, the non-verbal territory of our ongoing human observations takes primacy over our mathematical-verbal maps.

'Gods', like electrons, represent high-order abstractions, inferences about how the world works. However, unlike established present-day scientific formulations, theistic beliefs to a significant extent involve the intensional projection of our own motives, purposes, etc., onto the rest of the universe, e.g., faces in clouds, the 'man on the moon', etc. This personalization of the cosmos involves a reversal of the appropriate order of abstracting. We delusionally give primacy to religious maps when we read them onto the non-verbal world. This requires abandoning a scientific outlook (2003).

Religion as Primitive Science

The intensional personification of natural forces into 'spirits', 'Gods', and eventually one 'God' may initially have represented a primitive struggle toward science.[9] Such personification characterizes animistic, polytheistic and monotheistic religions. Early animistic religions gave everything its own particular 'spirit': trees, rivers, rocks, animals, etc. Eventually polytheism moved to a higher level of abstraction by replacing the spirits within natural processes with externalized 'Gods' who controlled these processes. These Gods could be placated through magic, prayer, sacrifice, etc. The monotheistic religions of Judaism, Christianity, and Islam went to a still higher level of abstraction, postulating a single 'God' separate from the world and often appearing to function in the manner of a dictatorial ruler.

From a naturalistic perspective, the literal belief in such an exclusive spirit ruling over the entire universe resulted from the intensional, elementalistic splitting of the creative order of the universe itself. A personal 'God'— a supernatural 'person' separate from the 'created world'—was formulated to explain the world's creative processes. If the creator 'God' (and his divinely-appointed representatives on Earth) are given higher value than the 'created world', this elementalistic split tends to encourage, at least for some monotheistic believers, a world-hating, anti-humanistic, authoritarian philosophy.

Even some pantheistic 'religions' may not be immune to an anti-humanistic, world-despising taint. Hinduism may appear polytheistic. However, from another point of view, Hinduism exists at an even higher level of abstraction than the monotheistic religions. In this pantheistic aspect it emphasizes the oneness and 'divinity' of everything. In this regard, some of its believers may still tend to personify natural forces and elementalistically split the world by overvaluing oneness and similarity, while denigrating multiplicity and differences as *maya* or illusion.

The tendency to explain things by imputing aspects of human personality to non-human aspects of the world has leaked out from religion to influence some naturalistic explanations as well. Such attempts have included Aristotle's physics and more recent attempts at biological explanation such as 'selfish' genes and memes.

Applying up-to-date scientific standards, anything more than minimal and tentative theistic belief, seems unwarranted by any evidence that I'm aware of. If a supernatural person called 'Allah' did exist, how would we know, following modern, extensional standards of evaluation? What observations or measurements could anyone make that could be explained better in terms of a supernatural 'God' or 'Allah' rather than by some naturalistic explanation?

My mother believed that there existed a 'something', some indecipherable purpose or intelligence that she thought might exist. I have known a few Deists, that is, theists who feel the need for some external purposeful intelligence to explain the cosmos. They admitted that they had no definitive evidence of this and were not dogmatic about it. Such minimal, tentative claims don't leave much, if anything, to dispute and do not conflict with a scientific attitude.

It seems most likely to me that, in the words of John Lennon's song *God*, a personal "God is a concept by which we measure our pain." Postulating a cosmic person named 'God'—white beard is optional—does allow some people to project a comforting gloss onto what seems to me for the most part an uncaring, impersonal universe. Perhaps that's useful sometimes. Though ironically—like those who fought the use of lightning rods—the degree of people's urgency to grasp onto such belief often seems proportional to their inability to deal constructively with the problems which they confront in life.

Illusory Revelations and False Holy Books

Different monotheistic faiths and believers have named and characterized their "Supreme Being" in different ways: "HaShem," "Deus," "Allah," "God," etc. In this book, I do not attempt to provide a thorough analysis of individual religions. Rather, I consider this discussion of religion a rough outline of some possibilities for further extensional study.

As part of this, I want to point out a mistake that both critics of religion and pious defenders of ecumenism sometimes make: overemphasizing the similarities among the deities, doctrines and ethical directions of different religions. In questioning the likelihood of what theists believe and the genuineness of 'Gods', 'Revelations', and 'Holy Books', I *do not* want to imply that I consider all theistic beliefs equally harmful.

The abandonment of extensional standards of evaluation seems quite evident in religious claims based on 'divine revelations'. Nowadays, most folks—even religious ones—will question the sanity of someone insistently claiming that 'God' or 'Allah' speaks to him. They will reasonably conjecture that a self-proclaimed Prophet of God's or Allah's word has some sort of psychiatric disturbance (delusions of grandeur) or is cynically trying to delude other people for personal gain.

The 'Prophet' may qualify as both since, as Lichtenberg noted, "the most successful and therefore the most dangerous seducers are the 'deluded deluders.' "[10] It seems curious that many otherwise-reasonable people fail to at least consider these possibilities in relation to the presumed founder of their favored religion, e.g., Muhammad, Joseph Smith, L. Ron Hubbard, etc.

Knowing the errors that can occur within the human abstracting process, we ought to eliminate other more probable alternative explanations, including hallucination and deception, before we accept the likelihood, let alone the unquestionable 'truth', of the revelations of 'divine messengers' found in 'holy books'. This rule of probabilistic judgment can be applied to conspiracy theories and extraordinary claims of all sorts proposed by both religious and non-religious 'true-believers'.

The Problem of Fundamentalism

Hume proposed that "there is a degree of doubt, and caution, and modesty, which, in all kinds of scrutiny and decision, ought for ever to accompany a just reasoner."[11] As I have already indicated, religious believers who non-absolutistically acknowledge an appropriate degree of doubt, caution, and modesty when advocating their views, minimize their conflict with a scientific attitude. This kind of tentative, humanistic, theistic belief exists on the other end of a continuum from less tentative forms sometimes called by the ambiguous term, "fundamentalism."

Fundamentalist religious beliefs are roughly characterized by fervent insistence on the complete and unquestionable correctness of their particular teachings. (The scope of the term has expanded from its original use which described American Christian sects that espoused a simplistic, literal interpretation of the Bible.)

However, to be useful, the term 'fundamentalism' requires indexing and dating since views characterized as 'fundamentalist' differ in kind and degree of absolutism. There have existed and exist many different forms of fundamentalism among different religions at different times. The basic beliefs, scriptures, practices, ethical values, etc., which have been accepted as unquestionable among different faiths are not by any means the same in all respects. In addition, what is accepted as 'literal interpretation' of Holy Scripture within any one religion may vary among different believers and factions.

Textual criticism and historical/archeological study of Jewish and Christian source material, including the Jewish and Christian versions of the Bible, have been going on for several hundred years. Many Christians and religious Jews have learned to modify their orthodoxies in order to accommodate themselves to historical findings which indicate that—whatever their 'divine inspiration'—the scriptures are not the direct or dictated word of 'God' or his 'angels'.

Rather, significant evidence indicates that the Hebrew and Christian Bibles are the historical products of fallible human hands constructed for human purposes over centuries of time. Even the historicity (actual historical existence) of Biblical figures such as Abraham, Moses, Jesus and others has been placed in doubt. As far as I know, no present-day Biblical scholars in Europe, the Americas or Israel have been threatened by Christians or religious Jews for their views.

Present-day Muslim fundamentalists respond much more defensively and, in some cases, dangerously to criticism. More recently-begun historical/archeological study of Islamic sources, the Koran and the Hadith (stories and sayings of Muhammad), indicate the likelihood that these documents were constructed many years after Muhammad was supposed to have lived. Textual analysis of the Koran and Hadith indicates internal contradictions as well as contradictions with both Jewish and Christian sources. Other historical/archeo-logical studies have challenged the historicity of Muhammad. Scholars and writers who have dared to even consider such views have been threatened and persecuted throughout the Muslim world. Some have been killed.

I don't assume that monotheism necessarily involves more humanistic values than either animism or polytheism. Indeed, anti-humanistic, coercive proselytizing has appeared as a significant factor in some monotheistic faiths, i.e., Christianity and Islam. Religionists from both creeds have traditionally tended to emphasize that there is no 'God' but our 'God' and no path to our 'God' except through our particular savior, prophet, etc. The greater such emphasis, the easier it may have been to conclude that "our religion is the only valid one, so believe as we do or suffer (and perhaps die)." Thus, Islam spread by the sword and bloody conquest, and Christianity often aggressively encouraged conversions. None-theless, oppressive intolerance of other faiths is not an absolute necessity of monotheism, as demonstrated by Jewish religionists who have traditionally taught that " 'God' is One," and have mostly discouraged converts and looked down upon proselytizing.[12]

Intolerant belief systems may have facilitated but can't fully explain wars of domination and political oppression amongst various religiously-related groups. Monotheism developed in the areas of the world where the agricultural revolution and domestication of animals in the Fertile Crescent of the Middle East had taken place. Small, nomadic, hunter-gatherer, tribal groups eventually expanded into stable, agriculture-based societies with larger populations. These societies allowed for a division of labor, including organized armies, and the development of hierarchical, authoritarian governments to manage (or mismanage) things. Desire for more land and loot, not necessarily religious fervor, often provided non-religious incentives for wars of conquest. Such wars could occur on a much larger scale with much greater bloodshed than previously known by smaller, tribal societies.[13]

However, the fervent monotheistic beliefs which sprang up in these same societies may have provided one factor which increased the probability of religious coercion and resultant bloodshed when one tribe or society sought to conquer another. Deliberately-crafted religious revelations and holy books of one supreme 'God' could be used to unify and motivate a conquering army and to justify the supremacy of one group over others. Within a society, such a religion could also be used by those in control (or seeking control) to manipulate public opinion and suppress enemies. The merging of religion and politics, resulting in varied intolerant and intolerable theocracies (government by religious authority), has turned out badly for democratic aspirations and humanistic values.

Again, religious absolutism, coerciveness and theocratic authority have all varied within and among the different monotheistic religions. At present, relatively tolerant, non-absolutistic forms of belief have come to flourish within Judaism and Christianity. Presently, even some Jewish and Christian fundamentalists show some moderation by accepting some of the value of living in a pluralistic, democratic society, with separation of religion from the state.

In the case of the Jews, whatever fundamentalism in their religion that they started out with, became attenuated by thousands of years of exile. Only a small percentage of world Jewry remained in the Palestinian Jewish homeland of Israel after the Jewish wars with the Romans. Living throughout the 'civilized' world as an oppressed or barely tolerated ethnic minority, the Jews developed a strong sense of community and created an enduring and exemplary humanistic culture apart from their specific religious beliefs and practices.[14]

In the world of Islam, however, the most severe and intolerant form of fundamentalism still widely prevails (2003). We have seen the most recent results of the most extreme form of Islamic fundamentalism. Other Muslims, as well as the rest of the civilized world, are among its victims. Moderate Muslim fundamentalists, Muslim moderates and skeptics often fear for their freedom, lives and safety in Muslim-ruled nations (and elsewhere) if they speak out for democratic values or if they criticize Muslim religious authorities in any way.

Since the origin of Islam, with Muhammad portrayed as both religious, military and political leader of his people, authoritarian theocracy has remained the traditional model for Muslim societies. Presently (2003) there are many Islamic republics around the world where freedom of religion and from religion does not exist. A not-insubstantial number of Muslim believers support extending Muslim theocracy throughout the world. To take an optimistic view, perhaps the Muslim world is now going through 'growing pains' as a result of its persistent inability to deal with the problems of modern life. We can hope that the pains will not be too severe for the rest of us.

The Will to Doubt

Extreme theistic fundamentalists, whether or not they support coercive violence, don't permit any doubt about the 'truth' of their religious maps. Less extreme believers may permit a slight possibility of doubt when using the Bible, Koran, Book of Mormon or other holy texts to support their views. Despite their questioning, they may, on the basis of faith, accept their revealed teachings as 'The Truth'.

Despite possible intentions to the contrary, William James appeared to encourage such formulating in his essay, "The Will to Believe." When we have insufficient evidence and the consequences seem beneficial, e.g., make us feel good, it seems all too easy for many of us to treat as 'truth' what ought to remain hypothesis. This seems unwise for those who want to follow extensional standards. The will to believe can transform into the ills of belief, as the residents of Jonestown, the Heaven's Gate group, and Islamic Jihadists world-wide, among others, have amply demonstrated. Regarding the will to believe, mathematician/philosopher of science, W. K. Clifford wrote:

> No real belief, however trifling and fragmentary it may seem, is ever truly insignificant; it prepares us to receive more of its like, confirms those which resembled it before, and weakens others; and so gradually it lays a stealthy train in our inmost thoughts, which may some day explode into overt action, and leave its stamp upon our character for ever.[15]

An extensional orientation encourages the will to doubt, question and inquire. If I accept an extensional system of values, then the sureness I give to the 'truth' of any claim will remain proportional to the quality and quantity of evidence I can bring forth to support it at-a-date. Although I may still at times make very firm commitments, I will seek to test my beliefs and revise them when necessary. Scientific, historical analysis of holy books such as the Bible, Koran, etc., demonstrates a large amount of likely fiction and questionable 'fact'. Applying extensional standards to them does not allow for totally unquestioned belief. A reasonable theistic believer can remember this in order to avoid extreme fundamentalist views. In this way he or she can cultivate a sane attitude toward his/her system of belief. The collision between religion and science does not have to lead to explosions.

Chapter 18
Probabilistic Atheism

The notion of a supernatural, personal 'God' is not as clear or factually certain as many believers think. Yet, lack of absolute certainty about the non-existence of this "Supreme Being who created and controls the Universe"[1] doesn't mean that one can't come to reasonable conclusions for oneself that go beyond the suspension of belief and disbelief.

According to the "Probability Continuum" below, we can characterize assertions about the world as having degrees of indeterminacy or uncertainty along a continuum from highly probably 'true' to highly probably 'false'. The realm of extensionally 'meaningless' or 'unknowable' statements exists outside the continuum. I also place absolute 'Certainty' off of the continuum to indicate that in keeping with the probabilistic view of general semantics, no statement about the world qualifies as absolutely certain—including this one.

	'True'		'False'
'Certainty'	Higher Probability		Lower Probability
	Observation		Beyond Observation
	'Fact'	Inference	Wild Guess

Figure 8 Probability Continuum

Arguments for the existence of a supernaturalistic 'God' or 'Allah' constitute inferences at a higher order of abstraction than statements of 'fact'. Based on a probability notion of degrees of 'truth', can you have the same kind of confidence about statements about 'God' as you do about scientific inferences, such as electrons ? Where do you place a supernatural 'God'?

However you answer, I assert that neither dogmatic the- ism or inflexible atheism is compatible with the orientation presented in this book. Rather, applying extensional standards seems to me most likely to yield some position within a hu- manistic range that goes from probabilistic atheism to agnos- ticism to some kind of non-dogmatic, moderate theism.

In this chapter I present a case for what I call "probabilistic atheism," non-belief in the personal 'God' of conventional the- istic religions. Probabilistic atheism seems to me the view toward a supernatural 'God' most consistent with the scientific standards of naturalistic humanism and general semantics. (I said "to me"— some general semanticists do believe in a personal 'God'.)

On a personal note: As a Jew, I was raised in the non-ortho- dox but traditional branch of Conservative Judaism. I have got- ten and continue to get much value from the study of Jewish re- ligious sources and from traditional ceremonial practices. De- spite my skepticism about a personal 'God', I remain a Jew. I have found that this confuses non-Jews, and even some Jews, who don't realize that the term "Jewish" most comprehensively designates a people, i.e., ethnic group. "Judaism" can refer to their multifaceted, evolving civilization (profoundly related to their re- ligion, no doubt). Judaism$_1$ as civilization is more inclusive than Judaism$_2$, the religion of the Jews.[2] A significant number of Jews qualify as tentative theists, or do not believe in a personal 'God' and qualify as religious and/or naturalistic humanists.[3]

Removing the Stigma of Atheism

The term 'atheism' derives from the Greek "atheos" for "godless."[4] As such, it has labeled a variety of forms of reli- gious non-belief and does not indicate in itself the intent or the reasoning behind that non-belief. (Indeed, every religious person reading this qualifies as a 'atheist' in regard to some one else's 'God' or 'Gods'.)

Atheism has traditionally been viewed with disfavor. One or two centuries ago, open admission of atheism was still dangerous and nearly unheard of in America and Europe. Today, 'atheism' is still considered a 'dirty' word by many, with associations to Communism and moral degeneracy, as well as implications of absolutistic hatred for any and all 'religions' and 'religionists'.

Some non-believers prefer other labels for their basically atheistic (non-theistic) views. But the atheism that I advocate is neither Communistic nor immoral nor hateful of all religions. It eschews the attitude and behavior of absolutistic, single-focus atheists. By using the term and explaining how I have come to a position of "probabilistic atheism," I hope to help remove some of the negative stigma from the term that some people may have given to it.

What Do You 'Mean' by 'God'?

An extensional, multi-'meaning' approach to language involves recognizing a particular word in a statement (a propositional function) as a variable with a range of possible 'meanings'. The specific 'meaning' given to the statement and the words within it depends on the language user, context, etc. Therefore, looking in a dictionary is not enough.

When someone says he or she believes or doesn't believe in 'God', we may 'jump' at their words assuming they 'mean' exactly how we interpret them. Or we can operate in a more extensional manner by delaying our immediate reaction and asking the person what he or she 'means' and/or examining his or her statements and behavior to discover this as best we can. Applying a non-absolutistic approach, we will seek to understand other people's views concerning 'God' before agreeing with them, criticizing them, or assuming that they understand that word in the 'same' way we do.

If you consider yourself religious and believe in 'God' as you understand that term, should you necessarily jump for joy at proposals to allow government-mandated prayers to 'God' in public schools and civic events? If you do, you might pause to consider this from the multi-'meaning' perspective. *Whose 'God'?* Hindus, Quakers, Liberal Christians, Evangelical Christians, Mormons, Muslims, Pantheists, religiously-observant Jews, Wiccans, and others, all have very different notions about what the word 'God' represents, although they may share some common general views. Whose definition and whose prayers do those who propose public prayers want to impose on other people—including non-believers—and their children?

Many if not most of our favorite terms are over/under-defined. They can often be over-defined (over-limited) intensionally by verbal definitions, with those definitions believed in as 'facts'. Concurrently, they can be under-defined extensionally by having insufficient specification in terms of non-verbal events that they are presumed to refer to. It is not that intensional definitions are 'bad', just that they often seem insufficient for extensional purposes. My efforts in previous chapters to specify the terms 'science', 'religion', etc., have been intended to reduce some of their over/under-defined quality, i.e., to extensionalize them, at least within the context of my discussion.

We can intensionally define the over/under-defined term 'God' as the one, supreme, transcendental, non-human person who made and rules the world, and whom Christians, Muslims, theistic Jews, and others, despite their differences, are supposed to worship. Does this 'God' have a non-verbal referent? Can we point to 'God' extensionally?

The Non-Verbal Referent of 'God'

Absolutistic believers in a personal 'God' point us to their favorite holy scripture, e.g., the Hebrew Bible, the New Testament, the Koran, the Book of Mormon, etc. Such believers assert the authority of their religious texts because of the accounts of prophetic revelations which they contain. Believers also make various theological arguments for the necessary existence of a personal 'God' (which have been refuted by many philosophers—at least to my satisfaction).

One argument that appears unique to Fundamentalist Islam is the claim that the existence of the holy book itself—the Koran in its 'perfection'—provides evidence that the prophecy of Muhammad must be 'true' and by implication that 'Allah' exists.[5] A passage from the Koran reads, "If you doubt what We have revealed to Our servant, produce one chapter comparable to this Book. Call upon your idols to assist you, if what you say be true." [6] English and other translations of the Koran are considered imperfect translations of this perfect and 'authentic' Arabic version.[7]

The 'perfect' Koran is full of passages which contradict each other as well as earlier Jewish and Christian religious sources and later historical studies. It contains foreign words, awkward and ungrammatical writing, as well as indications of deleted and added verses. Different versions in Arabic have existed, which also belies the claim of an utterly 'authentic' one. As ex-Muslim Ibn Warraq points out, "When a Muslim dogmatically asserts that the Koran is the word of God, we need only ask 'Which Koran?' to undermine his certainty." [8]

As for the claim that no human could ever write anything comparable to this 'perfect' document, there is growing historical evidence, already mentioned, that humans not only could write something comparable to it but actually did —the Koran itself. Historical studies of multiple, post-Muhammad, Koranic authors are, not surprisingly, unwelcome among fundamentalist Muslims.[9]

Inquiring Muslims and non-Muslims, however, should explore the literature of the by-no-means-unitary Muslim world, including that of Islamic heretics, and judge for themselves if they can find anything more beautiful and inspirational than the Koran. Even in the early days of Islam, there were free thinkers who found the Koran wanting in comparison to their own literary works. I'll let the incomparable Islamic skeptic Al-Maari (973-1057) have the last words here:

> So, too, the creeds of man: the one prevails
> Until the other comes; and this one fails
> When that one triumphs; ay, the lonesome world
> Will always want the latest fairy-tales. [10]

All of the purported 'evidence' for 'God' or 'Allah' remains on the intensional, verbal level. It points to no unequivocal, extensional, non-verbal referents for a personal 'God', the truth of prophecies, or the infallibility of holy books. Instead, it does point to—provide evidence of— the intensional orientations of those believers who, by dint of enough indoctrination by themselves and others, project their belief-maps onto the non-verbal world––a pathological reversal of the appropriate order of abstracting.

If we accept that those who assert something have the burden of 'proof' or of evidence, then absolutist advocates of a supreme, supernatural person who created/rules the universe have this burden. They have little, if anything, of extensional value to show. At this point, believers in a personal 'God' may ask us to have faith in the 'truth' of their claims until we *do* believe. To do this, they may ask us to allocate 'God' to the special region of *the unknowable*, an incoherent and extensionally 'meaningless' notion as already noted. Abandoning this, what are we left with? Insofar as we can 'know' the personal 'God' of Judeo-Christian-Islamic fame, he seems nowhere to be found outside the books and brains of believers.

Probabilistic Atheism

Some argue that this doesn't warrant an atheistic position, i.e., rejecting belief in 'God'. According to such views, since we don't seem to have enough evidence to decide, we don't have the right to 'deicide'. Rather, we ought to suspend judgement, neither believing nor rejecting 'God'. I'm not sure how many advocates of this kind of 'fence-sitting' agnosticism actually exist. Nonetheless, those who make this argument, claim that no one espousing the atheist position can positively prove that 'God' doesn't exist. Thus, believers and non-believers seem at a standoff.

Indeed, *no one* can prove that 'God' or 'Allah'—or the Easter Bunny, for that matter—doesn't exist. This does not, however, make the positions of believers and non-believers equivalent. In this matter, I agree with the probabilistic argument of Bertrand Russell:

> I think that in philosophical strictness at the level where one doubts the existence of material objects and holds that the world may have existed for only five minutes, I ought to call myself an agnostic; but for all practical purposes, I am an atheist. I do not think the existence of the Christian God any more probable than the existence of the Gods of Olympus or Valhalla. To take another illustration: nobody can prove that there is not between the Earth and Mars a china teapot revolving in an elliptical orbit, but nobody thinks this sufficiently likely to be taken into account in practice. I think the Christian [and Jewish and Muslim, etc.] God just as unlikely.[11]

If we take any argument as adequate for our belief because no one can prove it false—a fallacy called the *argumentum ad ignorantiam* (argument from ignorance)—we can convince ourselves and others to accept any kind of nonsense. Some people do. What a wonderful rationalization for believing whatever you want.

Intellectual honesty requires something different, something which Nietzsche wrote about:

> *As interpreters of our experiences.*—One sort of honesty has been alien to all founders of religions and their kind: They have never made their experience a matter of con-

science for knowledge. "What did I really experience? What happened in me and around me at that time? Was my reason bright enough? Was my will opposed to all deceptions of the senses and bold in resisting the fantastic?" None of them has asked such questions, nor do any of our dear religious people ask them even now. On the contrary, they thirst after things that *go against reason*, and they do not wish to make it too hard for themselves to satisfy it. So they experience "miracles" and "rebirths" and hear the voices of little angels! But we others who thirst after reason, are determined to scrutinize our experiences as severely as a scientific experiment—hour after hour, day after day. We ourselves wish to be our experiments and guinea pigs.[12]

Accepting the notion of the burden of evidence requires this kind of honesty. It doesn't require that we only have the either/or choice of evaluating statements as 'true' or 'false'. Rather, we can proportion our beliefs in terms of degrees of probability according to available evidence. This relates to the general principle of uncertainty in human knowledge.

Supernaturalistic theists have overwhelmingly failed logically or empirically to demonstrate the existence of their 'God', 'Allah', 'spirits', etc. Given this failure and the effectiveness of naturalistic explanations, it seems reasonable to me to consider theistic belief, when not extensionally 'meaningless', as not only indeterminate or uncertain *but also* probably false. Degrees of agnosticism exist. Some agnostics may want to 'get off the fence' and call themselves atheists—probabilistic atheists—in regard to a supernatural 'God'.[13]

Chapter 19
Beyond Belief In Belief

'Gods' and 'Unicorns'

Reviewing the main points I've made so far about religion: Fervent religious belief, with religion defined as supernaturalistic theism, does not seem consistent with a scientific orientation. The more fixed and less tentative the belief, the greater the likelihood of conflict. An extensional attitude may allow some range of viewpoints from moderate tentative belief to probabilistic atheism.

To analyze religious (and other) beliefs extensionally, I suggest the following questions: "What do you mean?" "How do you know?" and "What then?"

So first, one can ask believers "What do you mean?" when using important terms like 'God', etc. Given the multi-meaning nature of language, different people will give different 'meanings' to common terms.

Asking next, "How do you know?" involves us with the issue of over/under-defined terms. For an extensional analysis, we require—beyond verbalistic, intensional definitions— extensional definitions for terms that supposedly refer to some aspect of the non-verbal world. References to the 'unknowable' character of 'God' appear non-testable and therefore 'meaningless' in an extensional sense. Insofar as reference to a personal 'God' might have some extensional content, the evidence, which involves claims based on revelation, appears pretty slim. In addition, theological arguments for 'God's' existence lead to a logical, philosophical deadend. If we insist that advocates for theism have the burden of evidence for their claims, probabilistic atheism seems warranted. In this view, the existence of a supernatural, personal 'God' has a very low probability. What then?

On a wall of our home, my wife and I have a print of a tapestry of a unicorn—a fanciful, cute creature—enclosed in a fence. I like the 'unicorn', which represents a fiction. I don't believe it exists except in symbolic form, in pictures and words and in neuronal patternings in people's brains. If people don't appropriately allocate their symbolism, 'putting fences around their unicorns' by recognizing them as most probably imaginary rather than actual creatures, they risk evaluational havoc for themselves and others. What happens if we substitute the word 'God' for unicorn?

Perhaps you, the reader, have noticed: the world at large has not taken much notice of the 'news' of 'God's' likely non-existence. Many relatively sane people continue to persist in allocating to the external world the products of religious imagination.

Some people, scientists and philosophers included, feel reluctant to extend the extensional methods that they may use in limited ways elsewhere to the religious traditions that they grew up with or embraced in their quest for community, connection and life-meaning. Admittedly, some do choose to believe in 'God' tentatively. Thus, they can more or less maintain an extensional, humanistic perspective. However, for every one tentative believer, there are many more who succumb to more dogmatic levels of belief.

There is a potential cost to the isolation of religious imagination from critical intelligence. Religious involvement can sometimes provide a major source for personal and social unsanity and insanity by entrapping people within dysfunctional, authoritarian worldviews. "The sleep of reason produces monsters," as the artist Goya portrayed in the famous print of that name.[1]

Religions and Religions

Dogmatic religious believers—like other dogmatic believers—absolutistically avoid serious inquiry while defending the greatest possible 'certainty' for their claims. Therefore, their claims conflict with the scientific, extensional orientation at the root of naturalistic humanism. Here, I want to emphasize that *it's important to make distinctions among religions and among subsets within religions.* There are religions and religions. And they aren't all the same. Even some fundamentalists can stop short of extreme dogmatism, *if* they assert, for themselves and others, the right to question.

As already noted, systems of belief can be viewed on a continuum from closed and dogmatic to open and skeptical. The characteristics of closed-mindedness and dogmatism characterize what can be called the authoritarian or fundamentalist pole. Openness and skepticism constitute the humanistic, fallibilist pole. Systems of both theistic and secular belief may exist anywhere along this authoritarian-humanistic continuum.

I would seriously overgeneralize if I were to claim either that "all religions are equally authoritarian" or that "all secular beliefs are humanistic." On the contrary, as I have already noted, there exist varieties of theistic belief that partake of openness and skepticism and can be called humanistic religions. Secular ideologies can in turn function in closed, dogmatic ways and promote authoritarianism. Focusing on theistic systems, as I do here, it is necessary to index and date them. Remember that religion$_1$ is not religion$_2$. Religionist$_1$ is not religionist$_2$ or any other religionist. Remember also that people's beliefs change with time and circumstances.

Religionists may vary from the occasional church-goer who believes in some vague intelligent principle behind things, to the obsessive Bible-believer. The more that supernaturalistic beliefs are elaborated and emphasized by a religion or religious believer, the less humanistic and the more rigid, dogmatic and authoritarian, i.e., intensional, they tend to become. Insofar as religions or religious believers partake of humanistic values they minimize supernatural creeds.

Among the monotheistic faiths, the religion of the Jews, i.e., Judaism$_2$, even in some of its more fundamentalist forms, has demonstrated strong democratic tendencies throughout its history. Current varieties of Jewish religion (2003) exemplify the possibilities of questioning and doubt within theism.

The Roman destruction of the Second Jewish Commonwealth (in what the Romans came to call "Palestine") resulted in the widespread dispersion of Jews from their national homeland. Jewish religious teachings supported Jewish survival as a minority within countries with often hostile Christian and Muslim majorities. This survival depended in no small part on a tradition which had already been shaped by memories of prior exiles in Egypt, Babylonia and Persia.

The tradition was recorded in the Torah (the Hebrew Bible) and the Talmud, a collection of discussions and commentaries by rabbis, i.e., scholars and teachers of the tradition. The Talmud emphasized inquiry and discussion, the learned debates of fallible men. It focused more on observance and ethics than on beliefs and had significant secular elements. Literacy and study for everyone in the community was expected and encouraged. The tradition, although accepted as 'divinely given' in some sense, was open to some degree of questioning, varied interpretation, and vigorous debate. Thus it has had at least some chance to grow openly.

The evolving civilization of the Jews (Judaism$_1$) has been religiously-tinged to a significant extent.[2] However, the relative openness of the religion (Judaism$_2$)—and the more or less separate, secular-ethnic aspects of Jewishness—have generally led Jews to accept a diversity of beliefs and practices among themselves and others. For a long time, seeking converts has not played much of a part in Judaism$_2$. All individuals of whatever faith are accepted as having a place in 'the world to come' if they follow certain basic moral precepts.

The Jews have not been immune to the development of narrow outlooks—even at times fanaticism. Nonetheless, for the most part, Jews of all degrees of religious belief and non-belief have learned through more than 2000 years of exile and oppression to hate injustice and persecution. They have thus had little motivation to impose on other ethnic or religious groups the kind of suffering they've experienced themselves. The result of this has been a culture that respects democracy, diversity and modernity. Many Jews with moderate, minimal or no religious beliefs participate in and honor the wisdom and culture which grew within and alongside the explicit religious teachings of Judaism.

Among humanistic religious groups with Christian roots, the Religious Society of Friends, the Quakers, focus on what they formulate as the 'God' within each person, what they call the "Inward Light." They thus deemphasize dogmatic creeds and Biblical fundamentalism and allow considerable freedom for individual points of view. Quakers have a lay leadership, function democratically, and traditionally have been in the forefront of the fight for civil liberties, women's rights, and world peace. I consider the Quaker faith as, on the whole, a quite admirable humanistic religion.[3]

Although it has ancient roots, Islamism, the currently pre-vailing, highly vocal, totalitarian version of Islam—which has become such a threat to both the Muslim and non-Muslim worlds (2003)—is not the only version of belief possible within Islam. More humanistic, moderate forms of Islam, such as some of the Sufi orders, have existed and continue to have a small presence. In the future, humanistic forms of Islam and other religious and non-religious viewpoints have the possi-bility to grow in the Muslim world. In order for this to hap-pen, the Muslim world will need to embrace democracy, within which more than a handful of Muslims may find the courage to question and exercise the will to doubt.

Recognizing the spectrum of religious possibilities brings out a related point about the reasons why people might be 'religious'. Some people seem to need an absolute dependence on the utter rightness of a rigid belief system. Other 'religious' people may participate in a 'religious' community for reasons that have little to do with formal doctrines. These reasons may include family connections, friends, community involvement, ethnic identity, etc. Remembering that 'religion' constitutes an over/under-defined term unless specified, and thereby applying extensional devices and techniques during discussions of 'religion', will increase the possibility of making necessary distinctions and therefore making sense.

Religions and Sanity

Albert Elllis has emphasized the importance of scientific, extensional 'thinking' for psychological health. In an article entitled "Is Religiosity Pathological?" he hypothesized "...that unbelief, humanism, skepticism, and even thoroughgoing atheism not only abet but are practically synonymous with mental health; and that devout belief, dogmatism, and religiosity distinctly contribute to, and in some ways are equal to, mental or emotional disturbance."[4]

Suggesting such a notion seems like an unlikely way to gain popular approval. Since the majority of the world's population avows some form of supernatural belief, this implies the neurosis (unsanity), to a greater or lesser degree, of a large portion of humanity. This implies that the United States—which ranks among the highest in religious belief among industrialized nations—might also rank among the highest in religiously-induced psychological disturbances. Despite the discomforting possibilities, the relation of religion to 'mental' health requires further investigation.

In an article on "The Mental Health of Atheists," John F. Schumaker suggested that, contrary to Ellis's conjecture, "religion has a *positive sum effect* on mental health..." and that "...atheists...have 45 percent more symptoms of psychological disturbance than their religious counterparts." [5] Since Schumaker's conclusions were based on the results of a self-report paper and pencil test, his results may indicate not greater psychological disturbance among atheists but rather greater honesty about their problems than those religious people tested.[6] At least, these results seem equivocal.

Psychologist Ken Livingston, in a survey of some of the research which has been done on religiosity and good health, has concluded that "Whatever the outcome of future research in this area, it is clear that the current literature does not establish that religion is necessary for health and happiness in this world." [7]

Edmond D. Cohen, a researcher who has examined the relation of religion to psychological health, provides some support—though surely not definitive by any means— for Ellis' conjecture about the harmfulness of at least extreme religiosity. His study of the psychology of extreme fundamentalist Christianity in the United States, *The Mind of the Bible Believer*, provides some interesting material to ponder. Cohen, both a psychologist and lawyer, came from a nominally Jewish background. As an adult he gradually became enmeshed within the belief system of Evangelical Christianity (a form of fundamentalism) which, following John Calvin, takes the Christian Bible as the revelation of 'God's' purpose for humanity. Many such Bible-believers thus study it obsessively and make it the focus of their existence and their source for ethical and social guidance.

As a former Evangelical Christian, Cohen has provided an insider's view of Biblical Christianity as a "semantic labyrinth"[8] which gradually engenders psychological dysfunction in those who take it with uncritical literalness. People may initially get involved in Biblical Christianity with the hope of finding better ways to function in their everyday lives. Gradually, as they become more and more immersed in the Biblical

message, they may learn to distrust and discount nonbeliev-
ers, their own consciences, and their normal human impulses
for love, self-expression, etc.

Through the use of prayer, church-going, bible-reading,
witnessing, and other indoctrination methods, such Bible-
believers become "obsessively preoccupied with God all the
time...thinking about whether this or that prospective behavior broke any of the rules or not..."[9]

Cohen has argued that the New Testament, when taken as
'the gospel truth', implies a consistently world-disparaging,
reason-numbing message which discourages mature behavior and relationships. The benign and loving surface appearance of the Bible is mirrored in the superficially calm and
loving mask that the devout Bible-believer displays to the
world. According to Cohen, this calmness results from a strait-
jacketing of the believer's emotional life. However, this tenu-
ous suppression of 'thoughts' and 'emotions' doesn't get rid
of them. Instead, issues that don't get confronted become invested in dissociated complexes which well up again and again
in the Bible-believer's life. Cohen has found guilt and depression rampant among Bible-believing, fundamentalist, Evangelical Christians.

Then there is fear. Although some evangelicals may have
absolute conviction that they will go to heaven, many others
can never feel sure whether they are among the saved or the
eternally damned. 'Hell' is a 'real' place where sinners will
be "tormented with fire and brimstone in the presence of the
holy angels, and in the presence of the Lamb: And the smoke
of their torment ascendeth up for ever and ever: and they have
no rest day nor night..."[10] (Imagine the benign, lisping Linus,
of *Peanuts* cartoon fame, reciting this Biblical passage from
the Book of Revelations as the theme of "A Charlie Brown
Inferno.")

Cohen's analysis seems consistent with the general-semantics notion of neuro-evaluational, neuro-linguistic environments. A popular 'new age' view has been that "we create our own reality." No—we don't create our own 'reality'. Rather, we each abstract/construct our own view of 'reality' out of our transactions with our environments, which include our neuro-evaluational, neuro-linguistic environments. We then continue to participate in perpetuating those environments for ourselves and others using Bibles, Korans, etc., and how we choose to interpret them. In this way, we continually co-create our neuro-evaluational, neuro-linguistic environments or, as Timothy Leary called them, our "reality tunnels."

The Snark Principle

The Evangelical Christian reality tunnel provides a particularly potent example of what seems to occur in all reality tunnels, religious-to-secular, non-humanist-to-humanist. Human reality tunnels seem to operate in such a manner that "Whatever the Thinker thinks, the Prover will prove." [11]

This is another way of talking about logical fate. The 'Thinker' aspect of our neuro-evaluational functioning involves postulating, proposing and posing our premises, assumptions, presuppositions, etc. The 'Prover' aspect then produces the 'logical', behavioral, 'emotional' consequences. From premises, conclusions follow.

This does not occur in a vacuum. For the most part our 'Thinker' starts with what has been given and has become familiar to us in the culture we grow up and participate in. To a significant degree, we look to those around us to establish what we take as 'reality'. With "exposure and repetition" by ourselves and others, learning will occur for good and ill. [12] Thus, repeat something often enough with enough intensity and with the will to believe it and you may just begin to believe it. In addition, reinforcement from authorities and fellow believers, as well as isolation from non-believers and alternative sources of information (among other factors), will help to solidify the belief.

Norbert Wiener, coiner of the term "cybernetics" wrote "...the brain probably works on a variant of the famous principle expounded by Lewis Carrol in *The Hunting of the Snark*: 'What I tell you three times is true.' " [13]

> "Just the place for a Snark!" the Bellman cried,
> As he landed his crew with care;
> Supporting each man on the top of the tide
> By a finger entwined in his hair.

> "Just the place for a Snark! I have said it twice:
> That alone should encourage the crew.
> Just the place for a Snark! I have said it thrice:
> What I tell you three times is true." [14]

Forms of influence ranging from sales methods to 'hypnosis' to 'brainwashing' employ "the Snark principle." [15]

Belief in Belief

Part of what makes some reality tunnels (belief systems) potentially, if not actually, pathological can be understood in terms of orders of abstraction. A first-order belief may serve a useful function as a map. A belief system, i.e., reality tunnel, involving neuro-semantic, neuro-linguistic environments, consists of a more elaborate set of maps or models. No one can remain entirely free of such first-order beliefs and belief systems. Problems arise with our second-order beliefs about belief. Pathological belief systems share a common multiordinal structure, *belief in belief*—which goes to the heart of supernaturalistic religions, as well as secular authoritarian ideologies.

Second-order belief in belief involves an over-commitment to one's first-order beliefs. As Korzybski noted, "... belief in belief, makes fanaticism." [16]

When *belief* is *too strong*, although this is never justified according to the best modern knowledge, we very easily fall into indentification, delusions, illusions, and the like. It should be emphasized that the last-mentioned pathological states are always compound. They involve at least two components. One of these consists of some ignorance somewhere; the other of strong affective belief in the 'truth' of our mistaken notions. The stronger the affective tension is, the more dangerous the semantic disturbance becomes.[17]

Belief in belief makes a belief system more or less uncorrectable and difficult to escape from. According to the fallibilistic reality tunnel that I favor, sanity requires a higher-order evaluation system (a meta-system) which allows for checking the results of any particular 'Thinker-Prover' belief system against non-verbal, observational consequences. The meta-system of general semantics encourages such sane evaluating which is not final and which is subject to correction based on new data. Using it, you can escape from self-entrapment.

Second-order disbelief in your first-order belief/belief-system doesn't necessarily entail total skepticism. It includes the limited skepticism of usefully questioning your own maps, seeing them as maps and not 'it'. You can still retain some commitment to your first-order beliefs, assumptions, premises but remain open to new evidence that might refute or modify them.

Religion and the Quest for Certainty

Some seekers who don't yet have a particularly strong first-order belief system maintain a kind of generic second-order belief in belief. (This often seems to go along with the pious public acceptance of religion as an unqualified good.) Such seekers in the 'spiritual supermarket' maintain their quest for certainty beyond questioning by hoping that someone somewhere has 'the answer'. They may envy or emulate those who already strongly believe in their particular beliefs. Their quest makes them vulnerable recruits for the kind of 'mind'-control in which the more extreme Biblical and Koranic believers excel. Do I need to provide names and references? Look at the news.

Many humans seem prone to seek a supernatural realm and authority in order to make sense of things. This tendency seems unlikely to simply reside in a gene or set of genes. Neither does it likely reside in a specific brain module for religion. Nigh undoubtedly, as with any human behavior, genetic factors and neural aspects transact with environmental factors at multiple levels.

However, we cannot understand the prevalence of supernatural belief without looking at how it may derive, in part, from persistent cultural messages, created by and continuing to affect human nervous systems. For millennia, humans have been repeatedly told (Snark, Snark, Snark!) that a person needs to be religious and to believe in one or another holy book, accept one or another prophet, authority, etc., in order to be among the 'elect', have a sense of life-meaning and purpose, and have an ethical framework for living. *Is this so?*

Chapter 20
The 'Meanings' Of Life

What 'Is' 'The Meaning of Life'?

No, I'm not talking about the title of a Monty Python movie. Rather, I refer to what psychiatrist Viktor Frankl wrote about when he said that "concern about a meaning of life is the truest expression of the state of being human." [1] (By the way, I don't dismiss the Monty Python movie's relevance to this issue.)

Frankl was writing about something broader than the 'meanings' of words. He was referring to life-meaning, some larger view of the nature and purpose of one's life that gives one continued reasons for living. We humans seem inclined to attempt to make sense of events in our lives, to see how we connect to larger purposes. We want to know how to live and what to live for.

Undoubtedly, the human search for the 'meaning' of life has found powerful answers in the religious traditions of the world. Supernatural religions still provide many, perhaps most, humans with their explanations of the nature of the universe and with their ethical guidelines for living. Large numbers of people will probably continue to derive meaning from the personal and social rewards of their religious connections for some time to come. For many people, religions promote a sense of social cohesion and ethnic identity as they help individuals mark significant events with rites of passage from birth through marriage to death.

Yet the meaning-giving 'goods' of religion can come with an ever-increasing cost. Theistic explanations of the universe either have had to retreat from or to beat back the viewpoints of science—witness the 'antics' of anti-evolution creationists. In addition, the ethical-moral views of one or another ancient culture can serve as static, stultifying yokes in our ever-chang-

ing, multi-cultural world. Ethnic/social identity held together
by religious 'glue' has contributed to cultural clashes, political persecution, ethnic-cleansing, and resentment-fueled
jihads around the world.

Transforming the Question

Dissolving supernatural shadows requires non-theistic humanists to find paths to the open air and sunlight of a naturalistically meaningful life. Some general-semantics formulations can help in this endeavor. Using them let's perform a *general-semantics transformation* of the question, *"What is the
meaning of life?"*

To begin with, remember the notion of evaluational reaction in order to view yourself as an organism-as-a-whole-in-
an-environment responding to life in terms of its meaning,
value, significance, etc. No meaning, value, significance you
experience is given by anything other than your individually-
abstracting, evaluating nervous system. However, when we
talk about the 'meaning' of something, this has the strong
implication of something external to ourselves. We strongly
tend to project or allocate the sources of 'meanings' outside
of ourselves. For that reason, I'll use the extensional device
of single quotes around the term 'meaning', as a warning to
question that implication. In this way, the question becomes
transformed to, *"What is the 'meaning' of life?"*

To eliminate the "is of identity," which can obscure the
role of the abstracting human, I substitute the question, *"How
do I (you, etc.) define the 'meaning' of life?"* In addition, I
pluralize 'meaning' to indicate that more than one 'meaning'
can exist both within and among individuals. We are now in a
position to index different 'meanings' and thus remain open
to new possibilities. The question transforms to, *"How do I
(you, etc) define the 'meaning(s)' of life?"*

An individual may have a strong tendency to assume that

the rest of humankind must share his or her own exact individual meanings, values, etc. It seems easy to forget that each person makes his or her own 'meanings' for himself or herself—not for some generic 'Man' or 'Woman'. To emphasize this individualized aspect of 'meaning'-making, we can specify whose life we are referring to by adding "my", "for me", "myself", etc. Thus, *"How do I define the 'meanings' of my life?"*

In asking about 'the meanings of life' we can also question the allness of the 'the', which can imply an absolutistic single answer. We can replace it with "a" or "some," *"How do I define some 'meanings' of my life?"*

Acknowledging the world and ourselves as processes, we can apply some dating to the question, for example, *"How do I define some 'meanings' of my life right now?"*

To get even more extensional, perhaps the noun "meaning(s)" can be made into an adjective to modify more actional nouns such as "goals" or "purposes." Replacing "define" with different verbs might also make the question more action-oriented: *"How can I find/create more meaningful (for me) goals in my life right now?"*

In this example of a set of general-semantics transformations, the cosmic question of 'the meaning of life' has come down to earth. It now has potential not just to stimulate navel-staring but also to provide some extensional provocation for 'meaningful' activity.

Finding and Fashioning Flow

Albert Ellis and Robert Harper have written about the importance of developing goals for 'meaningful' activity:

> To some degree, human contentment seems almost synonymous with absorption in outside people and events, or what Nina Bull calls goal-orientation...the three main forms of vital absorption comprise: (a) loving, or feeling absorbed

in other people; (b) creating, or getting absorbed in things; and (c) philosophizing, or remaining absorbed in ideas. Feeling inert, passive, or inhibited normally keeps you from getting absorbed in any of these three major ways— and hence from truly living.[2]

Religious involvement surely provides one possible approach to such 'meaningful' activity but it is not the only approach and not necessarily the best. To the extent that their religion alienates them from important aspects of themselves and encourages uncritical evaluating, it may even impair believers' attempts to construct a 'meaningful' life for themselves on the basis of self-directed goals.

The notion of self-directed activity as a key to a 'meaningful' existence figures prominently in the work of psychologist Mihaly Csikszentmihalyi. With resonance to Goldstein's and Maslow's notion of self-actualization which I discussed earlier, Csikszentmihalyi has developed the formulation of *flow*. Flow refers to an "optimal state of inner experience...in which there is *order in conciousness*. This happens when psychic energy—or attention—is invested in realistic goals, and when skills match the opportunities for action."[3]

He also characterizes flow as "autotelic experience" which "derives from two Greek words, *auto*, meaning self, and *telos* meaning goal. It refers to a self-contained activity, one that is done not with the expectation of some future benefit, but simply because the doing itself is the reward."[4]

C. S. Read, writing about Csikszentmihalyi's work, abstracted four rules for developing the experience of flow:
1) set clear goals to strive toward,
2) become immersed in the activity chosen,
3) pay attention to what is happening, and
4) learn to enjoy immediate experiences.[5]

She pointed out how using general semantics can provide help in developing flow, particularly *practice* in "differentiating between orders of abstracting":

> If we are to differentiate between verbal and non-verbal orders, for example, we would need to be in closer contact with the silent levels, and commit ourselves to learning to focus our attention on them when we wish. Hence our inclusion of Sensory Awareness and awareness of 'feelings' at our general semantics seminar-workshops.[6]

As with "self-actualization," the notion of flow focuses on the possibilities for developing "full humanness." Finding and fashioning flow does not require acceptance of a theistic worldview. Flow provides an alternative formulation of 'meaningfulness' that avoids the possible supernatural implications of 'spirituality'. Social Psychologist Ellen Langer has developed the related naturalistic notion of "mindfulness" to describe something similar to the kind of intentional, i.e., purposeful, awareness discussed above. Practices such as meditation, yoga, tai chi, etc., that come out of religious or 'spiritual' traditions can be interpreted naturalistically in terms of flow or 'mindfulness' and thus used by non-religious as well as religious humanists to enhance the quality of their this-worldly experience.

Immortality and Time-Binding

Apart from finding enjoyment in our immediate experiences, developing a more meaningful existence also seems to require the ability to view our activities within a larger framework. In this way, supernaturalistic religions do provide believers with an opportunity to see their actions as part of a larger divine purpose. Indeed, by postulating a system of rewards in an afterlife, such beliefs can give a measure of relief to those who don't experience much immediate enjoyment in their lives. Naturalistic humanists have not found any discernable convincing evidence of survival of an individual's personality after death. They may seem at a disadvantage here.

However, there are downsides to fervent belief in an afterlife. For one thing, belief in a system of after-death rewards and punishments—drilled into sensitive nervous systems starting at an early age—makes it a whole lot easier to downgrade this life. Islamic suicide bombers are carefully taught——snark, snark, snark——and 'know with absolute certainty' that they will immediately be transferred to a heaven with flowing fountains and dazzling virgins. What an irretrievable waste of innocent victims and deluded bombers if this life constitutes the only one that any of us will ever have.

Fervent and detailed belief in heaven and hell also debases this life in other ways. It makes ethical behavior a function of 'God's' cosmic carrot-and-stick, not one of thoughtful consideration and dialogue about values and consequence, etc., by oneself and others. Of course, true believers actually respond to the symbolic carrots-and-sticks wielded by religious leaders who control their symbol-systems. In this way they too can be seen as 'victims'.

Do humanistic, naturalistic alternatives to traditional immortality exist? The human search for 'meaning' to a great degree represents the discovery/creation of connections, not only connections within ourselves and with other humans but also with the fellow creatures with whom we share this planet and with the rest of the natural world of which we form a part. This sense of connectedness with nature combined with the notion of conscious evolution through time-binding can provide a welcome recourse to the supernaturalist's afterlife— a naturalistic option which provides security without the need for absolute 'certainty'.

Naturalistic formulations and practices drawn from religious and non-religious humanist sources can help us recognize and strengthen the sense of connectedness and security for ourselves. For example, the poet Rainier Maria Rilke expressed the wish and feel of connectedness like this:

Ah, not to be cut off,
not through the slightest partition
Shut out from the law of the stars.
　　The inner—what is it?
　　if not intensified sky,
hurled through with birds and deep
with the winds of homecoming.[7]

In the vast scheme of the natural universe what each of us does in our daily lives may seem insignificant, but we can see our individual dramas as expressions of a larger nature, as conscious human forms of nature's own evolving power. Catholic humanist/paleontologist Pierre Teilhard de Chardin wrote, "The consciousness of each of us is evolution looking at itself."[8]

As time-binders, we can each attempt to play our small part in contributing to the evolution of a somewhat more conscious and, we hope, better world. Seeing ourselves as standing on the shoulders of those beings (not just humans) who came before us and providing the shoulders for future generations of beings to stand upon may help to give us a larger, more 'meaningful' context for our actions.

SECTION C
Time-Binding Ethics

A growing company
Of self-aware time-binders,
Explorers, discoverers, pathfinders,
...mindful of their debt to time,
Will ask how it can be repaid—
"What track will I have left behind
To guide who follows me?
What clearer vision of my mind
Will help another see?
What saving sign for humankind
Will I bequeath as legacy?"[1]

— Ted Daly

Chapter 21
An Approach to Humanistic Ethics

What results when consciousness of our time-binding connections and responsibilities gets applied to the field of ethics?
How can the conscious time-binding methodology of general
semantics be used to deal with both theoretical and practical
problems of humanistic ethics? In this chapter I show how general semantics intersects with, complements, and strengthens a
naturalistic humanist approach to ethical questions. In the next
chapter, as a case example, I apply some GS-related insights
and tools to analyze a continuing ethical dilemma for individuals
and society—the clash of values related to abortion.

The Ethical Animal

Human values and ethics do not have to come from a supernatural realm on high. Rather, we can understand our capacity to make value judgements and create ethical systems
as naturalistically deriving from our biological inheritance.
Concurrently, as evolutionary biologist Paul Erlich points out,
"…the actual ethics, morals, and norms of a society—the products of that ethical capacity—are overwhelmingly a result of
cultural evolution within that society." [1]

Humans make ethical choices based on considerations of
values. We judge things, ideas, ourselves and others in terms
of 'right' and 'wrong', 'good' and 'bad', etc. My late cat
Samantha, when sniffing around the dinner table, made choices
based on values too: lettuce was bad within her system of values, and tuna good—very good! Samantha did not verbalize
these judgements of value. I inferred them from observing her.

The process of valuation—evaluating—results from a
transaction between an organism and its environment. 'Values' as 'meanings' don't elementalistically exist separately
from an organism allocating them. As living creatures, both

cats and humans give value to objects, events and other creatures, etc., in relation to how we perceive that they satisfy our needs. Individual acts of valuing (evaluating) become organized into systems of value-based behavior involving aggression, altruism, curiosity, reverence, etc. These can be observed in species other than humans.[2]

Both human and animal nervous systems possess a limbic-brainstem system, concerned with intrinsic values, i.e., setpoints or reference levels for evolutionarily-derived physiological patterns. These intrinsic values, messages from "self," regulate the internal economy of the organism. A thalamo-cortical system also registers messages from "self" and from "non-self" (the external environment). The thalamo-cortical system ("cortex") coordinates with the limbic-brainstem system to produce so-called 'voluntary' behavior. The cortex is concerned with categorization of the world (creating systems of non-verbal and verbal abstractions) produced on a background of values—evaluation. Learning involves adaptive changes in behavior that can satisfy intrinsic values and generate the emergence of new values as well.[3]

The Human/Animal Difference

Behaving and changing behavior according to some set of values, then, is not unique to humans. And neither in animals nor in humans is behavior solely determined by genes. Like us, different animals have varying degrees of ability to learn from and build upon their own and others' experiences.[4] In doing so, some animals begin to approach the kind of behavior—most clearly seen in humans—that Korzybski characterized as "time-binding."

Whether or not animals can be said to time-bind, what distinguishes humans is our elaborated symbolic-linguistic ability. We can talk, and talk about our talking. The resulting generation of human time-binding (with accelerating, geometrical progression) allows us to formulate ethical systems—abstract standards and codes of behavior and judgement based on the values we hold.

In terms of fulfilling our values, how much of an advantage our symbolically-based abilities give us seems open to question. Samantha occasionally chased her tail or a beam of light reflected onto the carpet. However, she seldom seemed very confused about what she wanted and how to get it effectively. Although a 'naïve realist' without the capacity for human-like language, she also had immunity from belief systems involving 'gods', 'demons', 'heaven', 'hell', 'revelations', 'sin', and other means of symbolic tail-chasing. In this way she operated much more extensionally than many, if not most, humans. I've sometimes envied her and other animals.

An animal has limited abilities to abstract self-reflexively, that is, to symbolize its symbols, map its maps, etc. In this sense, its abstracting stops at a certain level. However, since an animal basically lives its life without human-like symbolic language, it normally can continue to remain in touch with the dynamic extensional world. Thus it can continue to dynamically abstract, adjusting for gradations of 'good' and 'ill' that happen in the process world. We don't usually worry about the sanity of an animal unless it has been interfered with by human trainers/owners who can create conditions that make it neurotic (or unless the animal nervous system becomes diseased 'on its own' through infection, trauma, etc.).

However, humans can easily stop their abstracting process in the sense that they become blocked by a static abstraction or set of abstractions. In this case, problems necessarily result. With such static abstracting, we cease behaving extensionally—responding freshly to the dynamic non-verbal world. We become 'mindless'. Our final conclusions become barriers that keep us stuck in old evaluations.

Noting this process, Korzybski wrote "When we come to a *stop*, and consider it 'final' or that we 'know all about it', we copy animals in our nervous reactions."[5] For a long time, I've felt dissatisfied with this characterization. It can seem to unfairly disparage animals for what essentially seems a human pathology. With static abstracting, humans artificially limit, block or stop their abstracting processes at a certain fixed point.

When humans commit mass murder in the name of a fixed, dogmatic religion or ideology, they are not acting like animals. Rather, their behavior seems human—all too human. Animals cannot and do not make such problems for themselves. Instead of defaming other creatures, we humans might do better to study and deepen our connections with them, learn to respect them, and thus discover what we can learn from them (including rats, hyenas, and vultures). Indeed, with some, we can reach some sort of companionship, communication, and empathy.

I fondly remember what Samantha (a beautiful brown, black, and white tabby cat) taught me. Many evenings, we spent time looking out of a ground-level window into the front yard of our house. We would watch the leaves shimmering in the wind, the colors of the evening light, a squirrel scurrying along a tree trunk, etc. We would listen through the screen to the crickets and feel the breeze. I would bring my head close to Sam, who liked to sit on the window ledge. She would turn to me for a moment and quietly meow. At those times, as I turned down the volume of words in my head more and more, I would enjoy the silence on the un-speakable level with Sam, who seemed deeply at ease there.

The consciousness of non-human animals, their capacity for feeling and for aesthetic values, and their abilities to learn from experience and to transmit what they have learned to others, should not be treated dismissively. The evidence for such capacities in animals is abundant. For example, science writer Dennis Flanagan reports:

Adriaan Kortlandt is a Dutch biologist who studies the be-havior of chimpanzees in the wild. Once he was in his observation blind at sundown on a clear day, watching a group of chimpanzees gathering papaws for their evening meal. A male in the group looked up and caught sight of the setting sun. The chimpanzee stopped dead in his tracks and watched the glowing red ball for a full fifteen minutes. By then it had got so dark he had to retire into the forest without gathering a papaw.[6]

We humans, by means of verbal self-intoxication, can impede our own abstracting processes. We can let animals re-mind us of the values inherent in silence on the un-speakable level. By shutting up verbally we can thereby open up non-verbally to the dynamic, unlabeled world.

Ethical 'Thoughts' and 'Thinking'

Among the values we share with other animals is the value of living with others in cooperative social life. Indeed, as Pe-ter Kropotkin emphasized in *Mutual Aid*, neither animal nor human life can be simply characterized as the ruthless com-petition of individuals. Rather, as Ashley Montagu wrote, "There is an unconscious force throughout the realm of liv-ing nature which is expressed as an unconscious mutualism which serves to produce greater survival values for every form of life than would otherwise be the case."[7]

Humans create symbolic systems of ethics by applying their linguistically-generated time-binding abilities to the value-based questions that primarily result from living with other creatures (human and non-human) who have their own values. Such questions may include: What should I do? What should we do? What "principles of conduct" ought to underly our individual and group behavior?

Robert Anton Wilson wrote about a distinction that I con-sider relevant to a naturalistic humanist, GS approach to val-ues and ethics:

Krishnamurti distinguishes between thinking, an active process, and thought, the result of past thinking filed away in the memory of the brain, or in a library or computer, etc. Thought contains all wisdom, and much of the folly, of the past; it's a great labor-saving device. Why does Krishnamurti regard thought as profoundly dangerous and the enemy of thinking? [8]

'Thought', in this sense, corresponds with what Ellen Langer calls 'mindlessness'. 'Thought'—I place single quotes around the term because "thought-felt" would more accurately label what's referred to—can involve a blocked or frozen abstracting process, i.e., static abstracting, which keeps us stuck in old evaluations, responding to events primarily in terms of previous abstractions we've made. In this way we respond in a more or less undelayed and unconditional fashion. In GS, we call this signal reacting, a common tendency in all of us and the habitual approach of authoritarian and dogmatic believers in belief. It characterizes an intensional orientation.

In contrast, 'thinking' (thinking-feeling) in the Krishnamurti sense, corresponds to Langer's 'mindfulness'. It involves an unblocked or unstuck abstracting process (dynamic abstracting) which includes seeing things anew, i.e., responding to events freshly by reevaluating previous abstractions and responses. This requires an "investigatory reaction" involving a "*delay in an immediate reaction* to a former stimulus"[9] in terms of what one thought-felt was going on. Using the tools of indexing, dating, silence on the unspeakable level, etc., you can think-feel freshly in response to new conditions. Less easy and habitual than signal reacting, delayed reacting/evaluating requires effort not to totally believe your own beliefs or those of others. It characterizes an extensional orientation.[10]

The field of ethics has been characterized by both 'thought'-based and 'thinking'-based approaches. Religious and non-religious dogmatists (or believers in belief) have created 'thought'-based ethical systems that have claimed 'final' solutions to questions of what humans ought to do.

In constrast, naturalistic humanists advocate ethical inquiry, creatical (creative-critical) evaluating that aspires toward never becoming totally stuck in one's own or other people's ethical belief systems. Promoting such ethical inquiry seems important in our ever-changing, process world. Paul Kurtz wrote: "The intransigent defenders of the status quo and of the unmodifiable, absolute commandments are unable to contemplate the stretching or revising of their principles. But this may be necessary in life." [11]

In philosophy, the tradition of ethical inquiry goes back at least as far as Socrates. As a philosophical field, ethics has been split into the areas of meta-ethics, concerned with more abstract questions of definition, theorizing, etc.; and normative ethics, which considers what we actually should do in particular situations. As a life-stance, the naturalistic humanist perspective seeks to take ethics beyond the area of armchair philosophizing by focusing on the second, practical aspect, taking theoretical meta-ethical questions into account insofar as they influence the practical decisions we make. Naturalistic humanists advocate ethical inquiry and seek to bring scientific knowledge and methods into the study of how to improve our decision-making.

General Semantics aligns with this naturalistic humanist view. It provides a basic ethical premise: to improve decision-making humans ought to develop their time-binding capacities to the fullest. This implies that each individual acknowledge her debt to previous generations for her cultural inheritance. This implies a dedication to questioning and improving upon this inheritance for one's own and others' benefit now and in the future—an imperative to 'think'.

It bears repeating that, in the GS view, we consider 'thinking' as inseparable from 'feeling', 'acting', etc. Totally separating 'thinking' and 'feeling', 'facts' and 'values', appears hopelessly elementalistic. We emphasize that human behavior involves evaluational transactions with environments, involving thinking-feeling-acting, etc. In this sense, value and ethical considerations permeate every aspect of life.

As humans, we're stuck with our humanness. Thrown into the human condition, we have the capacity to inform and/or delude ourselves and others with symbols. As symbolic-linguistic time-binders we can receive and transmit both ethical wisdom and nonsense. We undoubtedly do both. We cannot however, return and permanently function at the level of non-human animals.

Instead, we can consciously apply our enhanced human abstracting abilities to unblock our static abstractions. Self-reflexively we can take as data any particular static abstractions that we have produced at whatever level. Self-reflexively we can re-evaluate these in the light of new information, develop more useful abstractions, and share them with others. Such continuing dynamic, self-reflexive effort allows each one of us, in regard to ethical questions, to 'think' about our 'thinking', evaluate our 'values', etc.

Can Non-Believers Be Moral?

When a theistic acquaintance of mine discovered that I did not believe in his 'God', he seriously questioned me as to whether or not I could be a moral person. His concern reflects a widespread attitude that equates only supernaturalistic religion with 'moral' or 'ethical' behavior.

If, as naturalistic humanists contend, we humans discover/create our own 'meanings', values, purposes, etc., what basis do we have for behaving ethically? If naturalistic humanists reject supernaturally-based authority, does this make us complete relativists with no basis for ethics? Does anything go?

In this book, I've worked to distinguish among different religions and to qualify my criticisms by recognizing the continuum of attitudes toward critical 'thinking', non-dogmatism, etc., that exists among those who consider themselves 'religious'. Theistic believers who don't already do so might more accurately assess non-believers by similar criteria. Although there may exist some non-theists who consider that "anything goes," I have not met any among the secular humanists I know.

Rather than tar everyone with the same brush, we can recognize and index the gamut of ethical attitudes that exists among both religious and non-religious viewpoints. Starting at least with Kant, the autonomy of ethical judgements from religious authority has become a widely accepted notion among philosophers. This implies that religious people often have other reasons for their ethical behavior besides the 'fact' that the Bible or Koran tells them so.

The Common Ground of Human Ethics

Human ethics has a common ground in the exigencies—necessities of living—that every human shares. This derives from the trans-cultural 'fact' that humans, both religious and non-religious, share a common biological origin and have to live in a world of a certain structure, which includes society—the world of other people with whom we live and negotiate our lives. As a result, it seems reasonable to consider that both religious and non-religious people may go through similar stages of ethical development.

Do humans develop ethically as they learn to assess alternative courses of action and deal with the emerging consequences? The existence of some form of ethical, moral development across cultures would dispute the extreme ethical relativity that ethical absolutists seem to fear (more on different types of ethical relativity a little later).

Based on the behavioral observations and theorizing of Kohlberg, Piaget, Maslow and others, Paul Kurtz has postulated the following stages of ethical development: 1) "Infantile amorality"—If it feels good now, do it!; 2) "Obedience to rules"—I'll do it or I won't because mommy, daddy, or another authority says so and can reward or punish me; 3) "Moral feelings for others"—My actions toward you are guided by empathetically imagining myself in your situation. I take your viewpoint into account; 4) "The ethics of self-interest"—I make decisions based on estimating both short and long-term benefits for myself; 5) "Union of moral feeling and rational self-interest"—I expand my self-interest to include the group to which I belong; and 6) "Humanistic ethics." Kurtz has characterized humanistic ethics as follows:

> A fully developed ethical system involves a concern for the broader community on a more universalistic basis. It is able to transcend the level of small-group relationships, and has the following ingredients:
>
> —There is devotion to general ethical principles, and one does not break them without just cause.
>
> —There is an inward feeling of moral sympathy and beneficence, and a desire to not needlessly hurt other human beings.
>
> —Reason is used in guiding one's own conduct in terms of the excellences [standards of ethical excellence]. This may involve some consideration of self-interest, but it includes the interests of one's group as well.
>
> —There is in addition an ethical awareness of the need to extend ethical considerations beyond one's inner circle to a wider community of human beings. This ethical concern is for the preservation and well being of the world community and for humanity as a whole.[12]

I would add that humanistic ethics needs to widen the ethical circle to include the greater community of non-human beings that live on this planet.

Ethical Relativity

Kurtz's analysis, in keeping with other humanistic views, including general semantics, also entails a bio-psychosocial origin of values and ethics. It recognizes the individualistic nature of ethical judgements: values appear relative to whomever is making the evaluation. It also recognizes that values appear relative to cultures, i.e., different cultures, or 'reality tunnels', often espouse very different, even contradictory, value systems.

This does not warrant extreme or absolute ethical relativism, which implies that no system of values has any priority over another—"anything goes." Relativity and absolutism constitute multiordinal terms. Unqualified or absolute relativism thus becomes another absolutistic system, to be rejected by non-absolutists. To deny that standards exist for judging values assumes some standard of values for judging standards of value. Therefore the denial of any standards appears self-contradictory.

Relative relativism, on the other hand, provides a much sounder, more nuanced basis for humanistic ethics. While respecting all 'reality tunnels', general semanticists and other humanists don't judge all actions and qualities as equally good. Rather, in espousing a scientific attitude, we advocate a value system which we contend works better than appeal to authority, 'intuition', 'pure' logic, custom, etc., in discovering what we think is going on and what to do about it.

Science and Ethics

A scientific attitude constitutes a system of values and code of recommended behavior: an ethics of inquiry. It is based on an important injunction or 'ought': If you want to get reliable knowledge, then you ought to follow some set of procedures that includes experimenting, observing, describing, inferring, hypothesizing, revising and further testing by yourself and others.

Many philosophers of science now accept that value judgements pervade the practice of science. These include not only so-called extrinsic aspects like choice of topic, the ethics of human subject and animal experimentation, etc., but also so-called intrinsic aspects of science such as the choice of one theory over another.

Theoretical biologist C. H. Waddington agreed that, "The maintenance of a scientific attitude does in fact imply the assertion of a certain ethical standard." [13] This has serious implications for scientists, not only among their peers and within their own institutions but also within the larger social and political spheres in which they operate.

Werner Heisenberg worked on the Nazi atom bomb program. It is not so clear that a scientist can do this kind of thing without compromising the time-binding integrity upon which the whole scientific enterprise is built. Waddington noted that before World War II, "there was very remarkable agreement among scientists throughout the world that a system of thought such as Nazism is incompatible with the scientific temper and is, for that reason among others, to be ethically condemned." [14] Note: there are other less obvious ways in which scientists can violate the scientific temper.

The evolution of scientific knowledge can continue by emphasizing the appropriate order of abstracting—adjusting our verbalized beliefs to the non-verbal 'facts' rather than attempting to force 'facts' to fit our beliefs. Science, then, has an ethical basis in the sense that it has as its foundation a set of values concerning the importance of 'facts', 'validity', honesty, etc. Reversing this, can we find a scientific, naturalistic, extensional basis for ethics?

The Place of Value in a World of Fact

Paleontologist Stephen Jay Gould argued that, while science deals with 'facts', religion deals with life-meaning and ethics. For Gould, science and religion (including ethics) constituted "non-overlapping magesteria" (domains of discourse) which should stay out of each other's territory.[15] Although Pope John Paul II might agree, I see no adequate reason, from a naturalistic perspective, for accepting Gould's radical separation of scientific 'fact' from ethical 'value'.

Indeed, the name of the sub-heading above (which is taken from the title of a book by Gestalt psychologist Wolfgang Kohler) presupposes that 'value' as such does have a place in a world of 'fact'. Understanding this place has important implications for encouraging a naturalistic approach to ethical inquiry. The GS abstracting model below, first presented in Chapter 11, provides a framework for clarifying the distinctions and relations among 'fact' and 'value'.

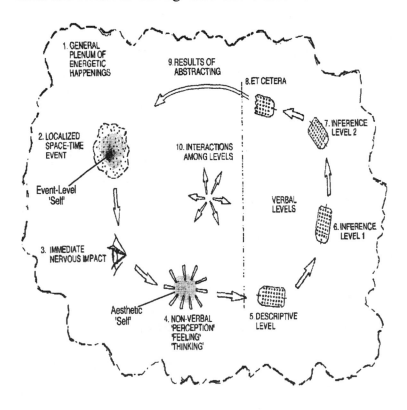

Figure 9 The 'Self'

Where is your 'self' located in the diagram of the abstracting process? According to this general-semantics model, everything, including each one of us, exists within what is labeled here as the "general plenum of energetic happenings"— the process universe. Each of us inescapably carries a part of this plenum, ourselves, around with us wherever we go. What is labeled here as a more or less "localized space-time event" consists of a field of an individual organism and the environment it transacts with at a given moment.

I have marked the "Event-Level 'Self' " in the diagram as a more specialized area within this field. The 'self' represents that bounded aspect of a more or less localized space-time event which can be specified as going on inside the skin of an organism, i.e., you, me, Smith$_1$, Smith$_2$, etc. Notice that the area around what is labeled 'Self' appears fuzzy, to indicate that it is distinguishable but not completely separate from its environment. According to the abstracting model, you can only infer and never experience your event-level self.

Each individual, then, constitutes part of the process universe from which she/he abstracts values. We don't abstract everything from our event-level selves. Much that goes on within us remains unregistered, with only a small portion getting conveyed into non-verbal awareness at any moment. I label this silent, un-speakable 'object' level awareness: the "Aesthetic Self," the non-verbal sensing-feeling of self.

This aesthetic self includes non-verbally experienced 'emotions', 'feelings', 'values', etc., which serve as filters for ongoing abstracting—background against which categorization of the 'external' world occurs. In addition, it's important to note that our object-level feelings, emotions, values, etc.— as we experience them—also provide material for our categorizations.

In neurological terms, the value messages from 'self', transmitted by means of the limbic-brainstem system, themselves provide 'grist' for thalamo-cortical categorization of values, which occurs on both non-verbal and verbal levels. The human sense of self (the symbolic self) involves such categorization of values involving the symbolic-verbal levels.

On these levels, statements about values, 'feelings', etc., can easily involve identification or confusion among orders of abstracting. Such confusion involves projecting onto the 'external' world what properly belongs to oneself. This occurs, for example, when someone says that "X is bad, evil, unnatural, immoral, unethical, etc." or that "Y is good, virtuous, moral, etc." Statements like these have the superficial appearance of descriptive reports, statements of fact about X or Y when I am actually stating my value-laden inferences (assessments, judgements) about X and Y.

For example, if I say "abortion is murder" or "abortion is evil," my statements seem like descriptions about abortion. But such uses of the ises of identity and predication describe more about me and my personal values than they do about abortion as such. In making these statements, I incorrectly project or allocate to abortion what more accurately pertains to myself. *In this way, I obscure my role in generating the evaluations (values) I make.* This provides the basis for many forms of absolutism, both religious and secular.

On the descriptive level, then, it seems more accurate to take responsibility for my own value judgements by saying that according to my system of values "I find X good," "I consider Y unethical," "I prefer Z," etc. Even saying, "X 'is' 'bad' to me" qualifies the assessment in a more factual way. Along these lines, it also seems more accurate to eschew terms like 'evil', 'unnatural', etc., which may project the source of my judgements onto some absolute quality allocated outside myself. In these ways, I can turn an uncritical inference into a statement of fact about my own values and preferences.

Rather than elementalistically splitting 'fact' from 'value', as some thinkers have done, it seems more accurate to recognize that, in making the assessment "I prefer or value Y over X," I make a statement both of 'fact' and 'value'. Since 'facts' and 'values' function multiordinally, at a higher-level of abstraction I can consider it a fact that "I prefer or value Y to X." I can also self-reflexively ponder whether I value or prefer my first-order preference or value. Do I like liking X, Y, or Z?

Taking ownership of your own values has important consequences for ethical decision-making because it provides an important first step for examining and possibly revising your values. To the extent that people can turn their uncritical value-laden inferences into descriptive statements about their own values, preferences, etc., they will probably generate more light and less heat in deliberations with others as well. Each of us abstracts differently. Each of us starts from more or less differing assumptions. Some conflict will occur. Although complete agreement may not be possible, greater agreement seems likely to occur if we can uncover and clarify our own values and help others to uncover and clarify theirs. Then conflict does not have to become a fight.

"Is" and "Ought"

Recognizing the distinction between statements of fact and those of inference also allows us to see how ethical conclusions can be derived from a given set of facts, which also includes one's values.

On the surface, this appears to violate the famous "is-ought distinction" which many philosophers attribute to Hume. The is-ought distinction involves the notion that what 'ought' to be done cannot be derived from what 'is' (facts). Failure to maintain the distinction between "is" and "ought" is said to involve what has been called the "naturalistic fallacy."

Philosopher Anthony Flew described the naturalistic fallacy in this way, "From the premise that all or most of us are thus or thus inclined, and hence that it is natural to us so to behave; it is immediately, but invalidly, inferred that such action is at best morally licit, if not obligatory." [16] Baldly stated—I agree on the importance of avoiding this fallacy.

My mother—a much better practical ethicist than many scientists and philosophers—did too. She plainly disputed my attempts to use the naturalistic fallacy when I begged her to let me do what all the other kids were doing. She would ask me, "Do you have to jump off a bridge because everyone else does?"

Of course, it seems useful to remember the distinction between assertions of 'fact' and inferential 'ought' statements (injunctions). As implied by Hume's distinction, to assert that "These apples 'are' bitter" doesn't automatically lead to "You shouldn't eat these apples!" However, while remembering the dangers of the naturalistic fallacy, it still remains possible to apply extensional methods to ethical decision-making. We can get to some conclusions about what we 'should' or 'shouldn't' do by a form of ethical reasoning called a practical syllogism. [17]

In a practical syllogism, factual statements connect with an injunction (an 'ought' statement) by means of an implication—a conditional if-then statement ("if x, then y"). The implication is based on values that someone holds: "If you don't want to get sick, you shouldn't eat bitter apples." The complete practical syllogism reads as follows: These apples 'are' bitter. Bitter apples can make you sick. If you don't want to get sick, you shouldn't eat bitter apples. You (I) don't want to get sick. So don't eat any of these apples!

Thus, from statements of facts (which include value-facts as I have described them), we can infer what we 'should' do. Paul Kurtz has called such ethical reasoning "act-duction" : "...we infer the actions that are most appropriate—we act-duce—given the valuation base at hand. On the basis of this, some choices may thus be said to be more reasonable in the situation than others." [18]

In terms of the abstracting model, recognizing the is/ought distinction and the naturalistic fallacy does not preclude arriving at a valid prescriptive inference about what I 'should' do, based on premises which include 'facts' of 'value'. My inference or conclusion ("I shouldn't eat bitter apples") exists at a different order of abstraction from the lower-order fact-value premises. ("These apples are bitter. Bitter apples can make me sick. If I eat bitter apples, I may get sick. I don't want to get sick.")

As indicated before, each of us can do this more extensionally by remembering to take responsibility for our own values instead of uncritically projecting them onto the rest of the world. Similarly, to operate extensionally each of us also needs to take responsibility for our ethical conclusions as *our* conclusions. Different individuals presented with a particular set of circumstances and their own particular values may arrive at different ethical inferences.

For example, what "ought" might result if in the above "bitter apple" sequence, the last sentence was "I don't care if I get sick because I like to try new tastes." Remaining conscious of abstracting, let us strive for agreement when we can reach it and accept when we don't.

Ethical Inquiry

The previous analysis provides a basis for applying a scientific attitude to ethical problem-solving and decision-making: ethical inquiry. Ethical inquiry can focus on some combination of what psychologists Cantril and Bumstead called "How-to-do" and "What for" questions:

When, in a problem situation, we ask ourselves: "What shall I do?" we may really be asking: "*How* should I perform a particular task, how achieve a particular goal already existing?" On the other hand, the question "What shall I do?" *may* mean, "*Why* shall I do a particular thing? Which of several goals is worth striving for? Which of two or more possible courses of action is right and good? [19]

"How-to-do?" questions predominate when people agree on what ends they want, what values they hold dear, but then disagree on the best means for achieving them. "What for?" questions predominate when people don't feel sure of their end goals or have conflicting ones.

If 'reason' cannot, except verbally, exist separately from 'emotion', then the use of reason has a function in providing answers to both kinds of questions. When we agree on values, "how-to-do" questions can lead us to study facts, consequences, etc., in order to find out the best means-at-a-date for accomplishing our purposes. (Of course, the criteria that different people hold for determining the 'best' means for a purpose will depend on their own particular values, which may in themselves differ, resulting in a higher-level value conflict. We can't escape individual differences and multiordinality.)

When we do not know what ends we want, or have a conflict of values within or among individuals, "what for" questions can lead us to examine ourselves and each other in order to find out the best ends-at-a-date for ourselves. (In this case, questions of fact may also have some relevance in deciding questions of value.)

Ethical inquirers should not elementalistically consider their so-called means and ends as entirely separate. One can get bogged down with a particular favored means (how-to-do?) and lose sight of the end (what for?) one wants to achieve. On the other hand, failure to properly apply necessary means, and/or 'success' in applying unnecessary means for an actual end, may lead to poor results and unintended consequences.

So far, I've indicated how science is based on ethical considerations and have demonstrated the possibilities of using general semantics to apply an extensional approach (generalized scientific attitude) to ethical problems. What kind of ethical system will result?

Absolutist Ethics

What kind of ethical system does my GS analysis of religion, science, and related issues suggest? The approach that I've presented leads to a middle ground between two extreme, absolutistic positions. At one extreme, ethical reasoning, although viewed as possible, is based on reified values allocated to an external source outside the individual, e.g., 'God', 'Natural Law', etc. Ethicist Joseph Fletcher called this approach absolutistic "rule ethics":

> In rule ethics we decide what we ought to do a priori according to some predetermined precept or categorical imperative. "You may not terminate this pregnancy because abortion, as such, is wrong." In effect, such rule ethics eliminates what we call conscience—that is, the responsible exercise of moral decision-making.[20]

Rule ethics, or legalism, can be viewed in GS terms as intensional ethics: Krisnamurti's 'thought'. Such absolutistic ethics depends on an external authority such as 'God', the Bible, the Koran, 'the State', etc., to provide basic values and rules for living. It involves a basic mistrust of each individual and may lead to hypocrisy since it mis-allocates the source of individual human values—individual humans.

Rule absolutists tend to present their viewpoints in two valued, either/or terms. For example, they may talk as if they have exclusive ownership of "family values," implying that those who don't agree with them couldn't have any. In a dispute, such absolutists talk as if only two alternatives exist: "Either you're for us or against us." They may view a particular action as all 'good' or all 'bad'.

At the other extreme from absolutist rule ethics exists what Fletcher called "antinomianism (literally, 'against law')." [21] While antinomians may allocate values to the individual, ethical reasoning is viewed as impossible or undesirable. Antinomianism appears close to what I previously characterized as the "anything goes," absolutistic relativist position.

Conditional Ethics

A humanistic viewpoint consistent with general semantics provides a balance between these extremes. This viewpoint allows one to see 'reason' and 'emotion' as compatible, indeed inseparable; hence ethical reasoning becomes possible. Such ethical reasoning derives from a non-absolutist framework that views the source of human values within individuals who live in society with others.

Any individual, living within a culture, inherits ethical teachings and principles based on the time-binding experiences of others. These teachings can serve as situational guidelines, not absolute rules. The non-absolutistic application of these guidelines remains relative to each individual with his/her own unique differences and circumstances.

In this approach, called "situation ethics" by Fletcher:
...the decision maker, judges what is best in the circumstances and in view of the foreseeable consequences. This is a posteriori rather than a priori—after the facts are known, not before. It is, indeed, an ethical strategy consistent with the scientific method. You choose the course of action which offers the greatest (nonmoral) benefit. [22]

In GS, we clearly advocate a situational approach, given our emphasis on the importance of developing conditionality in our reactions. We live in a dynamic, process universe. If we orient ourselves by static perceptual-conceptual maps, we can easily end up with hardening of the categories: responding to new conditions in terms of old and stereotyped (unconditional) behavior patterns. GS tools for revising our maps can help us develop more conditional responses: ways of evaluating more creatically and thus more suitably to changing conditions.

Some rule absolutists have turned "situation ethics" into a term of abuse by confusing it with antinomianism or absolutistic relativism. It should be clear by now that "situation ethics," as Fletcher described it, involves—not no standards——but flexible ones. To get away from the pejorative connotations, situation ethics can also be described as extensional ethics and/or conditional ethics, since it seems most consistent with a GS approach.

I especially want to emphasize here that not all theists qualify as absolutists. There exists no necessary contradiction between theistic belief and a non-absolutistic attitude toward ethical reasoning and decision-making. Religious people can follow a conditional approach to ethics and some do. Neither do all atheists or agnostics necessarily follow an extensional, conditional approach in their ethical lives. Some atheists I've known have nigh-definitely qualified as absolutists.

Some Consequences of Conditionality

From a GS perspective, assigning value to anything remains a human activity resulting from the abstracting processes of each of us. We discover-create-allocate value to objects, people, animals, fetuses, etc., as well as to higher-order abstractions such as principles, beliefs, and so-called abstract values. (This process is not entirely—or even mainly— conscious.)

The consequences of assigning values can be studied— we can become more conscious of the mechanism (how we do it). This may allow us to modify our values more consciously and perhaps more usefully. To acknowledge individuals as the measurers of their values, does not result in negating all values. Instead, maintaining flexible values and principles can allow each of us to encompass more of the complexities of human life than is allowed by an absolutistic approach to ethics.

Such flexibility involves a multi-valued orientation: not either/or; rather, both-and. The conditional decision-maker remains aware that different viewpoints can exist in a situation. Degrees of agreement may exist in a dispute. A particular action may have a number of consequences with varying degrees of 'goodness' and 'badness'.

Ultimately, preferences and values function as basic assumptions by which each individual lives his or her life. At bottom, these values may not agree with those of others. Different people will function with differing, sometimes contradictory, value assumptions. Conflict may not be avoidable. Yet if we desire agreement where possible, it seems important to understand these differences as clearly as possible.

A conditional approach to ethical problem-solving/decision-making with others depends upon each party making a committment to fruitful negotiating, which is not simply a matter of verbalistic exchange. It depends upon meeting the other in a dialogue, a relationship of I and Thou ("Ich und Du"), as Martin Buber called it.

Such a dialogue involves an openness to verbal and non-verbal levels (these are not separate after all). It involves openly putting one's assumptions, values and desires 'on the table'. Such dialogue also requires a willingness, not necessarily to agree, but to deeply listen to and understand the other person's views while not denying or withholding your own. The humanistic approach and tools of general semantics can contribute (along with other approaches) to such negotiations.

Chapter 22
When Values Clash: The Case of Abortion

Applying Conditional Ethics

Applied to ethical decision-making, an extensional approach leads to a conditional viewpoint: you consider the circumstances of a decision, which include your values and those of others. In addition, you evaluate the probable consequences of various alternative actions. With a conditional view, you consider principles as flexible guidelines.

To provide a case example of this approach to ethics, I'll use it to explore an ongoing 'explosive' ethical-social-political issue—the abortion debate.

'Abortion', 'babies', 'persons', 'murder'—The clash of evaluations between so-called pro-life and pro-choice viewpoints brings out profound differences in thinking-feeling about these words. The effects of this clash involve an individual woman's decision on whether or not to have an abortion. They also involve social policy decisions in which others decide the morality/legality of whether and/or when a woman can have an abortion. Those others (you and I) then create and/or support and/or enforce abortion-related laws.

Although some 'pro-life' GS students and humanists may disagree, I conclude that a consistent naturalistic humanist, extensional approach to this issue shows serious difficulties with the anti-abortion/'pro-life' perspective and leads to a pro-choice viewpoint.

In this chapter, I outline some key features underlying the pro-life view and elaborate a pro-choice perspective based on some relevant general-semantics and humanist formulations. These formulations also have relevance to the related issues of stem cell research, euthanasia, and other ethics issues, which I briefly touch upon at the end of the chapter.

The Abortion Issue

Those who consider themselves "pro-lifers" typically say that "abortion is murder." Many would legally ban abortion under any circumstances, with perhaps an exception to save the life of the mother. Some, still associating with a pro-life position, but less absolutely, make further exceptions in cases of rape or incest. Others, accepting a pro-choice position, may approve of abortion as the lesser of two 'evils' in some circumstances but may express ambivalence over the implications of destroying a fetus. Finally, those holding a strong pro-choice position view abortions as good under some circumstances, with the decision, in any case, up to the involved woman.

Before getting to the principal arguments of the 'pro-life' and pro-choice positions, I want to mention a couple of points about the main terms of the debate: "pro-life" ("right-to-life") and "pro-choice." It seems evident from a neuro-linguistic perspective that the terms by which one frames the debate may affect the conclusions drawn. To call anti-abortion advocates "pro-life" may imply that those opposed to their views 'are' "anti-life" and possess a blatant disregard for life, human values, etc.—clearly not so.

On the other hand, "pro-choice" does seem like a reasonable and neutral designation to me. It includes individuals who may personally object to abortion, but do not want laws that prevent women from exercising their own ethical judgements about an issue about which there is much disagreement among reasonable people.

Some 'pro-lifers' have turned "pro-choice" into an epithet implying a disregard for human values—equivalent to Nazi atrocities. Such excited absolutism seems ironic, since imposing the 'right' ethical view on everyone—the aim of the 'right-to-life' movement—was also central to Nazi totalitarianism.

(Nazi Germany banned abortions for 'Aryan' women while imposing involuntary sterilization, abortions, and worse, upon Jewish women and other 'undesirable' groups.)

I explicitly use single quotes around 'pro-life(r)' and 'right-to-life(r)' to indicate the specious nature of the 'pro-life' claim to possess the 'sole' criteria of value regarding life. As an alternative, I also refer to them as "anti-abortionists," "anti-choice" advocates, "compulsory pregnancy" patrons and "mandatory motherhood" promoters. The designation of "pro-abortionist" for pro-choice advocates may not be accurate, since not all of those who favor a woman's personal choice are necessarily for abortion in all or any cases, including for themselves.

In the following discussion, please note that, although I have abstracted broad commonalities which exist on each major side of the debate, variations exist within each of these viewpoints. In the United States, fundamentalist-style, Christian religionists seem to predominate among the most vocal and violent of the anti-abortionists. However, other Christian and non-Christian religious people can be found on a continuum from 'pro-life' to pro-choice viewpoints.

Also, although it may seem incompatible with conditional ethics, some non-theists, humanists and students of general semantics maintain vehement anti-abortion positions. For example, critic/columnist Nat Hentoff, a self-proclaimed "atheist civil libertarian," has for years ardently opposed abortion and supported the 'pro-life' movement. It is also important to note that not all anti-abortionists support, threaten or engage in killing and/or bombing abortion providers, although some unfortunately do.

The Right to Life

'Right-to-life' or 'pro-life' advocates oppose abortion as an option for unwanted pregnancies. They may argue that "unless rape or seduction is involved, a woman needn't become pregnant, but once the process begins, it is no longer a personal issue."[1] In their view, killing an embryo is wrong.

Although some may absolutely oppose abortion, others accept it only under severe restrictions (such as when the life of the woman is imperiled), in which case an argument might be made for the woman's self-defense. A common view among 'right-to-lifers' is that human life begins at conception, when the sperm and egg combine their genetic material, twenty three chromosomes each, to form a single fertilized cell.[2]

To reinforce the identity of the individual from fertilized egg to embryo to fetus to infant, 'pro-lifers' refer to the developing organism as a "baby," "unborn child," or "person." They point out how quickly it develops the external appearance and physiological functions of a recognizable human. According to them, this "little person" can feel pain and experience suffering.[3]

Even apart from this, abortion is said (especially by some openly religious 'pro-life' advocates) to involve the destruction of a human soul. According to Catholic philosopher Andrew C. Varga, S.J., for example, a human fetus possesses an underlying nature, an 'essence' or 'substantial form' that causes it to develop not into a tree or a bird but a human. Whether this essence constitutes the 'soul' and when this soul enters the organism seems a matter of controversy. Therefore, the most prudent course, for those 'pro-lifers' concerned about it, is to assume that the soul is present from conception and, hence, to ban abortions.[4]

The underlying intrinsic 'God-given' value of human life is emphasized in both the Catholic and Protestant anti-abortion arguments. Since the purpose of sex, according to 'God's natural law' is to ensure the development of life, chastity is the preferred method of birth control.[5] The use of contraceptives has been officially discouraged by the Catholic Church and other groups since, according to them, contraceptives separate the sexual act from its fundamental purpose.

'Natural law', or some other 'Will of God' surrogate provides a "more-than-human authority"[6] for the ethics of those
'pro-lifers'who consider themselves 'non-religious'. To me,
this makes them less 'atheists' than closet 'theists' of an extreme absolutistic sort. I substantially agree with Albert Ellis,
who wrote in his book, *Is Objectivism a Religion?*:

> I contend that any dogmatic, fanatical, absolutistic, anti-
> empirical, people-condemning creed is religious because
> there is no factual evidence on which it is based, and its
> adherents, in zealously sticking to it, strongly state or im-
> ply that some higher power or order of the universe de-
> mands that their views are right and that all serious dis-
> senters to their views are for all time wrong....that is the
> essence of...religiosity: deep abiding faith unfounded on
> fact—and often rigidly held in spite of the knowledge of
> contradictory facts.[7]

Of course, there are theists who may disapprove of abortion but don't demand that society make laws preventing others from following their conscience. Insofar as they eschew
dogmatism, absolutism and the need to impose their morality
on others, they eschew the extreme religiosity described above
and embody basically humanistic values.

Evaluating Abortion

Concern about the environmental impact of the expanding human world population—which by now (2003) has
topped six billion and is growing—at least ought to bring us
to question the pro-natalist bias of anti-abortionists. As biologist Garrett Hardin has asked, "Does God give a prize for the
maximum number of human beings?"[8]

The abortion issue has often been framed in terms of the
question, "How can we justify abortion?" Putting on neuro-
linguistic 'glasses', we can see the usefulness of reformulat-
ing the issue in terms of a different question. This may change
the focus of concern and lead to new and different answers.

Those concerned with the liberty of the individual may find it useful to change the question to, "How can we justify compulsory pregnancy?"[9]

This question acknowledges an important fact that anti-abortionists often neglect or downplay: For a woman with an unwanted pregnancy, the alternative to terminating her pregnancy is becoming a mother. Do the anti-abortion arguments provide overwhelmingly compelling reasons for restricting a women's ability to terminate her pregnancy? Let's see.

A sperm and egg each appears alive. It seems reasonable (without giving anything to the anti-abortion side) to also agree to call an initial cell or mass of cells, combined from sperm and egg, a living individual in some sense. When does this developing individual become a "baby," a "child," a "person"?

Here's where anti-abortion and pro-choice sides part company. As already noted, 'right-to-lifers' refer to even the initial mass of cells as a "baby" or "unborn child" to be given "personhood." Women and the abortionists who help them end even twelve-week or earlier pregnancies are thus called "baby-killers." Does this make sense?

Think of a baby. Cute, warm and cuddly. Repeating over and over (snark, snark, snark) that "embryos and fetuses are babies" can for some people almost hypnotically transfer some of those 'cute, warm and cuddly' evaluations to our notions of embryos and fetuses. (Whether anyone finds embryos and fetuses appealing or not remains irrelevant to the morality of forcing a woman to continue an unwanted pregnancy. For the record however, a several-weeks-old embryo doesn't look 'cute and cuddly' to me.)

'Pro-lifers' encourage people to overlook important differences among different stages of embryonic and fetal development. Thus, Dr. Bernard Nathanson can claim in the anti-abortion propaganda film *The Silent Scream* that the "human functions" of a twelve week old embryo "are indistinguishable from any of ours." [10] Does his word-map fit the fact-territory of human development?

Contrary to what anti-abortionists claim, a single fertilized cell does not contain the totality of everything we 'are' as developing organisms. A fertilized egg can be viewed primarily as a package of information, a genetic program—a map, not the territory, of a complete human. Biologist Charles Gardner notes that much that occurs in development is not contained in the genetic program. Rather, it depends on external factors such as "the positions and interactions of cells and molecules that will be formed only at a later time." [11]

What about brain development? Neuroscientists agree that human consciousness, e.g., 'thinking', 'feeling', 'perception', etc.—basic to many people's understanding of "personhood"—correlates with brain happenings. Does a twelve-week-old fetus have a brain "indistinguishable from any of ours"? There are no neurons, let alone a brain made up of them, before the fourth week of fetal development. Most neurons form between the second and fifth months and migrate to their final positions in the brain between the second and sixth months. Axonal and dendritic branchings begin to form after this migration has occurred. Synaptic connections between neurons begin to form around the third month and continue to form for years afterwards. This process occurs variably in different brain areas.

Movements of the fetus, noted at early stages of development and attributed by some anti-abortionists to conscious effort, result from early-developed spinal cord reflexes. No brain is necessary. So-called 'brain waves' attributed to twelve-week-old fetuses result from random electrical activity in developing nerve cells. Only much later in gestation does organized brain wave activity begin to occur. [12]

What about the 'pain' that the fetus is presumed to experience, say, at twelve weeks or even earlier—the first trimester of pregnancy? According to biologist Michael J. Flower, the possibility of any kind of organismic awareness—let alone pain—only begins to emerge around the twenty-first to twenty-third weeks of gestation. Before this time there are no connections between the developing neocortex and the thalamic neurons that link it to any possible source of external sensation.[13]

Compulsory pregnancy advocates tend to downplay these and other significant differences which exist at different stages of the developmental process. For example, Nat Hentoff emphasizes that "human life is a continuum—from fertilization to birth to death."[14] To Hentoff this continuum represents a single-valued entity which merits treating all of the stages of life the same.

From a more extensional viewpoint, the continuum of fetal development constitutes a multi-valued process. Human development involves a graded scale replete with differences. The significant differences that exist at different stages of development warrant evaluating those stages differently when weighing the pros and cons of compelling women to continue unwanted pregnancies.

'Pro-lifers' often convey their single-valued approach through their use of emotionally manipulative pictures and language. They use still or motion pictures of fetuses to focus attention on certain external similarities, like the outward shapes or movements of a fetus, which they then exaggerate to imply the sameness of different stages of human development.

This pictorial language combines with word usage which reinforces the static, single-valued, anti-abortion view. As noted, 'pro-lifers' refer to zygotes, embryos, and fetuses as "babies" or "unborn children." When discussing abortion with 'pro-lifers', pro-choice advocates should not accept those terms without question.

As Hardin has pointed out, it makes no more sense to talk about an "unborn child" than it does to talk about an "unborn voter" or an "unborn senior citizen" since the possible future manifestations of an entity simply do not yet exist. The terms constitute contrafactual maps without territories.[15] A one-celled fertilized egg is not yet a child, a voter, or a senior citizen. This evaluation is not intended to minimize the resistance, guilt, etc., that may be experienced by some pregnant women and their mates when faced with a potential abortion. These common (though not inevitable) reactions to losing an anticipated 'child' are understandable. Empathy and support seem in order.

The GS extensional devices of single quotes and dating may be useful here. We can put quotes around 'unborn child', 'baby', 'murder', when referring to anti-abortion arguments. We can date terms indicating the process of development: fertilized $egg_{day\,1}$ is not the same as $embryo_{6\,weeks}$ is not the same as $baby_{1\,day\,old}$, etc.

A related misevaluation involves the contrafactual statement that, "You wouldn't be here if your mother had had an abortion." In the same way, if their mothers had had abortions Beethoven (or Hitler) wouldn't have been here either. Since I am here, and you are here, as were Beethoven and Hitler, my answer to this contrafactual is—"So?" A logically coherent fiction/speculation about what might have happened—but didn't—just confuses levels of abstraction. It does not provide factual support against abortion. Except for those who think that humans have some 'God'-given duty to cram the planet with ever more human biomass, an argument about aborted 'Beethovens' has no merit.

Personhood

At what point does an individual become a 'person'? Even admitting the facts about differences at different stages of development, it still seems possible to argue that personhood exists at or near conception. This could derive from the previously mentioned 'essential nature' or 'substantial form', the 'soul'.

How can such a claim be examined extensionally? What possible observations could we make to test the existence of a 'spiritual essence' or 'soul' underlying human nature that determines personhood? None, as far as I know.

Such a belief ranks high on the scale of empty verbalism. The "substantial form" which causes the "orderly growth of the conceptus into a fully developed child" [16] is similar to the medieval "dormative principle." What causes people to sleep? The dormative principle! This response answers the question by rephrasing the subject of the question into a more impressive-sounding set of words. A one-word response would explain things just as well: "Because!" People sleep because they sleep. The conceptus grows because it grows. Such explanations don't extensionally explain anything, although they can superficially satisfy some people's search for explanations. Scientists rightly prefer to extensionally examine sleeping humans and growing fetuses to find out the causes of sleep and of human development.

Where does that leave 'personhood'? Pragmatically, that comes down to the practical consequences of calling or not calling someone or something a 'person'. In the case of a fetus, when, if ever, do we consider its life worthy of protection by the law? Whatever is decided, it is we as humans who decide the question, "When is a fetus a person?"

In his book *Humanhood*, medical ethicist Joseph Fletcher listed a number of standards by which humanness or personhood could be defined by us. These include the positive factors of:

1. Minimum intelligence...2. Self-awareness...3. Self-control...4. A sense of time...5. A sense of futurity...6. A sense of the past...7. The capability to relate to others...8. Concern for others...9. Communication...10. Control of existence...11. Curiosity...12. Change and changeability...13. Balance of rationality and feeling...14. Idiosyncrasy...15. Neocortical function. [17]

These standards, taken separately and together, admit of degrees. They allow us to get beyond a two-valued approach to defining personhood that says "something is either a person or it isn't." Evaluating personhood in terms of such a list suggests a multi-valued approach to the issue, which has applications to euthanasia, animal rights, and the rights of robots (which may become a pressing issue sooner than many people think), among other issues.

Accordingly, someone or something may be considered a 'person' to some degree. To the extent that this provides some basis for defining personhood, none of us has reached 100% of our potential for personhood. A developing fetus, similarly, can be considered much less of a person than any of you reading this, a one-day-old baby, or my cat (apply all of Fletcher's fifteen criteria here).

In considering the personhood of human fetuses, particular attention should be paid to number 15, neocortical function, which for humans provides a much more highly integrating and organizing role for the other functions than it does in other creatures.

According to developmental neurobiologist Dominick Purpura, neocortical function only begins in a recognizably human way after seven months of development, in the third trimester of pregnancy.[18] The guidelines established in Roe v. Wade, the 1973 Supreme Court decision which legalized abortion in the United States, steer abortions well away from this period.

The Right to Choose and Anti-Choice Obstacles

The 1973 U.S. Supreme Court decision in Roe v. Wade represents a standard for pro-choice views. It established the legal right of a woman to have an abortion based on a fundamental constitutional right to privacy. This legal right was not considered absolute. In the first trimester of pregnancy, the Court defined this right as unrestricted. However, it limited the right to choose, with considerations for a woman's health, to the beginning of the second trimester of pregnancy. Roe v. Wade also contained considerations for fetal life, at the beginning of the third trimester, when "viability," the fetus's potential to survive outside the womb, becomes an issue.[19]

Roe v. Wade seems consistent with the pro-choice view of women as ethical decision-makers. Each woman should, accordingly, be allowed to decide whether getting an abortion seems right or wrong for her, based on her individual situation, circumstances, anticipated consequences, etc.

Since 1973, various U.S federal and state government decisions have restricted women's access to abortions in various ways. An increasingly 'right-wing' Supreme Court has chipped away at previously established abortion rights with further decisions, such as the 1992 Planned Parenthood v. Casey decision. It was in this decision that, while five justices upheld "the right of the woman to choose to have an abortion before viability," three of the five noted that "the State has legitimate interests from the outset of pregnancy in protecting the health of the woman and the life of the fetus that may become a child." [20] Meanwhile, four dissenting justices recommended overturning Roe v. Wade completely. Presently(2003), a few new appointments to the Supreme Court could indeed tip the Court toward overturning Roe v. Wade.

Pro-choice advocates see this ongoing shift of the Court as supportive of anti-choice efforts to put obstacles in the way of women choosing abortion. New struggles both on state and national (as well as international) levels will be required to preserve and extend a woman's legal right to choose and to get an abortion.

For instance, recent controversy has been generated by horror stories of frequent late term abortions. Such anti-choice allegations have little relation to facts, however. In the year 2000, the U.S Centers for Disease Control and Prevention estimated that a majority of abortions occur within the first eight weeks of pregnancy. "Only 1.4% occur after 20 weeks." [21]

'Partial birth abortion' is not a medical term but rather a politicized label for "a specific surgical method of late abortion called intact dilation and extraction (D & X)." [22] Various legal attempts to ban this procedure have been used to bamboozle well-intentioned people into opposing all late-term abortions and then restricting all abortions.

Late-term abortions are performed under tragic circumstances—a woman whose life or health is at risk and/or a nonviable fetus. Again anti-choice propagandists have combined their excited rhetoric with graphic, out-of-context images to try to sway decisions that would be better made through thoughtful consideration of facts and circumstances.

Following a well-established standard for medical ethics—"First, do no harm"—the procedures used in late-term abortions ought not to increase the danger to the woman's health and life. This basic ethical guideline makes it irrelevant whether or not a given procedure such as a D & X might offend someone (including a physician) ignorant of the medical circumstances. This has long been recognized in Jewish law, for example, which shows that a religiously-permeated tradition does not necessarily have to oppose a sensible, humanistic approach:

> Halacha (Jewish Law) clearly permits, and even mandates, abortion in any case where there is danger to the mother's life, from conception at least until the head of an infant emerges in childbirth. A basic text for this stance is in the Mishna [a compendium of Jewish law at the core of the Talmud] : "If a woman has [life-threatening] difficulty in childbirth, one dismembers the embryo within her, limb by limb, because her life takes precedence over its life..."[23]

The consequences of legally defining a fertilized egg, embryo or fetus as a person with a 'right to life' have been seen where abortion has been made a crime, as happened in Romania during the dictatorship of Nicolae Ceausescu. In such circumstances, abortions don't stop. They simply become more dangerous for desperate women who will risk their health and lives with medically unsafe procedures in order not to be conscripted by the state into compulsory motherhood.

For those who want but don't get abortions because of legal obstacles, the consequences of bearing an unwanted child affect not only the women but society as well. Such consequences are well documented and may include child abuse and neglect which, associated with larger families and greater poverty, lead to many long-term social problems.[24]

Legal obstacles, such as mandatory parental consent for pregnant teenagers and twenty-four hour waiting periods that require 'pro-life'-slanted counseling before a procedure, may even result in a greater number of second-trimester abortions.[25] These have greater health risks for women than first trimester abortions, which remain much safer than childbirth.[26]

A Pro-Choice View

The notion of choice in relation to abortion opens up a frightening abyss for religious and seemingly 'non-religious' absolutists. Mother Theresa represented this view well when she asked, "If a mother can murder her own child, in her own womb, what then is left for you and me but to kill each other?"[27] Indeed, what then *is* left for you and me? As far as I know, Mother Theresa didn't stay for an answer.

'Pro-life' advocates seem to fear and reject the notion that we, as human beings, define personhood and its value. For them, the 'sacredness' and 'value' of life exists outside of us as 'God-given' properties. Their principles of conduct are spelled out by the Lord in the Bible, which they accept as their authority. So-called 'non-religious' 'pro-lifers' have their own favorite 'God'-substitutes and authorities.

The 'pro-life' viewpoint seems consistent with absolutistic rule ethics. For consistent anti-abortionists, "abortion is murder." Period and stop. Their absolutism blinds them from seeing how a woman might weigh her circumstances, the consequences, her own values and principles in order to reach a reasonable decision for herself about getting an abortion.

The underlying false or non-falsifiable premises of 'pro-lifers' ultimately rest on an appeal to authority that strongly tends toward attempts to silence or coerce those who do not share their beliefs. Intolerance of alternative ethical views seems basic to the 'pro-life' reality-tunnel. The bombings of abortion clinics; the stalking, threatening and shooting of doctors and clinic workers; etc., carry the rhetoric which sees abortion as 'violence', 'murder', and a 'holocaust' to its logical conclusion: killing the perpetrators.[28]

It seems wrong-headed to view the abortion controversy as "a clash of absolutes." Intolerance of other values appears central to the ethical absolutism of the typical 'pro-life' message, while the pro-choice position tolerates both decisions for and against an abortion, based on a woman's particular situation. In GS terms, the pro-choice position involves greater generality: it functions at a higher level of abstraction and provides for a wider range of actions than the 'pro-life' one.

For an individual woman, a pro-choice perspective includes the options of terminating or continuing a pregnancy based on the factors of her unique situation as an ethical decision-maker. From a socio-legal perspective, it views legal attempts to compel women to continue or terminate pregnancies as unacceptable.

A pro-choice advocate is not anti-life or necessarily pro-abortion. A particular abortion may be considered 'good' or 'bad' or somewhere in between depending on the circumstances. Primarily, the individual woman's values need to be considered. Thus a Protestant or devout Catholic woman who considers it wrong to end her unwanted pregnancy should not be compelled to do so and is not so compelled under Roe v. Wade. Given a pro-choice context—which honors ethical inquiry rather than ethical compulsion—she might change her view if given more of an option to do so without censure, harassment or legal obstacles; or she might choose not to change.

The availability of abortions appears socially beneficial. For many woman, abortion clearly serves as a positive good, "a humane, empowering, and morally licit option."[29] Readily-available access to legal and medically-safe abortion services remain a necessary part of a comprehensive approach to family planning. My analysis of the abortion issue finds the 'pro-life' view deficient and bolsters the more inclusive, positive, pro-choice position.

The Copernican Revolution in Ethics

This analysis has repercussions for other ethical issues involving stem-cell research, euthanasia, cloning, genetic engineering, animal rights, environmental ethics, etc. A humanistic transformation of human ethical standards, to which I believe GS can contribute, is afoot in these areas. Ethicist Peter Singer has referred to this as "another Copernican revolution."

In this shift away from traditional authoritarian religious viewpoints, humans are indeed the 'measure' of ethics in the sense that each of us is seen as ultimately responsible for our own ethical decisions. Nonetheless, humans are no longer seen "as the centre of the ethical universe" because the unconditional sanctity of any human life is no longer taken as an unquestionable given.[30] As Singer has written in relation to matters of life and death:

> When we consider how serious it is to take a life, we should look not at the race, sex, or species to which that being belongs, but at the characteristics of the individual being killed, for example, its own desires about continuing to live, or the kind of life it is capable of leading.[31]

It seems likely to me that the sanity, well-being and, perhaps, the survival of humans in the 21st century will depend in no small part on the success of this 'Copernican revolution', what GS-writer Kenneth Baldwin called the development of "a worldwide extensional ethic."[32]

Conclusion

Every man on the foundation of his own
sufferings and joys, builds for all.
— ALBERT CAMUS

Chapter 23
Sanity and Survival for the 21ˢᵗ Century and Beyond

In this concluding chapter, I return to the present mess of humanity, explore the possibilities of unifying the multiplicity of human interests under a humanist banner, and review the role of general semantics and related approaches in furthering a humanist agenda. I follow with discussion of how these approaches can promote human sanity and survival for the 21st century...and beyond.

Human Extinction and Evolution

Paleontologists, biologists who study the evolutionary history of life, note long-ago periods of mass extinction, one of which—about 65 million years ago—saw the destruction of the dinosaurs who had dominated Earth for hundreds of millions of years. The disappearance of the dinosaurs as a result of the impact of a huge comet saw the beginning of the ascent of our tiny shrew-like ancestors who had managed to survive the comet blast and ensuing bad weather. The age of the mammals, of primates, and of humans followed.

Some now think that we have entered a new age of mass extinction resulting from human activities. With our numbers exploding, the human 'footprint' on the Earth now affects the weather, geography, and the lives of just about every other species on the planet. This new mass extinction, some think, might also include us.

We seem to have reached a choice point in the cultural evolution of time-binders. The present lag of ethical wisdom in relation to technological development may lead to either breakdown and destruction or reorganization and survival at a higher, more adaptive level. The next hundred or so years should be 'interesting'.

Stanislaw J. Lec noted in his long out-of-print *Unkempt Thoughts*, "It is easy to populate the world, equally easy to depopulate it. What is the problem?" Nonetheless, perhaps you share with me the quaint and provincial notion that it would be nice for the human drama to continue for a while longer.

Our Sun may begin to burn out billions of years from now. It's a good bet that the Earth, if it still exists, will be destroyed in the ensuing conflagration. Will descendants of Earth-life have been able to get off the planet before then? Going extraplanetary will require that we survive on this planet at least long enough for a sufficient number of us to make the leap.

For humans, extraplanetary living also will likely require a leap in our abilities to relate to one another in some kind of harmony. We can expect inhospitable environments on other worlds. We will have to bring our own engineered environments with us and create them wherever we go. The contained environment of a starship may need to travel for generations before finding landfall on some other distant world. It seems probable that, for survival, ecological and human relations will need to be much better managed than is currently the case on spaceship Earth. What we do now to resolve or not resolve our present messes and avoid possible future ones depends at least in part on our attitudes.

One World Under 'God'?

SETI (Search for Extraterrestrial Intelligence) researcher Jill Tarter has suggested that a civilization that could survive long enough to communicate with other worlds or to travel to the stars would have to come under the sway of a single world religion. Either that or it would need to somehow find a new way of unifying itself which went beyond religion.[1]

Could Earth civilization become one world under any current orthodox (fundamentalist) theistic belief system? The history of conflicts among different groups of fundamentalist believers makes this outcome doubtful. One world under anyone's 'God' seems unlikely to develop. However, a great deal of blood may be shed by those who try to bring such a world about.

Islamists—fundamentalist Muslim believers who interpret their religion as a political creed for creating one world under Allah—currently (2003) appear to constitute the most widespread and serious movement for a religion-based, totalitarian world movement. Islamists dream of an ummah (Muslim world community) joined under a caliphate (Muslim political-religious leadership) ruled by Sharia (Islamic law). By no means fully united, Islamists divide on—among other things—the use of violence to achieve their aim.

One nation under the Islamist Allah (the Taliban's Afghanistan) didn't work—even for a predominantly Muslim country. One world under Allah won't work either. Despite this, the cost for the rest of us in defending ourselves against radical fundamentalist Islamism will be high.

Unfortunately Islamists represent a significant percentage of Muslims, although they do not represent all Muslims. Moderate Muslims, who have accepted democracy and the principle of separation of religion and state, will have to gain much greater influence in the Muslim world and will need all the help they can get from non-Muslims, to render Islamist coercion insignificant as a threat to world peace.[2]

Neither does any other religion seem likely to become the one world religion. At the same time, it seems unlikely that most people will cease being religious anytime soon. The multiplicity of religions throughout the world will nigh surely continue.

Thus, the religious unification of the world seems as unlikely as a non-fundamentalist, humanistic unification seems necessary. We can hope that more religious people will soon begin to realize that they *need not* give up all the comfort of their traditions in order to benefit from the leavening effects of humanistic concern.

The Humanist Leaven

Like the measure of yeast which makes dough rise, even a small injection of humanism, which involves placing the human individual and empathy for others before belief, can have a leavening effect on current humanity. By promoting the underlying unity of nations and religions, an evolution toward humanism increases the probability of human survival while not denying the variety of beliefs and ethnic/national identities that presently exist and divide us.

The purpose of *Dare to Inquire* has been to explore how people, whether religious or not, can find individual meaning and purpose, learn to live with others, and explore the world while letting go of fundamentalism—accepting the possibility of being wrong and the wisdom of uncertainty.

Humanism is not a substitute for religion. Rather, as a leavening agent for human belief systems, it encourages an attitude of questioning and inquiry in religious and non-religious realms. Humanism does not replace 'God' with humankind. The old way has often—though not always—been for 'God' to serve as a ventriloquist's dummy for the very human purposes of a few power-hungry 'prophets' and 'holy' men. Instead, by emphasizing this life, humanism makes individual human purposes primary for individual humans, whether religious or not.

The potential of humanism has barely been touched. For some individuals, the eclipse of the traditional, supernatural 'God' has led to an absence of 'light'—an eclipse of purpose and a loss of direction. This sense of loss may have been encouraged by restricted views of science and rationality favored by some scientists, philosophers and humanists.

In *Dare to Inquire*, I have taken up the challenge of showing how an attitude of inquiry (perhaps seen most clearly in the fields traditionally labeled "science") can be extended to apply to broader areas of personal and social life. This has already been done for centuries by isolated individuals and small groups.

General Semantics, emerging out of a scientific, humanistic background, is one such effort to make the attitude of inquiry explicit and teachable and thus to fulfull the ideal of humanism by making it workable.

General Semantics and Related Approaches

One of the most inadequate ideas we can have is that our present ideas are adequate. The consideration of allied viewpoints can help the advocates of different humanistic approaches to enlarge their perspectives and encourage a general evolution toward humanism.

General Semantics provides one of the most important systems developed so far for promoting an up-to-date and usable method of inquiry for science and daily life. Nonetheless it is not complete. Other viewpoints have been developed which supplement and complement GS. I discuss just a few examples below.

1. As Lou Marinoff, author of *Plato Not Prozac*, has noted, the work of philosophical practitioners has provided new ways to enrich scientific research and everyday life. For example, Fernando Flores, an organizational consultant, has merged existentialism with the linguistic philosophy of John Searle, and with biological studies of cognition. His work has been used by Matthew Budd, M.D., to create a health/wellness education program which focuses on teaching physicians and patients about speech acts—how we talk to ourselves and others. Quoting Heidegger, Budd notes that we humans "live in a house of language."[3] Our capacity for self-awareness can allow us to consciously remodel our neuro-linguistic 'house'. By talking to ourselves differently we can shift our mood, relationships and health in more desirable directions. Research on related cognitive-behavioral practices (such as meditation, guided visualization, awareness techniques, etc.) indicates that, as Korzybski contended, semantic (evaluational) factors are not only affected by, but can also in turn powerfully affect, mea-

surable neurological and other physiological functions. The confluence of this work with GS could help extend both approaches, as for example studying the role of extensional representation and standards in the various kinds of speech acts and cognitive-behavioral practices.

2. Korzybski considered Norbert Wiener's *Cybernetics*, "a turning-leaf in the history of human evolution and socio-cultural adjustment." [4] The work of William Powers, Richard Marken and others in Perceptual Control Theory (PCT) has extended cybernetics (negative feedback control theory) into a detailed research program for human psychology which emphasizes human autonomy, a phenomenological perspective, and the rigorous modeling of behavior. PCT's multi-leveled theory of purposeful behavior as the control of perception (abstracting) offers new approaches for further research into the spiral mechanism of time-binding that GS studies. PCT may provide a way to study the relationships of language use to perception and other aspects of behavior at levels of detail not previously conceived of. The study of GS by PCT researchers (and vice versa) could open up new avenues of research and application in both fields. [5]

3. Mutual enrichment could also occur between GS and the philosophy of science. Making more connections between the two fields could enhance the development of new scientific methods and extensional approaches. Some students of science have begun to acknowledge that "the scientific method"— as such—represents a fiction. Rather, for different areas of inquiry, different scientific methods may apply. [6] The neglect of the individual and of individual experience remains a profound failure of current conventional wisdom in much of the human sciences and medicine. General semantics provides an alternative viewpoint that extends a scientific attitude to individuals and provides a coherent base of assumptions for the development of new scientific methods:

> General semantics, Dr. [Douglas] Kelley [a student and
> colleague of Korzybski] pointed out, does not concern it-

self primarily with scientific method. He [Kelley] hit hard
at what he considered a serious defect in 'scientific
method'—the fact that it leaves out the individual. The
methods of GS include the individual. In fact, he maintained that is more basic than scientific method...[7]

PCT researcher Philip J. Runkel has proposed a name for scientific methods that study the behavior of individuals. He calls
such methods "specimen testing." The development and application of specimen testing methods will have greater importance as the importance of the science of the individual is
recognized—an important area for humanists to encourage.
One particular method of specimen testing, for example, is
called "the method of possibilities," which seeks to answer
the question, "What can be done?" As Runkel puts it, the
method of possibilities involves "a trial of a course of action
to find out whether it might be possible to bring it off." [8] The
method of possibilities remains important for personal research in one's own possibilties.

4. Finally, I want to mention the allied approaches of those
who have sought to develop naturalistic approaches to what
some people call 'spirituality', humanistic 'religion', and 'religious' humanism. I prefer not using these terms for my own
views as they have been associated for so long with theism,
supernaturalism, immateriality, unworldliness, etc. Some other
terms—e.g., connectedness, celebration, etc.—might serve
better for labeling the conscious, creative and non-supernaturalistic use of ritual, ceremony, meditation-awareness techniques, etc. Humanist celebrations/practices can be constructed for marking and solemnizing events of daily life, the
cycles of the week and year, important personal and communal historical events and lifetime rites of passage, such as
births, marriages, deaths and mourning, etc. Such methods for
both personal and communal use surely do not exclusively
belong to theists. They can be used by non-theistic, naturalis-

tic humanists to reinforce our deepest values, sense of awe, gratitude and reverence for life and to enhance our sense of relationship to deeper aspects of self, community and nature. Vitvan (Ralph deBit), a teacher who synthesized Western and Eastern wisdom traditions with science—by means of general semantics—made pioneering efforts toward the development of a naturalistic practical philosophy of connectedness. I have found his work stimulating, although he seemed to have not entirely escaped supernaturalism. Despite this caveat, I have learned much from his students at the School of the Natural Order. His work has much to offer those who want to go beyond over-intellectualized approaches to humanism.[9] My own explorations as a Jewish humanist have been enhanced by Vitvan's work, among other non-Jewish viewpoints, as well as by ongoing study of Jewish culture, history, sources, and traditions.

Wealth and IlIth

In the twenty-first century, humans face serious threats from over-population, environmental degradation, economic disparity and despair, intra-group and inter-group confict, etc. We humans have created the possibility of crippling or even destroying civilization, human life, and much, if not all, other forms of life on planet Earth by means of nuclear and other weapons of mass destruction or through ecological collapse. These human-created problems illustrate a basic dilemma: Does more time-binding always mean better?

Biologist Richard Dawkins coined the term "meme" in 1989 to indicate a basic unit of time-binding transmission. He derived it from the Greek word root for imitation and memory.[10] Analogous to the term "gene," "meme" refers to a "pattern of matter or information produced by an act of human intentionality." [11] The term caught on (a successful meme?) and has led to a discipline called "mimetics," journals, discussion groups, organizations and books.

Although the term obviously has a certain elasticity and vagueness, it does provide a convenient label for the products of human time-binding. Memes might include mathematical, scientific, and literary formulations; words, statements and doctrines; languages; songs; objects; inventions; media (memes for transmitting memes); artworks; fashions, forms of behavior, etc.

Beneficial memes, or the 'positive' products of time-binding, can be called *wealth*. Malign memes, the 'negative' products of time-binding, can be called *illth*, a term coined by nineteenth-century English writer John Ruskin. How do we distinguish wealth ('good' memes) from illth ('bad' memes)?[12]

The basic problem is not in our 'memes' but in ourselves. Although meme enthusiasts tend to talk as if 'memes' have a 'life' of their own, 'memes' require a human substrate for whatever 'life' they do take on. It helps to remember that. Distinguishing and creating wealth rather than illth will not result from blaming our 'memes' but from applying the best of our creatical intelligence to them.

To do this we need to take a multi-valued, conditional approach. This involves recognizing that the seemingly neat division of time-binding as either 'positive' (resulting in wealth) or 'negative' (resulting in illth) isn't so neat. Instead, there remains some fuzziness between the two categories, depending on the individuals involved, their number, the time scale considered, multiple effects, etc. For example, applying such a conditional approach makes it hard for me to absolutistically conclude that such things as bombs, swords, guns, and tanks always constitute 'illth'. At times, bombs, swords, guns and tanks can provide protection against 'illth'.

If we want to separate wealth from illth and thus increase the likelihood of human survival, a multi-valued, conditional approach requires considering the *personal and collective long-term and system-wide consequences* of present-day decision-making. This will involve what Hardin has called "the time-binding question." [13] "Every proposal of a plausible policy must be followed by the question 'And then what?' " [14]

A Time-Binding Approach to Human Survival

Asking the pragmatic question, *And then what?*, can help us to keep our awareness on a long-term and system-wide view. Such a view involves seeing ourselves as biological organisms—albeit, symbol-using, time-binding ones—highlighting our connections with other creatures.

Like wolves, deer, spotted owls, etc., we function in environments. We live in an ecological web. Our decisions affect that web and we are affected by it. We are not immune to regularities that have been observed to operate within and among other creatures.

In politics and economics, the conventionally-accepted methods of measuring success have largely prevented taking a long-term, ecological perspective. New business and social accounting methods need to go beyond the narrow view of short-term wealth for a few which may lead to long-term, system-wide illth for many.

Useful notions in ecology can be extended into economic and social decision-making. For example, the notion of carrying capacity, developed to refer to animal and plant populations in their environments, has been found useful in the fields of ecology and game management. According to Garrett Hardin:

> The carrying capacity of a particular area is defined as *the maximum number of a species that can be supported indefinitely by a particular habitat, allowing for seasonal and random changes, without degradation of the environment and without diminishing carrying capacity in the future.* [15]

It seems instructive to apply this notion to humans. Biologists Paul and Anne Erlich have concluded that:

...if the long-term carrying capacity of an area is clearly being degraded by its current human occupants, that area is overpopulated. *By this standard, the entire planet and virtually every nation is already vastly overpopulated.*[16]

I find it interesting that many present-day so-called 'conservatives' don't take more seriously this biological viewpoint. Thus, they may be discounting the future of humanity, hardly a prudent and 'conservative' thing to do in the long run.

Seeing humans as time-binding organisms *par excellence* makes it easier to neither discount nor to overemphasize the notion of "carrying capacity." As biological organisms, evolved from other animals, we are not immune to considerations about carrying capacity. On the other hand, as a time-binding class of life, we can creatively as well as degradingly affect our habitats in ways not possible for other organisms. As Korzybski pointed out, "We produce artificially [by artifice, but not unnaturally] because we are time-binders...Our numbers are not controlled by unaided nature, but can be increased considerably." [17]

This suggests that environmental Cassandras trumpeting inevitable doom and environmental Polyannas claiming inevitable progress are both probably wrong. The maximum possible human population that we can indefinitely support on our planet depends somewhat on human ingenuity. The state of environmental degradation that a given human population might produce at a given time also depends, among other things, not only on the population size but also on human ingenuity. To a significant degree, it is up to us humans to decide how many people we consider either too many or enough, what we consider environmental degradation, and how much of it we want to bear and at what price.

While avoiding Cassandrian alarmism, I prefer looking at things conservatively and prudently without Polyannaism. Korzybski suggested a criterion for decision-making about human population and the environment which takes into account our enhanced time-binding ability: "In a human class of life, which does produce artificially, production should satisfy the wants of all, or their number should be controlled until the wants can be filled." [18]

Accordingly, we should work at reducing either shortages of goods or, what Hardin calls, 'longages' of people. We should probably work at reducing both. Not meeting this criterion, in other words creating a situation of overpopulation, constitutes a "...threat [that] not only portends a continual deterioration of living standards virtually everywhere in time of peace, but also contributes to conflict between nations and thus increases the chances of nuclear war." [19]

A Saner Individual

The survival of humanity is not engraved in stone. It remains indeterminate, in the sense that the future has not yet happened and that alternative courses of events seem possible. The particular course of events that will occur will be determined, in part, by the choices we now make, both individually and collectively. These choices will involve the standards by which we judge human efforts.

We have already looked at the standard of the long-term survival of humanity. This seems like a basic good agreed upon by most people. Let us now look at the standard of human happiness. It can be defined in various ways while subsuming many if not most other human goals. For my purpose here, I will consider happiness as, at least, an important component of sanity, if not equivalent to it. What then?

From a humanistic perspective, the notion of flow—the absorption of consciousness while pursuing clear and worthwhile goals—seems to provide a key to the question of individual happiness as well as life's 'meanings'. This sense of flow, or self-directed experience, may be momentary or more lasting.

Although a suicide-bomber may experience momentary flow while skillfully evading capture and finding his way to murder the largest possible number of innocent victims, his activity will not lead to lasting happiness, either for himself, his family or social group (let alone his victims and theirs). A suicide-bomber wastes his own deluded life—as far as I know the only one he will ever have—and greatly increases the sum total of human misery. While still alive he has abandoned the possibility of a life of flow, of developing a self-directed personality or fuller humanness. Indeed, before he dies, the suicide bomber has actively reduced his own humanness to the level of an other-directed, religious fundamentalist robot.

A life of flow—a self-directed life of becoming more fully human—results, not from the collection of brief pleasures (even the pleasure, such as it is, of suicide-bombing) but from pursuing complex goals that both differentiate and integrate the different aspects of one's life. Such goals add harmony to the lives of both the individual and those around him or her. Glimpses of this harmony constitute what Maslow called "being-cognition," and "peak experience," locations along the road of self-actualization. A life of flow may also constitute an essential ingredient for human survival.

Long-term happiness, then, has something to do with individuals pursuing goals by which they can fulfill more of their potential, develop themselves, become more mature, self-directing, self-actualizing, etc. For adults, this involves a degree of personal time-binding: building upon previous experiences to create a more complex and harmonious self. Such a level of maturity or 'adulthood' seems rare but eminently worth working toward.

Such maturity seems to depend upon making use of an already-mentioned feature of the human nervous system: multiordinal self-reflexiveness. Maps have a self-reflexive quality: we can make a map of a map, a map of a map of a map, etc.—on verbal and non-verbal levels. So we can observe our observations, symbolize our symbols, talk about our talking. The "multiordinality of terms" refers to the self-reflexive aspect of language.

These multiordinal mechanisms can serve pathology, as in belief in belief, ignorance of ignorance, fear of fear, etc. They can also self-reflexively benefit us. They allow reasoning about reasoning, knowledge of knowledge, evaluation of evaluation, observing your observation, etc. Reversals of first-order effects can occur by means of doubt of doubt, hate of hate, etc. Perhaps some reversals of first-order effects need further refining. Better than hate of hate, would be refusal to hate. The second-order attitude should be less absolutistic than the first.

Long-term happiness involving self-actualization seems to require the ability not only to flow with the moment, to "follow your bliss" but also to "evaluate your bliss," i.e., to self-reflexively evaluate the values, evaluations, etc., related to it.[20] Those for whom goals, 'meanings', values, and ethics are fixed will not be able to correct their courses of action since they see no need to do so. Their belief in their beliefs results in their ignorance of their ignorance and an inability to change and to grow. Korzybski called this "adult infantilism."[21]

By contrast, chronological adults who function as 'adults' will continue to grow, to learn, to time-bind. They will retain a child-*like* attitude without behaving child*ish*ly.[22] They will not fix their goals, 'meanings', values, ethics, or themselves in the cement of certainty. Self-reflexively conscious of their abstracting, they will embody a creatical perspective, searching out opportunities to change course, if needed, by seeking knowledge of their ignorance.

A Saner Society

Expanding our focus, what might society look like if enough people developed such a creatical perspective? If enough adults were able to behave as *mature* adults, we would, I believe, live in a dramatically different society, and a much more humanistically-oriented one.

Government by instant opinion polls, focus groups and other marketing techniques would, for example, be recognized as demagoguery, not democracy. More people would be willing to say "I don't know" when confronted with complex questions regarding social-political-economic issues. There would be a greater demand, not only for information, but also for greater critical appraisal of its quality. Much greater use would be made of the potential of social/behavioral research to help us advance toward a more humanistic future.

One focus of activity would center around research, development and education in conflict resolution on interpersonal, group, societal and international levels. Force-based approaches may sometimes seem necessary. However, they are not sufficient for long-term solutions to conflicts at these various levels. In helping people and groups deal more effectively with conflicts, more work needs to be done on multiculturalism and diversity. How can we embrace the particularity of our own nationality/culture without falling into the tyranny of chauvinism? How can we accept the particularities of other ethnic/cultural groups while avoiding phony universalism, facile relativism, and a tolerance of intolerance which could lead to the death of open societies? What role does GS have to play in such work? [23]

The flames of interpersonal and inter-group conflict are fueled in part by 'emotional' immaturity and internal conflict within individuals. 'Emotional' education, such as is taught in Rational Emotive Behavior Therapy (REBT), seems essential in order to develop saner, more mature individuals and thus a saner, more mature society and world. Albert Ellis and his co-worker Ted Crawford have noted in their book *Making Intimate Connections* that reducing conflict and improving relationships and communication involves learnable skills. Chief among these is the skill of transforming absolutistic demands, 'shoulds', and 'musts' into non-absolutistic preferences and goals.

What would a society made up of 'emotionally mature', consciously self-reflexive, constructively self-questioning individuals look like? Such a society would develop as a learning society with self-studying institutions and a culture-studying culture. It would, I anticipate, unleash positive time-binding energies to a much greater extent than occurs at present.

In Greek mythology, Prometheus, one of the Titans (god-like beings), felt compassion for uncivilized humanity. Prometheus stole fire from the Gods of Olympus, and gave it, along with reason and civilization, to humans. For this and other 'sins', the chief God, Zeus, had Prometheus bound to a rock where an eagle fed on his liver. After untold ages, Hercules killed the eagle and freed the still rebellious Prometheus. Prometheus became a humanist symbol of defiance against unjust authority, and of reason and compassion for humanity.

Not Prometheus, but many promethean individuals through their time-binding efforts have provided every human living today with the wealth that we've inherited. Meanwhile, our inherited illth includes the beliefs and institutions that have bound and repressed the promethean power in each of us. Moving toward a humanistic future (the adulthood of humanity) will require that—with compassion—we each work to unleash our own power and, to the extent that we can, that of those around us. It will take each of us a lifetime. How long will it take humanity?

Visualizing the Adulthood of Humanity

With Korzybski, I accept that human survival depends on the extension of human sanity. I'm enough of a human chauvinist that I want the game to continue. Humans are more likely to avoid self-destruction and continue surviving as a species when a significantly large number of people begin to follow an extensional orientation—an attitude of inquiry—which promotes beneficial time-binding.

In the present world, most humans have more or less inappropriate, immature habits of evaluating. Our everyday unsane evaluating and associated unconscious language habits encourage us to confuse maps with territories. We thus fail to make the distinctions necessary for extensionally dealing with our everyday problems, relationships, etc.

Thus, in the present world, technological developments in the narrow areas that *do* have an extensional, scientific basis often make this a more dangerous world. Many so-called intelligent people simply have more powerful tools with which to behave more stupidly with disastrous results for themselves and others. Others control our symbol systems and thus control us. If this trend continues, we can expect more, and probably more devastating, human-caused disasters.

In a possible future, inquiry-oriented culture, most humans will have more or less appropriate, mature and sane habits of evaluating and associated conscious language habits. These will then help them to make the everyday distinctions necessary for decreasing difficulties and increasing well-being.

In this possible future world, broad areas of life, including personal and social decision-making, will be based on applying a generalized scientific attitude. Technological developments will make this a more creative, interesting, productive and sustainable world. Many more intelligent and sane people will have more powerful tools with which to act more effectively, individually and in common, with beneficial results for themselves and others. We each will control our own symbol systems better and thus better control ourselves. With such a trend, we can expect accelerating human advancement—a world-wide extensional ethic. We will have a more scientifically-and-humanistically-oriented world.

Such a non-aristotelian evolution will involve many more individuals who dare to inquire in their daily lives. An attitude of inquiry will necessarily be codified in everyday language use. We will talk differently. We will 'think' differently. We will 'feel' differently. We will act differently. We will see the world differently.

Can we bring it off?

Notes

Epigraph
1. Qtd. in Haack, p. 241

Preface
1. In a Sept. 2002 article entitled "The Camp David War," quoted in full below, historian Michael Oren describes the still current (January 2003) war which began in September 2000:

> Though Arabs and Israelis disagree not only on the names of their wars but also on their numbering, both sides recognize the last two years of bloodshed as a war in every respect, distinct from the previous intifada of the late 1980s. There can also be a neutral name for the struggle: the Camp David War. The Palestinians initiated the fighting after the Camp David summit meeting, during which they demanded the return of all refugees to Israel and Israel refused to commit demographic suicide. Rather, convinced that they had offered more-than-adequate concessions at the summit, the Israelis rallied together and successfully resisted Arafat's attempt to wage diplomacy by other means. Camp David also symbolized the climax of the Oslo process. Nine years of negotiations failed to produce peace and, after Camp David, devolved into a war in which both sides, Israeli and Palestinian, have suffered greatly. (*Jerusalem Post Internet Edition*, Special Supplement "Naming the War: Two Years of Violence" at www.jpost.com)

For details about how Arafat's Palestinian Authority (formerly Palestine Liberation Organization or P.L.O.) orchestrated the outbreak of violence that began the Camp David War, see "How the War Began" by Khaled Abu Toameh.

2. Qtd. from Silver, pp. 5, 38

Acknowledgements
1. In *The Joys of Yiddish*, Leo Rosten explained this term as follows: "**naches, nakhes** Pronounce NOKH-*ess*, to rhyme with "Loch Ness"— with the *kh* sound a Scot would use in pronouncng "loch." Hebrew: *nachat:* 'contentment.' 1. Proud pleasure, special joy—particularly from the achievements of a child...2. Psychological reward or gratification...See also KVELL." p. 257

Introduction
1. Marquis qtd. in Winoker, p. 141

Chapter 1
1. E. O. Wilson 2002, p. 86
2. Erlich and Ellison

3. Seckel and Edwards

4. Einstein 2000, "Physics and Reality," p. 247

5. Lamont, p. 207

6. Kurtz 1992, p. 125

7. See Kenneth G. Johnson 1992, 1986, and 1984.

Part I — The Humanist Tradition
1. Lec

Chapter 2
1. Webster's, p. 586

2. Hadas, pp. 18, 33

3. Qtd., in Lamont, p. 31

4. Merejkowski

5. Abraham, p. 3

6. Telushkin, pp. 118-119

7. See *The Golden Rule* for the Wiccan version and that of Muhammad. Jesus's version comes from Reese, p. 267.

8. Williams, pp. 276-280

9. Kant

10. Lichtenberg, p. 92

11. Schopenhauer 1951, p. 40

12. Qtd. in Corben, p. 59

13. Korzybski 1994 (1933), pp. 383-384

14. Reese, pp. 203-204

15. Epictetus, Section 5

16. Blake, p. 256

17. Stirner, p.163

18. Wright, pp. 109, 117

19. Qtd. in Warren Allen Smith, p. 571

20. Reiser 1940, p. 243

21. Kaufmann 1976, p. 98

22. Edwards 1995a and 1995b

23. White, Vol. 2, p. 393

24. Yutang, p. v

25. Baum, p. 16

26. Ibid, p. 44

27. Parikh, p. 21

Chapter 3

1. Lively humanist organizations outside of the United States, in England, Holland, Scandinavia, India, etc., all made important contributions to the development of an international humanist community. However, because of my personal experience with and knowledge of the humanist movement in the United States, most of my comments here pertain specifically to the U.S.

2. Qtd. in Lamont, p. 287

3. Radest, p. 5

4. Webster's, p. 995

5. Kurtz 1994a, pp. 75, 84-85

6. Kurtz 1994b, p. 330

7. Radest, p. 55

8. Toulmin 1990, p. 25

9. George A. Kelly, p. 15

10. Rokeach, pp. 73-80

11. Ibid

12. Reiser 1940, p. x

13. Warren Allen Smith, p. 552

Chapter 4

1. Toulmin 1988, p. 337

2. Toulmin 1990, pp. 200-201

3. Kurtz 1994a, pp. 200-201. Kurtz originally spelled the term "eupraxsophy" without the "s" as "eupraxophy." However, he added the "s" in 2000 to facilitate pronunciation (See Kurtz 2000).

4. Kurtz 1994b, p. 329

5. Stopes-Roe, pp. 8-9. Although Stopes-Roe didn't do so, I prefer to hyphenate the term as "life-stance."

6. Goodman 1962

7. Maslow 1954, pp. 199-234

8. Qtd. in Lamont, p. 288

Part II — General Semantics: Making Humanism Workable

1. Korzybski 1990a, p. 77

Chapter 5

1. C. S. Read 1990, p. 742. Unless otherwise referenced, biographical data in this chapter have been derived from this work in combination with "Chronology of Alfred Korzybski's Life."

2. A. W. Read 1984, p. 16

3. Korzybski 1947a, p. 18

4. Korzybski 2002 (1937), pp. 227-229

5. Korzybski, 1947a, p.19

6. Ibid, pp. 447-448

7. Ibid, pp. 58-59

8. Ibid, p. 42

9. Korzybski 1990a, "Science, Sanity, and Humanism," pp. 383-384

10. Korzybski 1947a, p. 213

11. Korzybski 1950 (1921), p. 2. See Barzun, pp. 82-85 for his views on the term "Man" as a neutral one for "human being." You can find differing views in Minnich and in Miller and Swift.

12. Ibid, p. 56

13. Ibid, p. 58

14. Qtd. in Montagu 1953, p. 11

15. Montagu 1953, p. 11.

16. Korzybski 1950 (1921), p. 227

17. Ibid, pp. 232-234

18. Ibid, p. 230

19. Ibid, p. 234

20. Korzybski 1994 (1933), p. 291

21. Ibid, p. 76

22. Cassirer, pp. 24-26

23. Qtd. in Van Doren 1967, p. 44

24. Korzybski 1950 (1921), p. 110

25. "The typical term of the progression is PR^T where PR denotes the ending progress made in the generation with which we agree to start our reckoning. R denotes the ratio of increase, and T denotes the number of generations after the chosen 'start.' The quantity, PR^T of progress made in the Tth generation contains T as an exponent, and so the quantity, varying as time T passes, is called an exponential function of the time." (*Manhood of Humanity*, pp. 110-111)

26. Wilson 1983, p. 88

27. Paulos 1991, p. 70

28. Stuart Mayper, Personal Communication

29. Korzybski 1950 (1921), pp. 147-148

30. Qtd. in Montagu 1955, p. 66. From James T. Shotwell 1942, "Mechanism and Culture." In *Science and Man*, Ed. By R. N. Anshen. New York: Harcourt, Brace & Co.

31. George, p. 507

32. Korzybski 1950 (1921), p. 115

33. Ibid, p. 115

34. Ibid, pp. 132-133

35. Ibid, p. 198

36. Janssen, p. 27

37. Janssen, p. 28

38. Korzybski 1990c, p. 630

39. Korzybski 1950 (1921), p. 11

40. Ibid, pp. 10-11

Chapter 6

1. Roethlesberger, pp. 70-71

2. Qtd. in *Manhood*, p. 207

3. Korzybski 1990a, "Time-Binding: The General Theory (First Paper), p. 75

4. Modified from Korzybski's logical fate diagram. Used with permission of the Institute of General Semantics and Korzybski's Literary Estate.

Chapter 7

1. Korzybski 1947b, "Mathematical Method as a Way of Life" (Unpublished Lecture)

2. Rothwell and Sudarshan, pp. 21-24

3. Gardner 1983, p. 341

4. Rukeyser, pp. 279-280

5. "If we consider, further, that 2/1=2, 3/1=3, *and so on*, are all *different, specific,* and *unique,* we come to an obvious and $\overline{A}$ [non-Aristotelian] semantic definition of number in terms of relations, in which 0 and 1 represent *unique* and *specific symmetrical* relations and all other numbers also *unique* and *specific asymmetrical* relations....numbers, in general, represent indefinitely many *exact, specific,* and *unique,* and in the main, *asymmetrical* relations..." (*Science and Sanity*, pp. 258-259). Contrast this with Bertrand Russell's definition of number, still widely used today: "The number of a class is the class of all those classes that are similar to it" (qtd. in *Science and Sanity*, p. 255). According to Korzybski "Mathematics consists of limited linguistic schemes of multiordinal relations capable of exact treatment at a given date" (*Science and Sanity*, p. 253).

6. Prigogine and Stengers, p. xxix

7. MacNeal, p. 127

8. Qtd. in *Science and Sanity*, p. 66

9. See Holton 1998a.

10. From Mayper 1980, p. 108. Used with permission of *General Semantics Bulletin* and the Institute of General Semantics.

11. Mayper 1980, p. 108

12. Korzybski 1994 (1933), p. 307

13. Ibid, p. 133

Chapter 8

1. Keyser, qtd. in Korzybski 1994 (1933), p. 188

2. Korzybski 1994 (1933), p. 99

3. Ibid, p. 194

4. Ibid, p. 99

5. Ibid, p. 194

6. Ibid, p. 99

7. Ibid, p. 50

8. Pula 1994, p. xvii

9. Pula 1978, p. 71

10. Korzybski 1994 (1933), p. 194

11. Ibid, p. 310

12. Korzybski 2002 (1937), p. 24

13. Korzybski 1994 (1933), p. 172. See also pp. 603-614.

14. Ibid, p. 605

Chapter 9

1. Bois 1957, p. 46

2. Korzybski 1948/1949

3. See Korzybski 1994 (1933), pp. 111, 456; Hauser; Mordkowitz 1990, p. 88; and Lewis.

4. Crick 1994b, p. 18

5. Damasio 1994

6. Robert Pula coined the memorable phrase, "the pain in sprain is mainly in the brain." (Lecture Notes). Pula has emphasized the importance of not turning the unity of the nervous system-organism into an undifferentiated 'mush'. He emphasizes rather its particularity (specificity) of structure. "Two main <u>descriptive</u> characteristics of the nervous system are plasticity and specificity of structure, all manifested as dynamic processes. Nervous system events do not happen 'all at once' but over localizable-temporal space-time" (Personal Note). This and other important structural facts about the human nervous system were also noted by Korzybski (Korzybski 1994 (1933), p. 161).

7. Figure 4 modified from Korzybski's Structural Differential Diagram. Used with permission from the Institute of General Semantics and the Alfred Korzybski Literary Estate.

8. Figure 5 used with permission of the Institute of General Semantics and *General Semantics Bulletin.*

9. Kendig 1950 a, pp. xxxiv-xxxv

Chapter 10

1. Penny Lee 1996, p. 87

2. Korzybski 1994 (1933), p. 90

3. Pinker 1994, p. 58

4. Ibid, p. 57

5. Korzybski 1994 (1933), p. xl

6. Whorf, p. 239

7. Lamb 2000

8. Sampson, p. 136

9. Qtd. in Vossler, p. 235

10. Pinker 1994, p. 18

11. Lamb 2000

12. Pinker 1994, p. 57

13. Ibid, p. 57

14. Ibid, pp. 61-63

15. Ibid. p. 63

16. Ibid, p. 64

17. Whorf, p. 210

18. Pinker gets his 'information' about this from original research by anthropologist Laura Martin (Martin, 1986) and an article on Martin's work by Geoffrey Pullum, entitled "The Great Eskimo Vocabulary Hoax." Martin's conclusions were later challenged by Stephen O. Murray. The term "hoax" implies a conscious act of deception. Pullum and Pinker abuse Martin's research. They have no actual evidence of conscious deception by Whorf or his colleagues.

19. Agar, pp. 69-71

20. See P. Kay and W. Kempton,"What is the Sapir-Whorf Hypothesis?" This research is discussed in Lakoff 1987, pp. 330-334.

21. See Kempton. Also see Minkel.

22. Morris, p. 283.

Chapter 11

1. Webster's, p. 582

2. Marks, p. 92

3. Allman, pp. 32-40

4. Korzybski 1990a, "The Role of Language in the Perceptual Processes," p. 704. Korzybski derived the notion of self-reflexiveness from philosopher Josiah Royce.

5. Charlotte Read suggested that:
"In learning to feel the deeper significance of the map-territory premise we can:
1. Be more awake to our own personal role in making our maps.
2. Increase our ability to make needed revisions as we check with the territory.
3. Realize, through continual experiencing, that we each live in our "as if" world, and develop awareness of this.
4. Gain greater appreciation of the other person's world and his/her way of expressing it.
5. If the temptation arises to say 'This is nothing new,' we can say 'This can be a new experience, newly experienced today.'
Perhaps it would be useful to state the premise as: 'The territory is not the map.' Would this make a difference? I don't know.
Many questions arise as we progress toward a more unified view of our universe and our place in it. The multiordinal map-territory analogy can remain a helpful guide, provided we are aware of Korzybski's third premise: The map is self-reflexive—the mapmaker is in the map—and provided we remember that the premises, like all premises, are only maps."
(Charlotte Read, "Living in an 'as if' World: Some Reflections on 'The Map Is Not the Territory' " p. 75)

6. See *Drive Yourself Sane*, pp., 69, 91.

7. Powers 1998, p. 17. See also Cziko, Marken, and the PCT website: http://www.ed.uiuc.edu/csg/ See also my *Back Pain Solutions*, which presents a specific application of GS and PCT to physical therapy.

8. Northrop 1946, pp. 447, 443

9. Wilson 1990, p. 173. Pula has noted 5 significant functional steps in the process of abstracting which are common to both animals and humans: 1) structurally determined selecting/filtering, 2) transducing, 3) integrating (preconscious), 4) projecting, and 5) self-reflexive processes. In humans, these non-verbal processes precede and underlie an additional step, i.e., 6) languaging (symbolizing, talking), which, in turn, affects the prior non-verbal steps. See Pula 1979, p. 20 and Pula 2000, pp. 9-11.

10. Watzlawick, p. 132

11. Schopenhauer 1995, pp. 3-5

Chapter 12

1. Berman 1989, pp.168-172

2. Lukasiewicz, pp. 66-67

3. Korner, pp. 414-415

4. Abel, p. 51

5. Korzybski 1994 (1933), p. 194

6. Adler, pp. 13,14, 32, 50; Gorman, pp. 86-87, 140

7. Gorman, pp. 135-136

8. Magee 2001, p. 14

9. Korzybski 1994 (1933), p. xli

10. My colleague, James D. French observes:

> I understand that logicians view this GS argument as naive, a confu-
> sion of symbol with referent. They would say " 'A is A' is not saying
> that the A on the left is the A on the right, anymore than saying 'John
> is that professor' is saying that the word 'John' is the words 'that pro-
> fessor'. 'John is that professor' is saying that the word 'John' and the
> words 'that professor' refer to the same person. 'A is B' is saying that
> 'A' and 'B' represent the same entity, and also 'A is A', of course." In
> rebuttal, we could say that it takes time to make a statement, as the
> second element always comes later; thus the underlying entity or pro-
> cess has changed just in the time it takes to hear or read the statement.
> Of more relevance perhaps is that our abstractions or reactions to the
> two symbols of a statement are also not identical in all respects. Dif-
> ferent evaluational (semantic) reactions occur on hearing the word
> "John" and hearing the word "professor." Context also plays a role.
> Our reactions to the As in "A is A" are not identical in all aspects sim-
> ply because the second A follows the first, and symbol and referent
> cannot be *entirely* separated in our reactions. In other words, we par-
> ticipate in the identity formulation because we only know it as our ab-
> straction. We *cannot not* abstract it; and every abstraction is to some
> extent unique. Thus non-identity. (Personal Note)

11. Popper 1966 (1943) a, p. 33

12. Korzybski 1994 (1933), pp. 10-11

13. Some people define 'identity' differently, e.g. "sameness in relevant
respects."

14. Reiser 1940, pp. 50, 69, 84 (You can find these references in Berman
1989, pp. 45, 59, 69.)

15. Hook 1934, p. 546

16. "This is not the 'is of identity' in logic, only perhaps in GS. If 'Dewey' were identical in all respects with 'philosopher', then Dewey and Plato, for example, would be the same person, but the statement is not making that kind of absolute identity. I would say here that an individual is being confused with the higher-order notion of class membership. He must by definition have the attributes of the class or all the attributes that the members of the class have. The label of class membership, i.e., 'a philosopher' is substituted for the person." (James D. French, Personal Note)

17. Allen Walker Read 1984, pp. 22-23

18. Korzybski 1994 (1933), p. 408

19. Abel, p. 51

20. Ibid, p. 51

21. Black 1969, p. 149

22. Ibid, p. 97. See Black 1949 for "Korzybski's General Semantics," Black's more detailed and supposedly 'definitive' critique of GS. My article "Contra Max Black," shows that Black's critique, far from definitive, results from a profound misunderstanding of GS.

23. Aristotle, *Metaphysics,* Book IV: Ch. 4, p. 743

24. Aristotle, *De Interpretatione*, Ch. 9, p. 48

25. Aristotle, *Nichomachean Ethics,* Book II: Ch. 7, pp. 959-960

26. Magee 2001, p. 39

27. Korzybski 1994 (1933), p. xciv

Chapter 13

1. Mayper (Personal Note), Pula (Personal Note)

2. Qtd. in Abel, p. 3

3. Gregory 1987

4. See Block and Yuker 1992 and Hoffman 1998.

5. Charlotte Schuchardt Read 1965/1966, p. 50

6. Korzybski 1994 (1933), pp. lix-lx

7. See Gelb for further suggestions on visualization including drawing, "mind-mapping," etc. See Wenger for advanced visualization methods, many of which are available online at www.WinWenger.com

8. Dawes, p. 412

9. Dawes, pp. 410, 411

10. George A. Kelly, p. 5. This applies to women, as well as men. Kelly wrote at a time when few thought about non-sexist terminology.

11. Polanyi 1966, p. 4

12. Wendell Johnson wrote, "The scientific method reduces essentially to three questions...'What do you mean?'...'How do you know?' [and] 'What then?'...I have discovered that these three are about the most liberating questions you can imagine." (Johnson and Moeller, pp. 37, 40). As an exercise, you can examine how the seven steps of personal inquiry map onto the logical fate model, Einstein's model of thinking, and the abstracting model.

13. You can obtain a wall chart of the Structural Differential from the Institute of General Semantics, 86 85th St. Brooklyn, NY 11209-4208. Phone: 718-921-7093. Email: institute@general-semantics.org Web: www.general-semantics.org

14. French 2002, p. 8

Chapter 14

1. French 1993, p. 331. Re rewording: When you say something differently, you say something different—and that may make an important difference.

2. Allen Walker Read 1985, p. 7

3. Ibid, pp. 11-12

4. Kodish and Kodish 2001, p. 210

5. Pula 1998, p. 83

6. See Pula 1998 and Kodish and Kodish 1995.

7. Of course, the language community as a whole plays a role and has an effect on the 'meanings' we give to words. The fact that something is a word indicates that some 'meaning' has already been ascribed or assigned to it. When people ask what a word 'means', they are often asking in part "What are the agreed-upon meanings that the language community gives to this word?" So to say that it has no 'meaning' may seem like nonsense to some people. However, while we do inherit broad categories of 'meaning', our individual 'meanings' will differ somewhat or greatly. And these individual differences in 'meanings' may make a great deal of difference in understanding and getting along with one another—or not.

8. Korzybski 1994 (1933), p. 437

9. Ibid, p. 506, 507. See also Pula's discussion of "Higher Order Functions" in *General-Semantics Glossary*, pp. 73-79.

10. Allan Watts qtd. in Krassner, p. 3

11. Wendell Johnson 1946, pp. 215-216

12. Bandler and Grinder, p. 61

13. In no way do I wish to 'give the green light' here to abusive speech or to incitement. People vary in their vulnerabilities to the neuro-

evaluational, neuro-linguistic environments around them. Nasty parents who verbally abuse their children may contribute greatly to human miseries; as may demagogues who incite their listeners to violent acts.

14. Wendell Johnson 1946, pp. 14-15

15. Korzybski 1990 a, "General Semantics, Psychiatry, Psychotherapy and Prevention," p. 205.

Part III- Implications and Applications

1. Dewey qtd. in Peter, p. 420

Section A-Applying a Scientific Attitude to Science

1. Sigmund Freud qtd. in Peter, p. 438

Chapter 15

1. Korzybski 1994 (1933), p. 485

2. Jennings qtd. in Korzybski 1994 (1933), p. 5

3. Robert Pula refers to the "(premature) specifying of what single genes 'cause' (behavior, diseases, etc.)" as "genetic phrenology" (Personal Note). For some challenges to Pinker's and others' simplistic version of 'evolutionary psychology', see Bower; Lewontin, Rose and Kamin; Montagu 1980; David S. Moore; Rose 1997; and Rose and Rose. For reliable data on brain evolution, see Allman. As examples of intelligent, non-elementalistic, enviro-genetic accounts of the evolution of human intelligence and behavior, see Erlich 2000, and Skoyles and Sagan. Also see Quartz and Sejnowski for their presentation of "cultural biology," which corroborates the early work of Bridges, Jennings and Korzybski and which may eventually replace current attempts at 'evolutionary psychology'.

4. Edward Fitzgerald, "The Rubaiyat of Omar Khayyam"

5. Popper 1976, p. 187

6. Ibid, p. 181

7. Popper and Eccles, p. 376

8. Korzybski 1994 (1933), p. 162

9. Popper and Eccles, p. vii

10. Popper 1976, p. 19

11. Popper 1965 (1963), p. 214

12. Popper 1976, p. 29

13. Ibid, p. 29

14. Popper and Eccles, p. viii

15. Eccles and Robinson, p. 43

16. Ibid, p. 36

17. Damasio 1999, p. 323

18. Chalmers, p. 92

19. Northrop 1949, pp. 196-197

20. Spinoza 1951, p. 185

21. Bunge, p. 11

22. Ibid, pp. 217-218

23. For example, see John McCrone's 1999 book *Going Inside*. See also his website, http://www.btinternet.com/~neuronaut/ . Although not a general semanticist, McCrone's dynamic, non-elementalistic approach to conscious brain functioning shows in much of his language use.

Chapter 16

1. Ellis 1996, p. 254. See Korzybski's discussion of 'pragmatism' (Korzybski 1994 (1933), pp. 109-110). This relates to Popper's "critical rationalism" (Popper 1966 (1943)b, pp. 237-238, 357).

2. Strahler, pp. 223-224

3. Ibid

4. Ibid, p. 238

5. Polanyi 1962 (1958), p. xiii

6. The Institute of General Semantics Teacher Certification Program provides a minimal set of standards for GS competency. Korzybski suggested the applicability of GS to interdisciplinary and transdisciplinary research in *Science and Sanity*, pp. lxxvii-lxxxi, 553-555,557-561, 569. Paul Erlich discusses the ongoing need for "interdisciplinary approaches to serious human problems" in his *Human Natures*, pp. 325-326.

Section B-Religion: An Extensional Approach

1. Montaigne qtd. in Peter, p. 69

Chapter 17

1. See O'Neal, "No dog tags for atheists: Now, where's my foxhole?"

2. Weaver, p. 164

3. See Larson and Witham which reports on religious belief among elite scientists, those elected to the Nation Academy of Sciences (NAS), and among other non-NAS-elected ones. They found that only 7% of NAS-elected scientists reported belief in a personal 'God'. Theistic belief rose to 40% among the non-NSA scientists polled.

4. Such question-begging (assuming what one wants to prove) provides the basis for the "argument from design" used to support belief in the existence of 'God'.

5. Einstein 2000, "Science and Religion," p. 214

6. Corben, p. 42

7. Einstein 2000, "Science and Religion," p. 214

8. Weaver, pp. 163-164

9. See Kramer and Alstad's *The Guru Papers: Masks of Authoritarian Power*, pp. 327-358.

10. Lichtenberg, p. 73

11. Hume 1988, p. 192

12. The history of Christian coercion against non-Christians and amongst various kinds of Christians is well-known. See Ibn Warraq on the history of the Islamic conquest and oppression of non-Muslims (pp. 214-240), religious skeptics, and Muslims with variant viewpoints (pp. 241-289). "Like Christianity, Islam is a universal faith that envisions the ultimate transformation of the world in its image. But unlike large parts of Christianity in our time, Islam has yet to consider the option of religious pluralism based on the equality of faiths" (Yossi Klein Halevi, "Islam's Outdated Domination Theology"). May many more Muslims pursue that option, for all our sakes.

Lest someone think that I'm totally whitewashing the Jewish religion and culture in regard to intolerance, I acknowledge that Jews have not always behaved like 'perfect angels'. Nonetheless, I generally agree with Rabbi Joseph Telushkin who points out that, "Judaism has never taught that one has to be Jewish in order to be saved" (*Jewish Literacy*, p. 591).

13. See Diamond's *Guns, Germs and Steel*.

14. See Silberger's *The Jewish Phenomenon*.

15. W. J. Clifford qtd. in A. J. Burger, "An Examination of 'The Will to Believe' " in A. J. Burger, *The Ethics of Belief*

Chapter 18

1. Epstein, p. 297

2. See Mordecai M. Kaplan's *Judaism as a Civilization*.

3. See Judith Seid's *God-Optional Judaism* and Matt Young's "How to Find Meaning in Religion."

4. *Webster's*, p. 112

5. Al-Ansari, p. 52

6. Sura 2, The Cow 2:23, qtd. in N. J. Dawood, trans. *The Koran*

7. Al-Ansari, p. ii

8. Ibn Warraq, p. 108

9. See Toby Lester's article, "What is the Koran?"

10. Al-Maari qtd. in Ibn Warraq, p. 283

11. Russell 1969, p. 6

12. Nietzsche 1974, p. 253

13. Einstein rejected a supernatural 'God' and clearly qualified as a probabilistic atheist by my definition. Still, he often used the term 'God' figuratively in his statements about physics, i.e. "God does not play dice." Einstein also espoused what he called a "cosmic religion," a kind of scientific pantheism, and could genuinely say "I believe in Spinoza's God who reveals himself in the orderly harmony of what exists, not in a God who concerns himself with fates and actions of human beings." Opinions differ as to the usefulness of such talk (Gilmore).

Chapter 19

1. Goya qtd. in Jordan, p. 22

2. Kaplan

3. Miller

4. Ellis 1988b, p. 27

5. Schumaker, p. 13

6. Watters, p. 17 and Ellis 1993a, p. 18

7. Livingstone, p. 47. Recent studies which appeared to show the efficacy of prayer in recovery from illness have questionable correlations which fail to control for naturalistic explanations such as the placebo effect.

8. Cohen, p. 379

9. Ibid, p. 178

10. The Book of Revelations 14:9-11, qtd. in Cohen, p. 354

11. Robert Anton Wilson 1983, p. 6

12. Pula 2000, p. 64

13. Norbert Weiner, pp. 145-146

14. Lewis Carrol, p. 735

15. "Hypnotism, debate, and countless other games have the same mechanism: *Invoke often* and *Banish often*." Shea and Wilson "The Tactics of Magic," p. 218.

16. Korzybski 1994 (1933), p. 440

17. Ibid, p. 716

Chapter 20

1. Qtd. in Klemke 1981b, Preface

2. Ellis and Harper, pp. 186-187

3. Csikszentmihalyi 1990, p. 6

4. Ibid, p. 67

5. Charlotte Schuchardt Read 1993, p. 88

6. Ibid, pp. 88-89

7. Rilke qtd. by Abrams, p. 261

8. Teilhard de Chardin, p. 220

Section C - Time-Binding Ethics

1. Daly, p. 83

Chapter 21

1. Erlich 2000, pp. 308-309

2. See Sagan and Druyen.

3. Edelman, pp. 118-120

4. See Dugatikin.

5. Korzybski 1994 (1933), p. 484

6. Flanagan, p. 173

7. Montagu 1951a, p. 25

8. Robert Anton Wilson 1988, p. 71

9. Korzybski 1994 (1933), p. 357

10. See Langer 1989 and Langer 2002. It's important to not elementalize Krishnamurti's distinction between 'thought' and 'thinking'. 'Thought' as I've characterized it constitutes precisely the time-binding residue *from which* we can do our present dynamic 'thinking'. So we can't entirely eliminate it and shouldn't try. I'm talking about *orientation* here.

11. Kurtz 1988, p. 175

12. Ibid, pp. 154-156

13. Waddington 1948 (1941), p. 32

14. Ibid, p. 33

15. Gould 1999

16. Anthony Flew qtd. in Strahler, p. 296

17. George H. Smith, p. 294

18. Kurtz 1992, pp. 297-298

19. Cantril and Bumstead, p. 168

20. Fletcher 1979, p. 3

21. Fletcher 1966, p. 22

22. Fletcher 1979, p. 3

Chapter 22

1. Juge, p. 104

2. Nurses for Community Education

3. Eccles and Robinson, p. 20

4. Varga, p. 61

5. Brunning, pp. 1-2

6. Calhoun, p. 158

7. Ellis 1968, pp. 173-174

8. Hardin 1982b, p. 195. Hardin, a biologist, studied general semantics.

9. Hardin 1978a, pp. 29, 34

10. Nathanson qtd. in Jaworski, p. 56

11. Qtd. in Tribe, p. 118

12. Details regarding brain development can be found in Jaworski.

13. Flower, p. 72

14. Hentoff, p. 16

15. Hardin 1982a, p. 142

16. Varga, p. 61

17. Fletcher 1979, pp. 12-16

18. Jaworski, pp. 59-60

19. Tribe, p. 11

20. Qtd. in Tribe, p. 280

21. Planned Parenthood, "Abortion After the First Trimester."

22. Allan Guttmacher Instititute, "Late Term Abortions: Legal Considerations."

23. Blumenthal

24. Russo

25. Stack

26. Alan Guttmacher Institute, "Induced Abortion (US)"

27. Hardin 1982a, p. 144

28. See Jerry Reiter's *Live from the Gates of Hell*

29. Flynn, p. 7

30. Singer 2000, "In Place of the Old Ethic, " p. 211

31. Ibid, p. xv

32. Baldwin, in Kodish, ed. 1998

Conclusion
1. Camus, qtd. in Peter, p. 456

Chapter 23
1. Tarter, p. 35

2. See Daniel Pipes' *Militant Islam Reaches America*. Regarding Islamism and other fundamentalist (or even non-fundamentalist) one-world visions, we would all do well to contemplate the following statement by Pula, "We're all one, but not the same one." (*Jottings*, available at www.general-semantics.org).

3. Budd, p.128.

4. Qtd. by M. Kendig in "Book Comments" GSB 1 & 2: 46.

5. See Cziko; Marken; Powers; and Runkel.

6. See Derry; Klemke, Hollinger and Kline; and Northrop 1949.

7. From "Reports from the Institute: Intensive Professional Weekend Seminar given by Douglas M. Kelley, M. D."

8. Runkel, pp. 175-176.

9. Of course, we need to be wary of under-intellectualized approaches as well. See Satriano's *Vitvan: An American Master* for more on the life and work of Ralph deBit. The School of the Natural Order's website is at http://www.sno.org

10. See Laurent, "A Note on the Origin of Memes/Mnemes."

11. Csikzentmihalyi, *The Evolving Self*, p. 120

12. Robert Anton Wilson 1983, p. 92

13. Hardin 1982c, p. 155

14. Hardin 1985, p. 221

15. Hardin 1977, p. 113

16. Erlich and Erlich, p. 39

17. Korzybski 1994 (1933), p. 548

18. Ibid

19. Erlich and Erlich, p. 171

20. "Evaluate your bliss" is Robert Pula's higher-level, cautionary counter to mythology scholar Joseph Campbell's "follow your bliss." (Class Notes).

21. Korzybski 1994 (1933), p. 305

22. See Montagu's *Growing Young*.

23. In our current conflict, a *"war* of *and* on *nerves"* (Korzybski 1994 (1933), p. lxxi) with militant Islamist totalitarians, I opine that

general semantics has a very important role to play in the "education for intelligence and democracy" (Ibid, p. lxxv), and related research, needed to combat terrorism. As Korzybski noted in relation to the battle with the Nazis: "...the totalitarians have exploited neuro-semantic and neuro-linguistic mechanisms to their destructive limit, the best they knew how, to date. Counteraction, reconstruction, and/or prevention are impossible unless such mechanisms are utilized *constructively* under the guidance of governmental specialists in the fields of anthropology, neuro-psychiatry, general semantics, etc., ...a permanent consulting board of specialists who would advise how to conserve and prevent the abuse of human nervous systems." (Ibid, p. lxxix)

Bibliography

Abel, Reuben. 1976. *Man is the measure: A cordial invitation to the central problems of philosophy*. New York: The Free Press/Simon & Schuster.

Abraham, Ralph H. 1994. *Chaos Gaia Eros: A chaos pioneer uncovers the three great streams of history*. New York: HarperCollins.

Abrams, David. 1996. *The spell of the sensuous: Perception and language in a more-than-human world*. New York: Vintage.

Abu Toameh, Khaled. Sept. 19, 2002. "How the war began." *Jerusalem Post Internet Edition*. www.jpost.com

Adler, Mortimer J. 1978. *Aristotle for everybody: Difficult thought made easy*. New York: Macmillan Publishing Co.

Agar, Michael. 1994. *Langage shock: Understanding the culture of conversation*. New York: William Morrow and Company.

Agassi, Joseph. 1968. *The continuing revolution: A history of physics from the Greeks to Einstein*. (The History of Science Series, edited by Daniel A. Greenberg.) New York: McGraw Hill Book Company.

Alan Guttmacher Institute. 2000. Induced abortion (U.S.). Available at www.agi-usa.org

Alan Guttmacher Institute. 1997. Late term abortions: Legal considerations. Available at http://www.agi-usa.org

Al-Ansari, Jalal. 1996. *Introduction to the systems of Islam*. London: Al-Khilafah Publications

Alford, Dan. 1980. A hidden cycle in the history of linguistics. In *Phoenix*, Vol 4, Numbers 1 & 2. Available at http://sunflower.com/~dewatson/dma-2.htm

Allman, John. 2000. *Evolving brains*. New York: Scientific American Library Paperbacks.

Aristotle. Ed. by Richard McKeon. 1941. *The basic works of Aristotle*. New York: Random House.

Baldwin, Kenneth L. 1998. Can we develop a worldwide *extensional* ethic? In *Developing sanity in human affairs (Contributions to the study of mass media and communications, number 54)*. Ed. Susan Presby Kodish and Robert P. Holston. Westport, CT: Greenwood Press. 420-426.

Bandler, Richard and John Grinder. 1979. *Frogs into princes: Neuro Linguistic Programming*. Moab, Utah: Real People Press.

Barber, Benjamin R. 1995, 2001. *Jihad vs. McWorld: Terrorism's challenge to democracy*. New York: Ballentine Books.

Barrow, John D. 1992. *Pi in the sky: Counting, thinking, being*. New York: Oxford University Press.

Barzun. Jacques. 2000. *From dawn to decadence: 500 years of Western cultural life 1500 to the present*. New York: HarperCollins.

Baum, Archie. 1958. *Tao Te Ching by Lao Tse: Interpreted as nature and intelligence*. New York: Frederick Unger Publishing Co.

Beattie, Paul H. 1985/86. The religion of secular humanism. *Free Inquiry* 6 (1): 12-17.

Berman, Sanford I. 1989. *Logic and general semantics: Writings of Oliver L. Reiser and others*. San Francisco, CA: International Society for General Semantics.

————. 1969. *Why do we jump to conclusions?* Concord, CA: International Society for General Semantics.

Berra, Yogi with Dave Kaplan. 2001. *When you come to a fork in the road, take it!: Inspiration and wisdom from one of baseball's greatest heroes*. New York: Hyperion.

Bickerton, Derek. 1990. *Language & species*. Chicago: U of Chicago Press.

Black, Max. 1969. *The labyrinth of language*. New York: Mentor.

————. 1949. *Language and philosophy: Studies in method*. Ithaca, NY: Cornell University Press.

Blake, William. 1946. Selected and arranged by Alfred Kazin. 1946. *The portable Blake*. New York: Viking Press.

Block, J. Richard and Harold E. Yuker. 1992. *Can you believe your eyes?: Over 250 illusions and other visual oddities.* New York: Brunner/Mazel.

Blumenthal, Jacob. The abortion controversy: Jewish religious rights and responsibilities. *United Synagogue of Conservative Judaism*. Available at http://uscj.org/ Enter "abortion" in search engine.

Bois, J. Samuel, ed. by Gary David. 1966,1996. *The art of awareness: A handbook on general semantics and epistemics*. Fourth Edition. Santa Monica, CA: Continuum Press & Productions.

————. 1957. *Explorations in awareness.* San Francisco: International Society for General Semantics.

Boston, Robert. 1993. *Why the religious right is wrong: About separation of church & state.* Buffalo, NY: Prometheus Books.

Bourland, D. David and Paul Dennithorn Johnston, eds. 1991. *To be or not: An E-Prime anthology*. San Francisco: International Society for General Semantics.

Bower, Bruce. 2002. Evolutionary upstarts: Theoretical alternatives blossom in the garden of evolved minds. *Science News* 162 (12) Sept. 21: 186-188.

Brian, Denis. 1995. *Genius talk: Conversations with Nobel scientists and other luminaries*. New York: Plenum Press.

Bronowski, J. 1973. *The ascent of man*. Boston/Toronto: Little, Brown and Co.

Brooks, Charles V.W. 1974. *Sensory awareness: The rediscovery of experiencing.* New York: The Viking Press.

Brunning, Gerald J. 1987. *Top secret*. Thaxton, VA: Sun Life.

Buber, Martin. 1970. (trans. by Walter Kaufmann.) *I and thou*. New York: Scribners.

Budd, Matthew and Larry Rothstein. 2000. *You are what you say: A Harvard doctor's six-step proven program for transforming stress through the power of language*. New York: Crown.

Bullock, Alan. 1985. *The humanist tradition in the west*. London: Thames and Hudson.

Bunge, Mario. 1980. *The mind-body problem: a psychobiological approach*. Oxford, UK: Pergamon Press.

Burger, A. J., ed. 2001. *The ethics of belief: Essays by William Kingdon Clifford, William James, A. J. Burger*. Roseville, CA: Dry Bones Press, Inc. Also at http://ajburger.homestead.com/ethics.html

Calhoun, Don. 1957. The illusion of rationality. In *Life, language, and law: Essays in honor of Arthur F. Bentley*, ed. Richard W. Taylor, 155-167. Yellow Springs, OH: The Antioch Press.

Campbell, Joseph with Bill Moyers. 1988. *The power of myth*. Ed. Betty Sue Flowers. New York: Anchor Books.

Cantril, Hadley and Charles H. Bumstead. 1960. *Reflections on the human venture*. New York: New York University Press.

Caro, Isabel and Charlotte Schuchardt Read, eds. 2002. *General Semantics in psychotherapy: Selected writings on methods aiding therapy*. Brooklyn, NY: Institute of General Semantics.

Carroll, Lewis. 1965. *The works of Lewis Carrol*. Ed. Roger Lancelyn Green. London: Paul Hamlyn, Ltd.

Cassirer, Ernst. 1944. *An essay on man*. New Haven, CT: Yale University Press.

Chalmers, David J. 2002. The puzzle of conscious experience. *Scientific American, Special edition-The hidden mind* 12 (1): 90-100.

Chronology of Alfred Korzybski's Life. In *Alfred Korzybski Collected Writings*, 907-908.

Churchland, Patricia Smith. 1986. *Neurophilosophy: Toward a unified science of the mind/brain*. Cambridge, MA: The MIT Press.

Cialdini, Robert B. 1985. *Influence: Science and practice*. Glenview, IL: Scott, Foresman and Company.

Cohen, Edmond D. 1986, 1988. *The mind of the Bible-believer*. Buffalo, NY: Prometheus Books.

Comment: Alfred Korzybski. 1950. *The American Journal of Psychiatry* 106 (11). Reproduced in *General Semantics Bulletin* 3: 32.

Corben, Herbert C. 1991. *The struggle to understand: A history of human wonder & discovery*. Buffalo, NY: Prometheus Books.

Crick, Francis. 1994a. *The astonishing hypothesis: The scientific search for the soul*. New York: Scribner.

————. 1994b. "Francis Crick on the Workings of the Brain." *Free Inquiry* 14 (4): 18-21.

Csikszentmihalyi, Mihalyi. 1993. *The evolving self: A psychology for the third millennium*. New York: HarperCollins.

————. 1990. *Flow: The psychology of optimal experience*. New York: Harper Perennial.

Cziko, Gary. 2000. *The things we do: Using the lessons of Bernard and Darwin to understand the what, how, and why of our behavior*. Cambridge, MA: MIT Press.

Daly, Theodore P. 1980. Manhood of humanity (an imaginative interpretation). *General Semantics Bulletin* 47: 82-83.

Damasio, Antonio R. 1999. *The feeling of what happens: Body and emotions in the making of consciousness.* San Diego, CA: Harvest/Harcourt, Inc.

———. 1994. *Descartes' error: Emotion, reason, and the human brain.* New York: Avon Books.

Davis, Philip J. and Reuben Hersh. 1986. *Descartes' dream: The world according to mathematics.* Boston: Houghton Mifflin.

Dawes, Milton. 1996/1997. An approach to everyday living: A note regarding the calculus. *ETC:. (Et Cetera) A Review of General Semantics* 53 (4): 406-412. A version of this available at http://dfwcgs.net/milton/md_calc.html

Dawood, N. J., trans. 1974. *The Koran.* Hammondsworth, UK: Penguin.

Derry, Gregory Neil. 1999. *What science is and how it works.* Princeton, NJ: Princeton UP.

Dewey, John and Arthur F. Bentley. 1949. *Knowing and the known.* Boston: Beacon Press.

Diamond, Jared. 1999. *Guns, germs, and steel: The fates of human societies.* New York: W. W. Norton.

Doerr, Edd and James W. Prescott. eds. 1989, 1990. *Abortion rights and fetal 'personhood'.* Second Ed. Long Beach, CA: Centerline Press.

Dugatkin, Lee Alan. 2001. *The imitation factor: Evolution beyond the gene.* New York: Simon & Schuster.

Durant, Will. 1926, 1954. *The story of philosophy: The lives and opinions of the great philosophers.* Second Ed. New York: Simon and Schuster.

Eccles, John and Daniel W. Robinson. 1985. *The wonder of being human: Our brain and our mind.* Boston & London: Shambhala.

Edelman, Gerald M. 1992. *Bright air, brilliant fire.* New York: Basic Books.

Edwards, Paul. 1995 a. Freud. *The 1995 Prometheus Books Lecture Series.* (Personal Notes). New School for Social Research, New York City.

———. 1995 b. Reich. *The 1995 Prometheus Books Lecture Series.* (Personal Notes). New School for Social Research, New York City.

———. 1967. Reich, Wilhelm. In *The encyclopedia of philosophy.* Edited by Paul Edwards. Offprint. New York: The Macmillan Company & The Free Press.

Einstein, Albert. 2000. *Albert Einstein in his own words (Two complete books – Relativity and Out of my later years).* New York: Portland House.

Einstein, Albert and Leopold Infeld. 1938. *The Evolution of physics: The growth of ideas from early concepts to relativity and quanta.* New York: Simon and Schuster.

Elgin, Suzette Haden. 2000. *The language imperative.* Cambridge, MA: Perseus Publishing.

Ellis, Albert. 1996. *Better, deeper, and more enduring brief therapy: The Rational Emotive Behavior Therapy approach.* New York: Brunner/Mazel.

———. 1993 a. Are atheists really more psychologically disturbed than religionists? *Free Inquiry* 13 (3): 18-19.

————. 1993 b. General Semantics and Rational-Emotive Therapy. *General Semantics Bulletin* 58: 12-28.

————. 1988 a. *How to stubbornly refuse to make yourself miserable about anything yes anything!* Secaucus, NJ: Lyle Stuart Inc.

————. 1988 b. Is religiosity pathological? *Free Inquiry* 8 (2): 27-32.

————. 1968. *Is Objectivism a religion?* New York: Lyle Stuart.

Ellis, Albert and Robert A. Harper. 1975 (1961). *A new guide to rational living.* Hollywood, CA: Wilshire Book Co.

Ellis, Albert and Ted Crawford. 2000. *Making intimate connections: Seven guidelines for great relationships and better communication.* Atascadero, CA: Impact Publishers, Inc.

Epictetus. Trans. by Elizabeth Carter. *Enchiridion.* The Internet Classics Archive© by Daniel C. Stevenson. Available at http://classics.mit.edu/Epictetus/epicench.html

Epstein, Isidore. 1959. *Judaism.* Middlesex, England: Penguin.

Ericson, Edward L. 1985. *The free mind through the ages.* New York: Unger.

Erlich, Paul R. 2000. *Human natures: Genes, cultures, and the human prospect.* Washington, D.C.: Island Press/ Shearwater Books.

Erlich, Paul R. and Anne H. Erlich. 1990. *The population explosion.* New York: Simon and Schuster.

Erlich, Paul R. and Katherine Ellison. 2002. "A looming threat we won't face." *Los Angeles Times* Sunday, Jan. 20: M6.

Evans, Don. ed. 1999. *Humanism: Historical and contemporary perspectives.* Washington. D.C.: Washington Area Secular Humanists.

Feyerabend, Paul. Ed. by Bert Terpstra. 1999. *Conquest of abundance.* Chicago: The University of Chicago Press.

Fischbach, Gerald D. 1992. Mind and brain. *Scientific American* Sept., 1992: 48-59.

Fitzgerald, Edward. 1929. Rubaiyat of Omar Khayyam of Naishapur. In *British Poets of the nineteenth century,* 2d Ed. by Curtis Hidden Page and Stith Thompson. New York: Benj. H. Sanborn & Co.

Flagg, Allen. 1973. Actualizing our potentialities: Multiordinality for self-actualization and health. *General Semantics Bulletin* 38,39, 40: 104-118.

Flanagan, Dennis. 1988. *Flanagan's version: A spectators guide to science on the eve of the 21st Century.* New York: Alfred A. Knopf.

Fletcher, Joseph. 1979. *Humanhood: Essays in biomedical ethics.* Buffalo, NY: Prometheus Books.

————. 1974. *The ethics of genetic control: Ending reproductive roulette.* Garden City, NY: Anchor Books.

————. 1966. *Situation ethics: The new morality.* Philadelphia: Westminster.

Flower, Michael J. 1989, 1990. Neuromaturation and the moral status of human fetal life. In *Abortion rights and fetal 'personhood,* Second Ed., ed. Edd Doerr and James W. Prescott, 65-75. Long Beach, CA: Centerline Press.

Flynn, Tom. 1991/1992. "Pro-choice": Wrong turn for abortion rights? *Free Inquiry* 12 (1): 6-7.

Ford, Brian J. 1999. *The secret language of life: How animals and plants feel and communicate.* New York: Fromm International.

Frazier, Kendrick. 1998. A mind at play: An interview with Martin Gardner. *Skeptical Inquirer* 22 (2): 34-39.

French, James D. 2002. Editor's essay 2001. *General Semantics Bulletin* 65-68: 8-10.

———. 1993. The prime problem with general semantics. *ETC: A Review of General Semantics* 50 (3): 326-335.

Fromm, Erich. 1966. *Man for himself.* New York: Holt, Rinhart and Winston.

Gardner, Martin. 1983. *Order and surprise.* Buffalo, NY: Prometheus Books.

———. 1952, 1957. *Fads and fallacies in the name of science.* 2nd edition. New York: Dover.

Gelb, Michael J. 1998. *How to think like Leonardo da Vinci: Seven steps to genius everyday.* New York: Delacorte Press.

Gelwick, Richard. 1977. *The way of discovery: An introduction to the thought of Michael Polanyi.* New York: Oxford UP.

George, Henry. 1929 (1879). *Progress and poverty.* New York: The Modern Library.

Gilmore, Michael R. 1997. Einstein's God: Just what did Einstein believe about God? *Skeptic* 5 (2): 62-64. Available at www.skeptic.com/archives50.htm.

Gleick, James. 1987. *Chaos: making a new science.* New York: Viking Penguin.

Goicoechea, David, John Luik and Tim Madigan. Eds. 1991. *The question of humanism: Challenges and possibilities.* Buffalo, NY: Prometheus Books.

The Golden Rule. http://www.fragrant.demon.co.uk/golden.html

Goodall, Jane. 1986. *The Chimpanzees of Gombe: Patterns of behavior.* Cambridge, MA: Harvard UP.

Goodman, Paul. 1962. *The society I live in is mine.* New York: Horizon Books.

Gorman, Margaret. 1962. *General Semantics and contemporary Thomism.* Lincoln, NE: University of Nebraska Press.

Gould, Stephen Jay. 1999. *Rocks of ages: Science and religion in the fullness of life. (Library of Contemporary Thought).* New York: Ballantine Books.

Gregory, R. L. with the assistance of O. L. Zangwill. 1987. *The Oxford companion to the mind.* New York: Oxford UP.

Gregory, Richard L. 1987. Benham's Top. In *The Oxford companion to the mind*, 78-79.

Haack, Susan. 1997. "The first rule of reason." In *The rule of reason: The philosophy of Charles Sanders Peirce*, ed. Jacqueline Brunning and Paul Forster, 241-261. Toronto: University of Toronto Press.

Hadas, Moses. 1960. *Humanism: The Greek ideal and its survival.* New York: Harper.

Haney, William V. 1986. *Communication and interpersonal relations: Text and cases.* Fifth Edition. The Irwin Series in Management and the Behavioral Sciences. Homewood, IL: Irwin.

———. 1961/1962. The uncritical inference test—applications. *General Semantics Bulletin* 28 & 29: 26.

———. 1955. Measurement of the ability to discriminate between inferential and descriptive statements: Precis of a doctoral thesis, Northwestern University, 1953. *General Semantics Bulletin* 16 & 17: 49-51.

Hanna, Thomas, ed. 1979. *Explorers of humankind.* San Francisco: Harper & Row.

Hardin, Garrett. 1993. *Living within limits: Ecology, economics, and population taboos.* New York: Oxford UP.

———. 1985. *Filters against folly: How to survive despite economists, ecologists, and the merely eloquent.* New York: Viking.

———. 1982 a. Biological insights into abortion. In *Naked emperors,* 131-147.

———. 1982 b. Conservation's secret question. In *Naked emperors,* 190-195.

———. 1982 c. Ecology and the death of providence. In *Naked emperors,* 147-159.

———. 1982 d. *Naked emperors: Essays of a taboo-stalker.* Los Altos, CA: William Kaufmann.

———. 1978a. Abortion–or compulsory pregnancy. In *Stalking the wild taboo,* 28-40.

———. 1978b. *Stalking the wild taboo. Second Edition.* Los Altos, CA: William Kaufmann.

———. 1977. Ethical implications of carrying capacity. In *Managing the commons,* 112-125. Hardin, Garrett and John Baden, eds. San Francisco: W. H. Freeman and Company.

Hauser, Ernst A. 1950. Korzybski's relation to colloid chemistry. *General Semantics Bulletin* 4 & 5, pp. 6-8. Available at http://www.general-semantics.org

Hentoff, Nat. A pro-life atheist civil libertarian. *Free Inquiry* 21(4): 16-17.

Hobson, J. Allan. 1999. *Consciousness.* New York: Scientific American Library.

Hoffer, Eric. 1951. *The true believer.* New York: Perennial Library.

Hoffman, Donald D. 1998. *Visual intelligence: How we create what we see.* New York: Norton.

Holton, Gerald. 1998 a. Einstein's model for constructing a scientific theory. In *The advancement of science and its burdens,* 28-56.

———. 1998 b. *The advancement of science and its burdens.* Cambridge, MA: Harvard University Press.

Hook, Sidney. 1985/1986. Pluralistic humanism. *Free Inquiry* 6 (1): 19-20.

———. 1973. The snare of definitions. In *The humanist alternative,* ed. Paul Kurtz, 31-34. Buffalo: Prometheus Books.

———. 1934. The nature of discourse. *Saturday Review of Literature* 10 (March 10): 546-547.

Horgan, John. 1996. *The end of science: Facing the limits of knowledge in the twilight of the scientific age.* Reading, MA: Addison Wesley.

———. 1999. *The undiscovered mind: How the brain defies replication, medication and explanation.* New York: Free Press.

Humanist Manifesto I, 1933. In *The philosophy of humanism* Seventh Edition, Revised and Enlarged (1990), Corliss Lamont, 285-289. New York: Continuum/Unger.

Hume, David. Ed. by Anthony Flew.1988. *An enquiry concerning human understanding*. La Salle, IL: Open Court.

Ibn Warraq. 1995. *Why I am not a Muslim.* Amherst, NY: Prometheus Books.

Ingersoll, Robert G. 1944. *Ingersoll's greatest lectures: containing speeches and addresses never before printed outside of the complete works*. Authorized Edition. New York: The Freethought Press Association.

Innaiah, N. and G. R. R. Babu.1994. *The humanist way*. Chirala, India: Hema Publications.

James, William. 1896, 1963. The will to believe. In *Pragmatism and other essays*, 193-213. New York: Washington Square Press.

Janssen, Guthrie E. 1951. Time-binding: Functional basis of democracy. *General Semantics Bulletin* 6 &7: 25-30.

Jaworski, Patricia. 1989, 1990. Thinking about *The Silent Scream: an audio documentary*. In *Abortion rights and fetal 'personhood,* Second Ed., ed. Edd Doerr and James W. Prescott, 55-63. Long Beach, CA: Centerline Press.

Johnson, Kenneth G., ed. 1992. *Graduate research in general semantics*, Revised Edition. Englewood, NJ: Institute of General Semantics.

————, ed. 1991. *Thinking creatically: A systematic, interdisciplinary approach to creative-critical thinking*. Englewood, NJ.

————. 1991. Harnessing self-reflexiveness for creatical thinking. In *Thinking creatically*, 3-16.

————. 1986. What research tells us about the effects of general semantics teaching. *General Semantics Bulletin* 53: 48-56.

————. 1984. Korzybski on research: Suggestions from *Science and Sanity*. *General Semantics Bulletin* 51: 43-59.

————. 1982. Self-reflexiveness in therapy and education. In *General Semantics Bulletin* 48: 84-94. Lakeville, CT (Now Brooklyn, NY): Institute of General Semantics.

Johnson, Wendell. 1946, 1989. *People in quandaries*. San Francisco: International Society for General Semantics.

Johnson, Wendell with Dorothy Moeller. 1972. *Living with change: The semantics of coping*. New York: Harper & Row.

Jordan, Stuart. 1999. Science and secular humanism. In Don Evans, ed. *Humanism: Historical and contemporary perspectives* 17-28. Washington, D.C.: Washington Area Secular Humanists.

Juge, Ron. 1997. Letter to the editor. *General Semantics Bulletin* 64:104.

Kant, Immanuel. 1997 (1784) Was ist Äufklarung? (What is Enlightenment?). Modern History Sourcebook.© Paul Halsall. Available at http://www.fordham.edu/halsall/mod/kant-whatis.html

Kaplan, Mordecai. 1994 (1934). *Judaism as a civilization: Toward a reconstruction of American Jewish life*. Philadelphia: Jewish Publication Society.

Kaufmann, Walter. 1976. *Existentialism, religion and death: Thirteen essays.* New York: Meridian/New American Library.

———. 1974. *Nietzsche: Philosopher, psychologist, antichrist.* Fourth Edition. Princeton, NJ: Princeton University Press.

———. 1973. *Without guilt and justice: From decidophobia to autonomy.* New York: Peter H. Wyden, Inc./Publisher.

Kay, Paul and Willett Kempton. 1984. What is the Sapir-Whorf hypothesis? *American Anthropologist* 86 (1) March.

Kelly, George A. 1955, 1963. *A theory of personality: The psychology of personal constructs.* New York: W. W. Norton & Company.

Kempton, Willett. 1991. Whorf and color. *Lingua List* Newsgroup 2.700 Oct. http://www.umich.edu/~archive/linguistics/linguist.list/volume.2/no.651-700

Kendig, M. [Marjorie Mercer]. 1950 a. A memoir: Alfred Korzybski & his work. In *Manhood of humanity*, Korzybski, xvii-xxxix.

———. 1950 b. Book comments. *General Semantics Bulletin* 1 & 2: 46.

Kendig, M., ed. 1943. *Papers from the Second American Congress on General Semantics, University of Denver, August, 1941: Non-aristotelian methodology (applied) for sanity in our time.* Chicago: Institute of General Semantics.

Klein Halevi, Yossi. 2002. Islam's outdated domination theology. *Los Angeles Times.* Commentary, Wed. Dec. 4. 2002, B 13.

Klemke, E. D. 1981a. Living without appeal: An affirmative philosophy of life. In *The meaning of Life*, ed. E. D. Klemke, 162-174.

———. 1981b. *The meaning of life.* New York: Oxford UP.

Klemke, E. D., Robert Hollinger, A. David Kline, eds. 1988. *Philosophy of science.* Revised Edition. Buffalo: Prometheus Books.

Kodish, Bruce I. 2001. *Back pain solutions: How to help yourself with posture-movement therapy and education.* Pasadena, CA: Extensional Publishing.

———. 1997 a. Evaluating abortion: A general-semantics analysis. *General Semantics Bulletin* 64: 96-101.

———. 1997 b. Contra Max Black: An examination of critiques of general-semantics. *General Semantics Bulletin* 64: 24-44.

Kodish, Susan Presby and Bruce I. Kodish. 2001. *Drive yourself sane: Using the uncommon sense of general semantics.* Pasadena, CA: Extensional Publishing.

———. 1995. Fuzzy logic and general semantics in everyday life. *General Semantics Bulletin* 62: 16-22.

Kodish, Susan Presby and Robert P. Holsten, eds. 1998. *Developing sanity in human affairs.* Contributions to the study of mass media and communications, number 54. Westport, CT: Greenwood Press.

Korner, S. 1972. Laws of thought. In *The encyclopedia of philosophy, Vol. 4.*, ed. Paul Edwards, 414-417. New York: Macmillan.

Korzybski, Alfred. 2002 (1937). *General Semantics seminar 1937: Transcription of notes from lectures in general semantics given at Olivet College*. Third Edition, edited by Homer J. Moore. Brooklyn, NY: Institute of General Semantics.

————. 1994 (1933). *Science & sanity: An introduction to non-aristotelian systems and general semantics*. Fifth Edition. Preface by Robert P. Pula. Brooklyn, NY: Institute of General Semantics.

————. 1990 a. *Collected writings: 1920-1950*. (Collected and arranged by M. Kendig. Final editing and preparation for printing by Charlotte Schuchardt Read with the assistance of Robert P. Pula.) Brooklyn, NY: Institute of General Semantics.

————. 1990 b. What I believe. In *Collected writings*, 645-663.

————. 1990 c. Time-binding and human potentialities: A lecture by Alfred Korzybski. In *Collected writings*, 625-633.

————. 1950 (1921). *Manhood of humanity*. Second edition. Brooklyn, NY: Institute of General Semantics.

————. 1948/1949. *Intensive seminar*. Audio tapes, unedited. 37 hours, recorded Dec. 27, 1948-Jan 2, 1949. Brooklyn, NY: Institute of General Semantics.

————. 1947 a. *Biographical material*. Recorded by Kenneth Keyes, July 1947. Transcribed by Roberta Rymer Keyes. Indexed by Robert P. Pula. Unpublished.

————. 1947 b. Mathematical method as a way of life. 1947 lecture at Columbia University. Transcription of a tape recording. Unpublished.

Kosko, Bart. 1993. *Fuzzy thinking: The new science of fuzzy logic*. New York: Hyperion.

Kramer, Joel and Diana Alstad. 1993. *The guru papers: Masks of authoritarian power*. Berkeley, CA: Frog, Ltd., North Atlantic Books.

Krassner, Paul. *Impolite interviews*. New York: Seven Stories Press.

Kuhn, Thomas S. 1988. Objectivity, value judgement, and theory choice. In Klemke, Hollinger and Kline, 277-291.

————. 1979. *The structure of scientific revolutions*. Second Edition, Enlarged. International Encyclopedia of Unified Science, 2 (2). Chicago: The University of Chicago Press.

Kurtz, Paul. 2000. On entering the third decade: Personal reminiscence: A humanistic journey. *Free Inquiry* 20(2).

————. 1994 a. *Living without religion*. Buffalo, NY: Prometheus Books.

————. 1994 b. *Toward a new enlightenment: The philosophy of Paul Kurtz*. New Brunswick, NJ: Transaction Publishers.

————. 1992/1993. Remembering John Dewey: America's leading humanist philosopher. *Free Inquiry* 13 (1): 16-18.

————. 1992. *The new skepticism: Inquiry and reliable knowledge*. Buffalo, NY: Prometheus Books.

————. 1991 a. *The transcendental temptation*. Buffalo, NY: Prometheus Books.

————. 1991 b. The two humanisms in conflict: Religious vs. secular. *Free Inquiry* 11 (4): 49-51.

―――. 1990. *Philosophical essays in pragmatic naturalism.* Buffalo, NY: Prometheus Books.

―――. 1989. Libertarianism or socialism: Where do secular humanists stand? *Free Inquiry* 9 (4): 4.

―――. 1988. *Forbidden fruit.* Buffalo, NY: Prometheus Books.

Kurtz, Paul, ed. 1973. *The humanist alternative.* Buffalo, NY: Prometheus Books.

Kurtz, Paul and Timothy J. Madigan. 1989. Eupraxophy, ethics, and secular humanism. *Free Inquiry* 9 (2): 4-5.

Kurtz, Paul and Timothy J. Madigan, eds. 1994. *Challenges to the enlightenment: In defense of reason and science.* Buffalo, NY: Prometheus Books.

Lakoff, George. 1996. *Moral politics: What conservatives know that liberals don't.* Chicago: University of Chicago Press.

―――. 1987. *Women, fire, and dangerous things: What categories reveal about the mind.* Chicago: University of Chicago Press.

Lakoff, George and Mark Johnson. 1999. *Philosophy in the flesh: The embodied mind and its challenge to western thought.* New York: Basic Books.

―――. 1980. *Metaphors we live by.* Chicago: University of Chicago Press.

Lamb, Sydney M. 2000. Neuro-cognitive structure in the interplay of language and thought. In *Explorations in linguistic relativity*, Edited by M. Pütz and M. Verspoor. Amsterdam/Philadelphia: John Benjamins Publishing Company. Also available at http://www.ruf.rice.edu/~lamb/lt.htm.

―――. 1998. *Pathways of the brain: The neurocognitive basis of language.* Amsterdam/Philadelphia: John Benjamins Publishing Company.

Lamont, Corliss. 1949, 1990. *The philosophy of humanism.* Seventh Edition, Revised and Enlarged. New York: Continuum/Unger.

Langer, Ellen J. 2002. Creativity and the evolution of culture. *General Semantics Bulletin* 65-68: 31- 42.

―――. 1989. *Mindfulness.* Reading, MA: Addison-Wesley.

Larson, Edward J. and Larry Witham. 1999. Scientists and religion in America. *Scientific American* 281 (3): 88-93.

Laurent, John. 1999. A note on the origin of meme/mnemes. *Journal of Memetics - Evolutionary Models of Information Transmission*, 3. Also at http://jom-emit.cfpm.org/1999/vol3/laurent_j.html

Lec, Stanislaw J., trans. by Jacek Galazka. *Unkempt thoughts.* Available at http://www.geocities.com/Athens/Forum/5344/lit/lecengl.html

Lee, Irving J. 1949/1950. On the varieties of research in general semantics. *General Semantics Bulletin* 1 & 2: 10-16.

―――. 1941. *Language habits in human affairs.* New York: Harper & Brothers. Second edition 1994. Edited by Sanford I. Berman. Concord, CA: International Society for General Semantics.

Lee, Penny. 1997. Language in thinking and learning: Pedagogy and the new whorfian framework. *Harvard Educational Review* Fall 1997: 430-471. Cambridge, MA.

———. 1996. *The whorf theory complex: A critical reconstruction.* Amsterdam/ Philadelphia: John Benjamins Publishing Company.

Lennon, John. 1970. God. *Plastic Ono Band.*

Lester, Toby. 1999. What is the Koran? *The Atlantic Monthly* 283 (1): 43-56. available at www.theatlantic.com

Lewin, Roger. 1992. *Complexity: Life at the edge of chaos.* New York:Macmillan Publishing Company.

Lewis, Steven. 1995. Jacques Loeb's influence on Korzybski. http://www. kcmetro. cc. mo.us/pennvalley/biology/lewis/loeb.htm

Lewontin, R. C., Steven Rose and Leon J. Kamin. *Not in our genes: Biology, ideology, and human nature.* 1984. New York: Pantheon Books.

Lichtenberg, Georg Christoph. (trans. and ed. Franz H. Mautner and Henry Hatfield.) 1959. *The Lichtenberg reader: Selected writings of Georg Christoph Lichtenberg.* Boston: Beacon Press.

Lieber, Lillian R., drawings by Hugh Gray Lieber. 1942. *The education of T.C. MITS (The celebrated man in the street): What modern mathematics means to you.* New York: W. W. Norton & Company, Inc.

Livingstone. Ken. 2001/2002. Reason, faith, and the good life: Does strong doubt permeate good health? *Free Inquiry* 22 (1): 42-47.

Lukasiewicz, Jan. 1967. On the history of the logic of propositions. In *Polish logic: 1920-1939,* edited by Storrs McCall, 66-87. London: Oxford University Press.

Mackie, J. L. 1982. *The miracle of theism: Arguments for and against the existence of god.* Oxford, UK: Oxford University Press.

MacNeal, Edward. 1994. *Mathsemantics: Making numbers talk sense.* New York: Viking Penguin.

Madigan, Timothy J. 1992/1993. John Dewey and *A Common Faith. Free Inquiry* 13 (1): 24-25.

———. 1991. Afterword: The answer of humanism. In *The questions of humanism,* ed. by Goicoechea. Luik and Madigan, 326-338.

———. 1989/1990. Moral education and critical thinking: The humanist perspective. *Free Inquiry* 10 (1): 4.

Magee, Bryan. 2001. *The story of philosophy.* New York: DK Publishing Inc.

———. 1997. *Confessions of a philosopher: A personal journey through western philosophy from Plato to Popper.* New York: The Modern Library.

———. 1987. *The great philosophers: An introduction to western philosophy.* Oxford, UK: Oxford University Press.

Maloney, Martin. 1956. How to avoid an idea. *Etc.: A Review of General Semantics.* XII (3): 214-224.

Marinoff, Lou. 2002. *Philosophical practice.* San Diego, CA: Academic Press.

————. 1999. *Plato, not Prozac: Applying philosophy to everyday problems.* New York: HarperCollins.

Marken, Richard S. 1992. *Mind readings: Experimental studies of purpose.* Chapel Hill, NC: Control Systems Group/New View Publications.

Marks, Robert W. 1964. *The new mathematics dictionary and handbook.* New York: Bantam Books.

Martin, Laura. 1986. Eskimo words for snow: A case study in the genesis and decay of an anthropological example. *American Anthropologist* 88 (June): 418-423.

Martin, Michael. 1996. *The big domino in the sky: And other atheistic tales.* Amherst, NY: Prometheus Books.

Maslow, Abraham H. 1968. *Toward a psychology of being.* Second Edition. New York: Van Nostrand Reinhold.

————. 1954. *Motivation and personality.* New York: Harper & Brothers.

Maturana, Humberto R. and Francisco J. Varela. 1987. *The tree of knowledge: The biological roots of human understanding.* Boston: Shambhala Publications, Inc.

Mayper, Stuart A. 1990. Reforming the language. *General Semantics Bulletin* 55: 19-23.

————. 1988/1989. General Semantics as a religion? *General Semantics Bulletin* 54: 9-12.

————. 1984. Korzybski's science and today's science. *General Semantics Bulletin* 51: 61-67.

————. 1984. Wu Li thinking about physics. *General Semantics Bulletin* 51: 68-82.

————. 1980. The place of aristotlelian logic in non-aristotelian evaluating: Einstein, Korzybski, and Popper. *General Semantics Bulletin* 46: 106-110.

————. 1962. Non-aristotelian foundations: solid or fluid? *Etc.: A Review of General Semantics* 18: 427-443.

McCrone, John. 1999. *Going inside: A tour round a single moment of consciousness.* New York: Fromm International.

McNeill, Daniel and Paul Freiberger. 1993. *Fuzzy logic: The discovery of a revolutionary computer technology—and how it is changing our world.* New York: Simon & Schuster.

McNeill, David and Susan D. Duncan. 1998. Growth points in thinking-for-speaking. *Cogprints* at http://cogprints.ecs.soton.ac.uk/archive/00000664/

Meerloo, Joost A. M. 1956. *The rape of the mind: The psychology of thought control, menticide, and brainwashing.* Cleveland, OH: The World Publishing Company.

Merejkowski, Dmitri., trans. Bernard Guilbert Guerney. 1928. *The romance of Leonardo Da Vinci: The gods resurgent.* New York: Random House.

Mill, John Stuart. Edited by Alburey Castell. 1947. *On liberty.* New York: Appleton-Century Crofts, Inc.

Miller, Casey and Kate Swift. 1976. *Words and women: New language in new times.* Garden City, New York: Anchor Press/Doubleday.

Miller, Richmond P. 1955. What is a quaker? In *Religions of america,* ed. Leo Rosten, 121-132.

Minkel, J.R. 2002. A Way with words. www.scientificamerican.com/explorations/2002/032502language/

Minnich, Elizabeth Kamark. 1990. *Transforming knowledge*. Philadelphia: Temple University Press.

Montagu, Ashley. 1981. *Growing young*. New York: McGraw-Hill Book Company.

———. 1980. *Sociobiology examined*. New York: Oxford University Press.

———. 1971, 1979. *The elephant man: A study in human dignity*. Second Edition. New York: E. P. Dutton.

———. 1955. *Immortality*. New York: Grove Press.

———. 1953. On time-binding and the concept of culture. *General Semantics Bulletin* 12 & 13: 9-16.

———. 1951 a. *On being human*. New York: Henry Schuman.

———. 1951 b. *On being intelligent*. Westport, CT: Greenwood Press.

Montaigne, Michel Eyquem de. Trans. and ed., Donald M. Frame. 1943. *Selections from the essays*. Arlington Heights, IL: Crofts Classics/Harlan Davidson.

Moore, David S. 2001. *The dependent gene: The fallacy of "nurture vs. nature."* New York: Henry Holt.

Moore, John A. 1993. *Science as a way of knowing: The foundations of modern biology*. Cambridge, MA: Harvard University Press.

Morain, Lloyd and Mary Morain. 1954,1998. *Humanism as the next step*. New Revised Edition. Amherst, NY: Humanist Press.

Morain, Mary, ed. 1980. *Classroom exercises in general semantics*. San Francisco: International Society for General Semantics.

———. 1969, 1977. *Teaching general semantics: A collection of lesson plans for college and adult classes*. San Francisco: International Society for General Semantics.

Mordkowitz, Jeffrey A. 1990. Korzybski, colloids and molecular biology. *General Semantics Bulletin* 55: 86-89. Available at http://www.general-semantics.org

———. 1985. Listener's guide to Alfred Korzybski's 1948-49 seminar. *General Semantics Bulletin* 52: 51-76.

Morris, Charles. 1946. *Signs, language and behavior*. New York: Prentice-Hall.

Murray, Stephen O. 1987. Snowing canonical texts. *American Anthropologist* 89 (June): 443-444.

Nadler, Steven. 1999. *Spinoza: A life*. Cambridge, UK: Cambridge University Press.

Nagel, Ernest. 1934 a. Untitled review of *Science and Sanity*. *Journal of Philosophy* 31: 80-81.

———. 1934 b. Untitled review of *Science and Sanity*. *New Republic* 80: 327.

Niebuhr, Gustav. 1994. Pious in public and proud of it. *New York Times* Dec. 4: 6E.

Nielsen, Kai. 1985. *Philosophy and atheism*. Buffalo, NY: Prometheus Books.

Nietzsche, Friedrich. ed. and trans. by R. J. Hollingdale. 1977. *A Nietzsche reader*. New York: Penguin.

————. ed. and trans. by Walter Kaufmann. 1974. *The gay science.* New York: Vintage.

————. 1954. *The portable Nietzsche.* ed. and trans. Walter Kaufmann. New York: Penguin.

Northrop, F. S. C. 1955. Mathematical physics and Korzybski's semantics. *General Semantics Bulletin* 16 & 17: 7-14.

————. 1949. *The logic of the sciences and the humanities.* New York: The Macmillan Company.

————. 1946. *The meeting of east and west: An inquiry concerning world understanding.* New York: The Macmillan Company.

Nurses for Community Education. Undated. *All about you.* (pamphlet) Cincinnati, OH.

O'Neal, Daniel. 2001/2002. No dog tags for atheists: Now, where's my foxhole? *Free Inquiry* 22 (1): 58.

Oren, Michael. Sept., 2002. The Camp David war, in Special supplement on naming a war. *Jerusalem Post Internet Edition,* www.jpost.com

Parikh, Indumati. 1994. Humanism - Need of the third world (with special reference to the Indian subcontinent). in *The Humanist Way,* ed. by N. Innaiah and G. R. R. Babu, 13-22. Chirala, India: Hema Publications.

Paulos, John Allen. 1991. *Beyond numeracy: Ruminations of a numbers man.* New York: Vintage.

————. 1988. *Innumeracy: Mathematical illiteracy and its consequences.* New York: Vintage.

————. 1985. *I think, therefore I laugh: An alternative approach to philosophy.* New York: Vintage.

Paulson, Ross Evans. 1983. *Language, science, and action: Korzybski's general semantics—a study in comparative intellectual history.* (Contributions in Intercultural and Comparative Studies, No. 9.) Westport, CT: Greenwood.

Peat, F. David. 1997. *Infinite potential: The life and times of David Bohm.* Reading, MA: Helix Books/Addison-Wesley.

Pecker, Jean-Claude. 1994. From Aristotle to the new age. In *Challenges,* ed. by Kurtz and Madigan, 144-156.

Peter, Laurence J. 1977. *Peter's quotations: Ideas for our time.* New York: Quill/ William Morrow.

Pinker, Steven. 1997. *How the mind works.* New York: W. W. Norton.

————. 1994. *The language instinct: How the mind creates language.* New York: Morrow.

Pipes, Daniel. 2002. *Militant Islam reaches America.* New York: Norton.

Planned Parenthood. Abortion after the first trimester. Available at http:// www.plannedparenthood.org/library/facts/abotaft1st_010600.html

Polanyi, Michael. 1966. *The tacit dimension.* Garden City, NY: Doubleday.

————. 1962 (1958). *Personal knowledge: Towards a post-critical philosophy.* New York: Harper & Row.

Pope cautions Jesuits against straying from dogma. 1995. *Baltimore Sun* Jan. 6: 7A.

Popper, Karl R. 1976. *Unended quest: An intellectual autobiography.* Glasgow: Fontana/Collins.

————. 1968 (1959). *The logic of scientific discovery* (first edition published as Logik der Forschung in 1934). New York: Harper Torchbooks.

————. 1966 (1943) a. *The open society and its enemies: Volume I – The spell of Plato.* Fifth Edition, Revised. Princeton, NJ: Princeton University Press.

————. 1966 (1943) b. *The open society and its enemies: Volume II – The high tide of prophecy: Hegel, Marx, and the aftermath.* Fifth Edition, Revised. Princeton, NJ: Princeton University Press.

————. 1965 (1963). *Conjectures and refutations: The growth of scientific knowledge.* New York: Harper Torchbooks.

Popper, Karl R. and John C. Eccles.1977, 1981.*The self and its brain.* Berlin: Springer International.

Powers, William T. 1998. *Making sense of behavior: The meaning of control.* New Canaan, CT: Benchmark Publications.

Presby, Susan. 1982. General semantics and the process of psychotherapeutic exchange. *General Semantics Bulletin* 49: 115-123.

Prigogine, Ilya and Isabelle Stengers. 1984. *Order out of chaos: Man's new dialogue with nature.* New York: Bantam Books.

Pula, Robert P. Contra-Korzybski: An evaluation of Margaret Gorman's *General Semantics and Contemporary Thomism.* In *Knowledge, Uncertainty and Courage* by Robert P. Pula. To be published. Brooklyn, NY: Institute of General Semantics.

————. 2000. *A General-Semantics glossary: Pula's guide for the perplexed.* Concord, CA: International Society for General Semantics.

————. 1998. . General-semantics and fuzzy logic/sets: Similarities and differences. In *Developing sanity in human affairs (Contributions to the study of mass media and communications, number 54).* Ed. Susan Presby Kodish and Robert P. Holston. Westport, CT: Greenwood Press. 82-95.

————. 1996. Alfred Korzybski, 1879-1950: A bio-methodological sketch. *Polish American studies: A journal of Polish American history and culture,* LIII (2): 57-105. Chicago: Polish American Historical Association.

————. 1994. Preface to the Fifth Edition, 1993. In *Science and sanity: An introduction to non-aristotelian systems and general semantics* by Alfred Korzybski. Fifth Ed. Brooklyn, NY: Institute of General Semantics.

————. 1979. Knowledge, uncertainty and courage: Heisenberg and Korzybski. *General Semantics Bulletin* 46: 10-25.

————. 1978. Change thinging. *General Semantics Bulletin* 44 & 45: 71.

Quartz, Steven R. and Terrence J. Sejnowski. 2002. *Liars, lovers, and heros: What the new brain science reveals about how we become who we are.* New York: William Morrow & Co.

Quine, W. V. 1987. *Quiddities: An intermittently philosophical dictionary.* Cambridge, MA: Harvard University Press.

Quine, W. V. and Yasuhiko Tomida. Interview between Willard Quine and Yasuhiko Tomida. Available at http://sortes.hs.h.kyotou.ac.jp/quine.html#qpragmatism

Radest, Howard B. 1990. *The devil and secular humanism: The children of the enlightenment.* New York: Praeger.

Rauch, Jonathan. 1993. *Kindly inquisitors: The new attacks on free thought.* Chicago: The University of Chicago Press.

Read, Allen Walker. 1986. General Semantics. In *Encyclopedic dictionary of semiotics,* ed. Thomas A. Sebeok. 280-282. Amsterdam: Mouton de Gruyter.

———. 1985. Language revision by deletion of absolutisms. *ETC.: A review of general semantics.* Spring 42 (1): 7-12. Available at http://general-semantics.org/

———. 1984. Changing attitudes toward Korzybski's general semantics. *General Semantics Bulletin* 51: 11-25.

Read, Charlotte Schuchardt. 1998. Living in an "as if" world: Some reflections on "the map is not the territory." In *Developing sanity in human affairs (Contributions to the study of mass media and communications, number 54).* Ed. Susan Presby Kodish and Robert P. Holston. Westport, CT: Greenwood Press. 71-76.

———. 1993. Review of *Flow: The psychology of optimal experience,* by Mihali Csikszentmihalyi. *General Semantics Bulletin* 57: 87-89.

———. 1990. *Alfred Habdank Skarbek Korzybski: A biographical sketch.* In *Korzybski collected writings,* 739-748.

———. 1988/89. The Institute of General Semantics: A brief historical survey. *General Semantics Bulletin* 54: 62-68.

———. 1965/1966. Exploring relations between organismic patterns and korzybskian formulations. *General Semantics Bulletin* 42: 7-12.

Reese, William L. 1999. *Dictionary of philosophy and religion: Eastern and western thought.* Expanded Edition. Amherst, NY: Humanity Books.

Reiser, Oliver L. 1958. *The integration of human knowledge: A study of the formal foundations and the social implications of unified science.* Boston: Porter Sargent Publisher.

———. 1940. *The promise of scientific humanism: Toward a unification of scientific, religious, social and economic thought.* New York: Oskar Piest.

Reiter, Jerry. 2000. *Live from the gates of hell: An insider's look at the anti-abortion underground.* Buffalo, NY: Prometheus Books.

Reports from the Institute: Intensive professional weekend seminar given by Douglas M. Kelley, M. D. 1951 *General Semantics Bulletin.* 6/7: 101.

Roethlesberger, F. J. ed. by George F. F. Lombard. 1977. *The elusive phenomena.* Boston: Division of Research, Graduate School of Business Administration, Harvard University.

Rokeach, Milton. 1960. *The open and closed mind: Investigations into the nature of belief systems and personality systems.* New York: Basic.

Rose, Hilary and Steven Rose, ed. 2000. *Alas, poor Darwin: Arguments against evolutionary psychology.* New York: Harmony Books/Random House.

Rose, Steven. 1997. *Lifelines: Biology beyond determinism.* New York: Oxford UP.

———. 1992. *The making of memory.* New York: Anchor Books.

Rossi, Alice S., ed. 1973. *The feminist papers: From Adams to de Beauvoir.* New York: Bantam Books.

Rosten, Leo. 1972. *Leo Rosten's treasury of Jewish quotations.* New York: Bantam Books.

———. 1968. *The joys of Yiddish.* New York: McGraw-Hill.

Rosten, Leo, ed. 1955. *Religions of america.* New York: Simon and Schuster.

Rothman, Tony and George Sudarshan. 1998. *Doubt and certainty.* Reading, MA: Helix Books.

Rukeyser, Muriel. 1942. *Willard Gibbs.* Garden City, NY: Doubleday, Doran & Co., Inc.

Runkel, Phillip J. 1990. *Casting nets and testing specimens: Two grand methods of psychology.* New York: Praeger.

Russell, Bertrand, (eds., Barry Feinberg and Ronald Kasrils). 1969. *Dear Bertrand Russell...: A selection of his correspondence with the general public 1950-1968.* Boston: Houghton Mifflin Company.

———. ed. Paul Foulkes. 1959. *Wisdom of the west.* New York: Crescent Books.

———. 1957. *Why I am not a Christian: And other essays on religion and related subjects.* New York: Simon and Schuster.

———. 1955. What is an agnostic? In Rosten, ed. 1955, 149-165.

———. ed. Lester E. Denonn. 1952. *Bertrand Russell's dictionary of mind, matter and morals.* New York: Philosophical Library.

———. 1948. *Human knowledge: Its scope and limits.* New York: Simon and Schuster.

———. 1945. *A history of Western philosophy.* New York: Simon and Schuster.

Russell, Charles G. 1999. *Culture, language and behavior.* Concord, CA: International Society for General Semantics.

Russo, Nancy Felipe. 1992. Abortion and unwanted childbearing: The impact of Casey. *Psychology of women: Newsletter of Division 35, American Psychological Association* 19 (4): 1-4.

Sagan, Carl. 1996. *The demon-haunted world: Science as a candle in the dark.* New York: Random House.

Sagan, Carl and Ann Druyan. 1992. *Shadows of forgotten ancestors: A search for who we are.* New York: Random House.

Sampson, Geoffrey. 1997. *Educating Eve: The 'language instinct' debate.* London: Cassell.

Satriano, Richard. 1977. *Vitvan: An American master.* Baker, NV: School of the Natural Order.

Schick, Theodore Jr. 1995. Do extraordinary claims require extraordinary evidence? A reappraisal of a classic skeptic's axiom. *Skeptic* 3 (2): 30-33.

Schopenhauer, Arthur. David Berman, ed., Jill Berman, trans. 1995. *The world as will and idea. Abridged in one volume.* London: Everyman.

———. 1951. A few words on pantheism. In *Essays from the parerga and paralipomena.* Translated by T. Bailey Saunders. London: George Allen & Unwin.

Schumaker, John F. 1993. The mental health of atheists. *Free Inquiry* 13 (3):13-15.

Seckel, Al and John Edwards. 1986. The revolt against the lightning rod. *Free Inquiry* 6 (3): 54-55.

Seid, Judith. 2001. *God-optional Judaism: Alternatives for cultural Jews who love their history, heritage and community.* New York: Citadel Press/Kensington Publishing.

Shah, Idries. 1964. *The Sufis.* New York: Anchor Books.

Shea, Robert and Robert Anton Wilson. 1975. *Leviathan: Illuminatus, part III.* New York: Dell Publishing.

Silberger, Steven. 2000.*The Jewish phenomenon: Seven keys to the enduring wealth of a people.* Atlanta, GA: The Longstreet Press.

Silver, Samuel M. 1964. *A treasury of Jewish ihoughts.* New York: Ktav.

Singer, Peter. 2000. *Writings on an ethical life.* New York: HarperCollins.

———. 1994. *Rethinking life and death: The collapse of our traditional ethics.* New York: St. Martin's Griffin.

Skoyles, John R. and Dorion Sagan. 2002. *Up from dragons: The evolution of human intelligence.* New York: McGraw Hill.

Sloan, Don with Paula Hartz. 1992. *Abortion: A doctor's perspective—a woman's dilemma.* New York: Donald I. Fine, Inc., 1992.

Slobin, Dan I. 2001. *Language and thought online: Cognitive consequences of linguistic relativity.* Draft Version. Available on author's website at http://ihd.berkeley.edu/slobin.htm

Smith, George H. 1979. *Atheism: The case against god.* Buffalo: Prometheus Books.

Smith, Warren Allen. 2000. *Who's who in hell: A handbook and international directory for humanists, freethinkers, naturalists, rationalists, and non-theists.* New York: Barricade Books.

Spinoza, B., ed. by Dagobert D. Runes. 1951. *Spinoza dictionary.* New York: Philosophical Library.

Spinoza, B., ed. by Joseph Ratner. 1926. *The philosophy of Spinoza.* New York: The Modern Library.

Stack, Barbara White. 1994. New state law may mean fewer abortions. *Pittsburgh Post-Gazette* Mar. 20: A-1, A-13.

Stirner, Max. trans. by Steven Byington. ed. by David Leopold. 1844, 1995. *The ego and its own.* Cambridge Texts in the History of Political Thought, Cambridge, UK: Cambridge University Press.

Stopes-Roe, Harry. 1987/1988. Humanism as a life stance. *Free Inquiry* 8(1): 7-9, 56.

Strahler, Arthur N. 1992. *Understanding science: An introduction to concepts and issues.* Buffalo: Prometheus.

Tarter, Jill. 2000. SETI and the religions of the extraterrestrials. *Free Inquiry* 20 (3): 34-35.

Taylor, Richard W., ed. 1955. *Life, language, and law: Essays in honor of Arthur F. Bentley*. Yellow Springs, OH: The Antioch Press.

Teilhard de Chardin, Pierre. Bernard Wall, trans. 1959 (1955). *The phenomenon of man*. New York: Harper & Bros.

Telushkin, Joseph. 2001 (1991). *Jewish literacy: The most important things to know about the Jewish religion, its people, and its history*. New York: William Morrow.

Tolstoy, Leo. 1981. My confession. In *The meaning of life*, ed. by E. D. Klemke, 9-19.

Toulmin, Stephen. 1990. *Cosmopolis: The hidden agenda of modernity*. New York: The Free Press.

————. 1988. The recovery of practical philosophy. *The American Scholar* 57 (Summer): 337-352.

Tribe, Laurence H. 1990, 1992. *Abortion: The clash of absolutes*. New York: Norton.

Van Doren, Charles. 1991. *A history of knowledge*. New York: Ballantine Books.

————. 1967. *The idea of progress*. New York: Praeger.

Varga, Andrew C. 1980,1984. *The main issues in bioethics*. Revised Edition. Ramsey, NJ: Paulist Press.

Vitvan. 1982. *Self-mastery through meditation*. Baker, NV: School of the Natural Order.

————. 1952. *The problem of good and evil*. Baker, NV: School of the Natural Order.

Vossler, Karl. Trans. by Oscar Oeser. 1932. *The spirit of language in civilization*. London: Routledge & Kegan Paul Ltd.

Waddington, C. H. 1977. *Tools for thought: How to understand and apply the latest scientific techniques of problem solving*. New York: Basic Books.

————. 1948 (1941). *The scientific attitude. Revised second edition*. West Drayton, UK: Penguin Books.

Watters, Wendell W. 1993. A response to Schumaker. *Free Inquiry* 13 (3): 17-18.

Watts, Alan. 1998 (1959). Impolite interview with Alan Watts. In *Impolite Interviews* by Paul Krassner (with additional questions by Robert Anton Wilson), pp. 1-10. New York: Seven Stories Press.

Watzlawick, Paul. 1990. *Münchausen's pigtail: Or psychotherapy & "reality" essays and lectures*. New York: W.W. Norton.

Weaver, Warren. 1955. Can a scientist believe in God? In *Religions of America*, ed. by Leo Rosten, 158-165.

Webster's Ninth New Collegiate Dictionary. 1987. Springfield, MA: Merriam Webster.

Weinberg, Harry L. 1959. *Levels of knowing and existence*. New York: Harper and Row; Second edition 1973. Lakeville, CT (now Brooklyn, NY): Institute of General Semantics.

Wenger, Win and Richard Poe. 1996. *The Einstein factor: A proven new method for increasing your intelligence*. Roseville, CA: Prima Publishing.

White, Andrew D. 1896, 1993. *A history of the warfare of science with theology in Christendom.* (Two volumes in one) Great Minds Series. Buffalo, NY: Prometheus.

Whitlow, Maynard. 1950. Max Stirner and the heresy of self-abundance. *ETC.: A Review of General Semantics,* VII (4): 277-286.

Whorf, Benjamin Lee. ed. by John B. Carrol. 1956. *Language, thought & reality: Selected writings of Benjamin Lee Whorf.* Cambridge, MA: M.I.T. Press.

Wiener, Norbert. 1961 (1948). *Cybernetics: Or control and communication in the animal and the machine.* Second Edition. New York: MIT Press and John Wiley & Sons, Inc.

Wiener, Phillip P., ed. 1958. *Values in a world of chance: Selected writings of Charles S. Peirce (1839-1914).* Garden City. NY: Doubleday Anchor Books.

Williams, Raymond. 1983 (1976). *Keywords: A vocabulary of culture and society.* Revised Edition. New York: Oxford University Press.

Wilshire, Bruce. 1990. *The moral collapse of the university: Professionalism, purity, and alienation.* Albany, NY: State University of New York Press.

Wilson, Edward O. 2002. The bottleneck. *Scientific American.* Feb. 2002: 82-91.

———. 1998. *Consilience: The unity of knowledge.* New York: Alfred A. Knopf.

Wilson, Robert Anton. 1993. *Cosmic trigger II: Down to earth.* Phoenix, AZ: New Falcon Publications.

———. 1990. *Quantum psychology.* Phoenix, AZ: New Falcon Publications.

———. 1988. *Coincidance.* Phoenix. AZ: Falcon Press.

———. 1986. *Natural law or don't put a rubber on your willy.* Port Townsend, WA: Loompanics Unlimited.

———. 1983. *Prometheus rising.* Phoenix, AZ: Falcon Press.

Wilson, Robert Anton, with Miriam Joan Hill. 1998. *Everything is under control: Conspiracies, cults, and cover-ups.* New York: HarperCollins.

Winetrout, Kenneth. 1967. Review of *Humanistic pragmatism: The philosophy of F. C. S. Schiller,* ed. by Reuben Abel. *Etc.: A Review of General Semantics* 24 (1): 119-122.

Winokur, Jon, ed. 1987. *The portable curmudgeon.* New York: New American Library.

Wright, Frances. 1973. Of free inquiry. In *The feminist papers,* ed. by Alice S. Rossi, 108-117.

Young, Matt. 2002. How to find meaning in religion without believing in God. *Free Inquiry* 22 (3) Summer, pp. 44-46.

Yutang, Lin. 1937. *The importance of living.* New York: John Day/Reynal & Hitchcock.

Zadeh, Lotfi A. 1995. Fuzzy logic: Issues. contentions and perspectives. 1994 Alfred Korzybski Memorial Lecture. *General Semantics Bulletin* 62, pp. 12-15.

Ziman, John. 1988. What is science? In *Philosophy of science,* ed. by Klemke, et al, 28-33.

Index

List of Figures

THE WORLD'S NEED

So many gods; so many creeds,
So many paths that wind and wind,
While just the art of being kind
Is all the sad world needs.

— ELLA WHEELER WILCOX

About the Author

Bruce I. Kodish, Ph.D., P.T. has studied general semantics since 1965 and has worked as a member of the teaching staff of the Institute of General Semantics since 1986. He received his advanced degree in Applied Epistemology/General Semantics from the Union Institute and University in 1996. Bruce lectures and teaches widely and is the author of *Back Pain Solutions: How to Help Yourself with Posture-Movement Therapy and Education.* With his wife Susan Presby Kodish, Ph.D., he wrote *Drive Yourself Sane: Using the Uncommon Sense of General Semantics.* A physical therapist and teacher of the Alexander Technique, Bruce maintains a practice in posture-movement therapy and education in Pasadena, California.

With Susan, he founded the Los Angeles Center for General Semantics (LACGS), which provides coaching and consulting services to individuals and organizations and offers a wide range of presentations and workshops.

You can find further information on their website: www.driveyourselfsane.com

You can contact Bruce and Susan at driveselfsane@aol.com. You may write to them in care of Extensional Publishing, P.O. Box 50490, Pasadena, CA 91115-0490.

Secure online ordering of *Dare to Inquire, Drive Yourself Sane*, and *Back Pain Solutions* is available at www.driveyourselfsane.com. These books are also available at Amazon.com and can be purchased or ordered at bookstores. You may also order them directly from Extensional Publishing.